MORE SAIL TRIM

Trademark

A second anthology of articles concerning
efficiency in sailing

Edited by Anne Madden

Foreword by Jeremy Howard-Williams

ADLARD COLES
8 Grafton Street, London W1

Adlard Coles
William Collins Sons & Co. Ltd
8 Grafton Street, London W1X 3LA

First published in the United States by Sail Books Inc. 1979
First published in hardback in Great Britain by
Adlard Coles 1979
Paperback edition 1990

With acknowledgment to the editorial staff of SAIL Magazine and especially
Charles Mason, the editor responsible for SAIL's techniques articles. Their
expertise contributed greatly to this effort.

British Library Cataloguing in Publication Data

More sail trim.
  1. Sailing. Seamanship
  I. Madden, Anne, *1948–*
  623.88223
ISBN 0-229-11875-5

Printed and bound in Great Britain

Contents

2 BALANCE

3 DOWNWIND

Foreword

Plus ça change, plus c'est la même chose. Alphonse Karr was right when he wrote that over 150 years ago. Much has, indeed, changed in sails during the period since this book was first published in 1975, but when I was asked whether I would contribute a Foreword to its British reissue I was interested to note that almost all its original articles are still very much to the point.

There is therefore much basic common sense between these covers, from definition of sail trim to factors which affect sail power; from the use of tell-tales to spinnaker technology; and from theory to practice. The list of authors reads like a mini *Who's Who* in

yacht racing: Colgate, Twiname, Bertrand, Knights, Bouzaid, Bainbridge, Doyle and Ulmer, to mention but a few. If you only take on board half of what they have to say, you will be well on the way to understanding how to get the best out of your boat.

During the course of a quarter of a century closely connected with sails and sailmaking, both racing and cruising, I have read and discussed much about the subject. I have no hesitation in saying that this book, in conjuction with its sister volume *The Best of Sail Trim*, represents a distillation of sailing wisdom which it would be hard to equal.

Jeremy Howard-Williams
Warsash, Hampshire

Sail Control

"Sail Trim" Defined

The basics of learning how to correct poorly set sails　　　　Steve Colgate

Before we talk about basic sail trim, let's make sure the word *trim* is clearly understood. We often hear about the *trim* of a boat, and here trim refers to whether it is level in the water. The painted waterline shows when it's level. It may be trimmed *bow down,* meaning that weight in the bow is causing the waterline to be submerged in the bow, or *stern down* which indicates the opposite.

We also say *trim the sails,* which means to pull them in tighter. But (sail) trim, when it is used as a noun rather than a verb, indicates the overall relationship of the wind direction to the various sails on a sailboat. This is the subject we are going to discuss.

Very simply, if the sails are angled too far into the wind they flutter in the breeze and this is called *luffing.* If a sail luffs, it is losing power because the wind is no longer filling it completely. A luff is cured (one way) by trimming or pulling the sail in tighter. Of course there's a point beyond which the sail can no longer be trimmed because it is in as far as it can come. When that point is reached, and the sail continues to luff, it means the boat itself is pointing too close to the wind. The solution is to turn the boat away from the wind to fill the sail.

The opposite of a luffing condition is *stalling.* If the sails are trimmed in too flat relative to the wind direction, air will not be able to flow on the leeward side of the sail. Turbulent flow is the result and sails lose their *lift* just as surely as an airplane wing loses its lift when it becomes stalled.

A luff is easy to see because the sail flutters, but a stall is very hard to detect. Yet a stall is far more detrimental to boat speed than is a luff. In fact, there are times when a boat will sail faster with a slight luff in her sails than she would if there were no luff. But she will *always* sail slower with a sail that is stalled.

Your real problem, therefore, is how to detect a stall. It has become popular to sew a piece of wool through the jib (and mainsail too) at various levels along the luff. These often are placed at points one-quarter, one-half, and three-quarters of the way up the sail. It is important that they be located so the helmsman can see the lower one or two pieces of wool. In addition, the wool should not be able to touch a seam where it can catch its hairs on the threads. Nor should it be able to touch the leading edge of the sail.

Though opinions vary on just how to locate the wools, a good general rule is that they should be located in the area of maximum draft (depth) of the sail. This means you ought to place them in the middle of a panel of cloth about one-third of the way aft of the leading edge of the sail with about six to eight

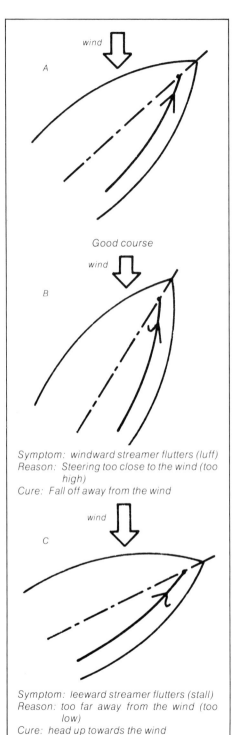

Symptom: windward streamer flutters (luff)
Reason: Steering too close to the wind (too high)
Cure: Fall off away from the wind

Symptom: leeward streamer flutters (stall)
Reason: too far away from the wind (too low)
Cure: head up towards the wind

Figure 1: Close hauled

inches of wool lying on either side of the jib.

Thread a needle with three feet of wool and push it all through the sail except for the last six inches. Cut it so a similar amount hangs out from the other side; then repeat the process in two other locations. There are many other techniques and locations, but this is adequate for daysailing, and using one long piece of wool saves threading the needle more than once, sometimes a time-consuming process itself. To keep the wool from pulling out, tie a small overhand knot in the wool very close to the sail on either side. The sail clotn is translucent enough to see both pieces of wool through the sail from the windward side in most lighting conditions. Some sailors use ribbon streamers rather than wool because they feel they're easier to "read" but it's really just personal preference.

In Figure 1 situations A, B and C show three trim possibilities when sailing close hauled. Because the sails are trimmed in tight in all three examples, it's up to the helmsman to correct the condition by altering course if one or the other piece of wool flutters.

If the windward one flutters, the helmsman is sailing *too high* (too close to the wind) and must fall off. When the leeward one flutters he is sailing *too low* and must head up.

In Figure 2 situations A, B and C show how to read wools on a reach, assuming the boat is sailing on a steady heading and the crew is adjusting the sails to the wind direction. If the windward streamer flutters, the sail must be trimmed in. If the leeward one flutters, indicating a stalled and turbulent airflow, the sail must be eased out until the fluttering stops.

Remember though, these wools or streamers are meant only as a reference and they are not absolute. For example, on a very windy day you may have a constant flutter in the windward wools in order to reduce the heeling force.

One other important reason we place streamers at three or more levels in a jib is to determine proper jib lead position. When we are sailing close hauled and turn our boat slightly into the wind,

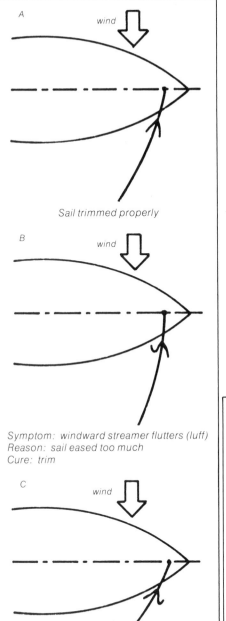

Figure 2: Reaching

A

wind

Sail trimmed properly

B

wind

Symptom: windward streamer flutters (luff)
Reason: sail eased too much
Cure: trim

C

wind

Symptom: leeward streamer flutters (stall)
Reason: sail trimmed in too tight
Cure: ease it out

thereby causing the sail to luff, we want it to luff along its entire length at the luff of the sail at the same time. When this happens, it means the wind is hitting the sail at the same angle at the head as it is at the foot, and this is proper sail trim for most types of jibs.

All wools on the jib should flutter at the same time on the windward side of the sail. If, for example, the top wool flutters first (Fig. 3), the jib lead is too far aft, the jib sheet angle is too low and is pulling more along the foot of the sail than it is along the leech. This results in the top part of the sail twisting, falling off to leeward, and luffing first. To cure it, move the jib lead (the block on the deck through which the jibsheet passes) forward.

If the bottom windward streamer flutters first, the jibsheet angle is too high and you should do just the reverse and move the jib lead aft.

Also remember that, with any change of course, sail trim also should be changed. Sail trim also should be adjusted for any change in wind direction. No one, to the best of my knowledge, has really improved on the old axiom,

Symptom: top streamer flutters first as
you luff
Reason: jib lead too far aft
Cure: move jib lead forward

Figure 3

13

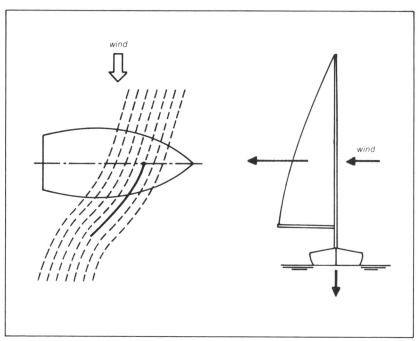

Figure 4

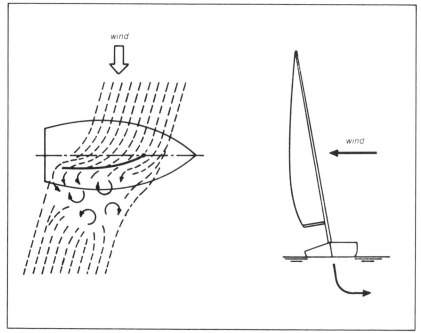

Figure 5

"Let the sail out until it luffs, then trim it in just enough so it doesn't."

If the sails are overtrimmed, however, not only do you stall the sails and lose lift, you cause the boat to heel more. Figure 4 shows a boat sailing on a reach with the mainsail properly set. The drive of the sail is in a forward direction, shown by the arrow. Because the force is more or less in the direction of the boat's travel, there is very little heeling produced. If anything, the force is pushing the bow down into the water, which is the reason crews usually move their weight aft when reaching.

But if you trim the mainsail in flat (Fig. 5), airflow becomes stalled on the leeward side, all the force becomes sideways, and the result is almost nothing but heeling. As the boat heels, a number of things happen. There is more of the leeward side of the hull exposed to the water so the boat is *plowing*, rather than cutting through the water. This is called wave-making, and because the leeward side of a boat is curved, the bow tends to be forced by this wave resistance in the direction of the curve, and the bow must inevitably turn to windward.

Furthermore, because the mast now is leaning over the water, any *forward* force on the sails tends to rotate the boat toward the wind. Because the boat wants to turn into the wind, it now has what is called *weather helm* and the helmsman has to resist it to keep the boat on a straight course. He does this by turning the rudder to leeward, or pulling a tiller to windward.

Not only is this tiring, in the case of very strong weather helm, it is virtually impossible to do because rudders can only turn so far before they too stall and lose their effectiveness. At that point you lose control of the boat and it will turn into the wind whether you like it or not. This whole scenario could be saved just by easing the mainsheet and keeping the force headed forward.

Always be conscious of proper sail trim. If things are not set properly, you will be able to see it in the wools, and feel it in the sailing angle of the boat and in the feel of the helm.

A Quick Guide to Shape

General appraisals of proper sail trim   Jeremy Howard-Williams

Dinghy sailors have long been acutely conscious of the importance of well-shaped sails for the business of going faster. Appreciation of this importance by keelboat sailors, both inshore and offshore, has grown enormously in the last 10 years as owners strive to achieve more speed and efficiency be it ever so fractional.

To cater to this awakening of interest, boat builders, riggers and sailmakers all have provided a positive plethora of sail controls, each with its own particular part to play. Do they work or are they a waste of time, serving only to confuse and distract? Well, if we remember that we are only seeking small increases (if a boat that averages five knots over a five-hour race increases her speed by one percent, or one 20th of a knot, she will save three minutes), then *any* time de-

voted to achieving better sail shape—which sometimes can increase speed by as much as one whole knot—will be time well spent indeed.

First, and most important, remember that sails ought to be set by how they look when they are properly trimmed with the wind blowing across them while under way. You may think this is pretty vague advice in this day of scientific instrumentation, but in the final analysis there is no substitute for good personal judgment. Don't therefore, be content merely to pull up on the main halyard until you hit the black band, and go out on the outhaul until you cannot haul any farther. Have a look at what is happening to the sail as you pull.

Woven sail cloth stretches when it is pulled at an angle to the threadline be-

Learn to use trimming devices and practise getting proper sail shape such as one used on leeward Fireball. Boat has less heel and is pointing higher

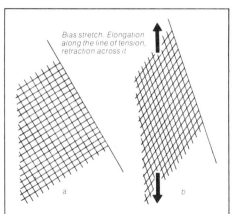

Figure 1: Woven cloth will distort under tension and the little squares formed by the weave will change into little diamonds. The cloth stretches along the line of tension and narrows across it. If pull is along the threadline however, no such distortion takes place and stretch is almost eliminated

cause the little squares formed by the weave distort into little diamonds. If, on the other hand, the tension is parallel with the threadline, no distortion takes place and stretch becomes minimal (Fig. 1). This is why sail cloth usually is shaped to strike the leech at right angles, for this is where you want a flat surface. You want none of the belly, sag or hook that is caused by stretching sail cloth.

A basic fact of life, as far as sails are concerned, is that wind does cause stretch. And as the wind increases in strength, it tends to blow the draft aft in the sail, and it takes on an inefficient shape.

But what is the ideal shape we want? There is enough material for discussion on this subject to fill a book (in fact I *have* filled a book about it), but what is a quick guide to the shape we are seeking, without necessarily going too

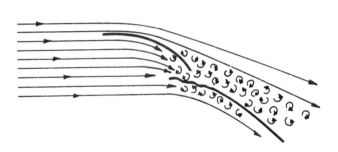

Figure 2A: Bellied headsail leech deflects wind into lee side of mainsail

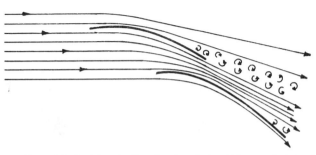

Figure 2B: Both headsail and mainsail should be parallel at exit so wind can pass through with minimum disturbance

deeply into details or reasons?

When the *apparent* wind is forward of the beam, you want the mainsail and genoa to form one smooth airfoil with a slot between them. This slot should be unobstructed and correctly angled, which is to say the headsail leech should be absolutely flat and should parallel the lee side of the mainsail at the slot exit (Fig. 2). The slot should be big enough to pass the amount of air the wind conditions are producing. When, for example, the wind increases towards 20 knots, the existing slot may well need to be larger. A genoa with more hollow to its leech, possibly even a smaller sail as well would become more efficient.

Under such conditions you might also think about moving the headsail fairlead farther outboard to produce a wider slot. This can be done with barber haulers or twin sheets (Fig. 3).

I have said that increasing wind strength tends to force the draft aft in a sail. This puts a belly or hook in both the genoa and mainsail leeches, and prevents a free runoff for the wind and it acts as a brake on the boat. Furthermore, wind that is deflected from the genoa leech into the lee side of the mainsail, causes the luff of the main to lift and the sail to lose drive. This means, of course, that we need to draw the draft forward again, particularly in

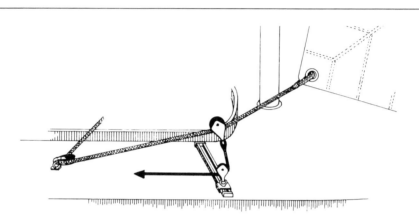

Figure 3A: Barber hauler with genoa sheeted well aft. Note how barber hauler is mounted on a transverse traveler (which normally would have control lines to govern its movement)

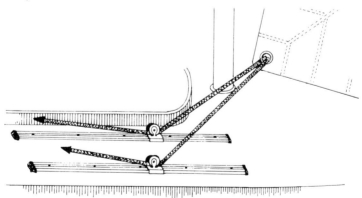

Figure 3B: Twin sheets genoa sheets are taken to fairleads on each track and clew can be adjusted between them (weather sheets have not been drawn in for simplification)

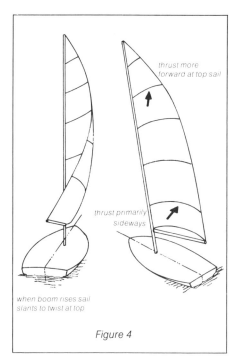

thrust more forward at top sail

thrust primarily sideways

when boom rises sail slants to twist at top

Figure 4

A sail that has excessive twist will be inefficient because the lower half of the sail has to be pulled in a long way if the upper half isn't going to float when the wind gets behind it. This means that the bottom of a sail will have its thrust going largely sideways instead of forward (Fig. 4). Secondly, a sail that is trimmed too far inboard in strong winds will tend to heel the boat to excess even though some boats can accept a surprising amount of inboard trim of both mainsail and genoa if the conditions are right, particularly in very light winds.

For reaching and running, the boom vang normally should be pulled down as hard as reasonable purchase will get it in order to keep twist at a minimum. If you haul in the mainsheet until the boom is hard down and then strap down the vang, you probably will have it too tight and you won't have much shape in the sail; you should allow just a little give so there's some shape left in the sail.

Some boats without a boom vang rig a tackle from the main boom to the rail cap when reaching. This does the same job as the boom vang (i.e., keeps the boom down) but more efficiently, for the purchase usually is greater. It has to be adjusted as the mainsheet is eased or hardened, and of course it has to be taken right off before tacking or gybing.

I'd like to finish this article where we started: sails should be set by how they look. Develop and train your own eyes to assess the shape of the sails and try to look at the mainsail and genoa as one airfoil with an all-important slot between them.

Remember though, you can read all you want about correct shape but unless you go out and try to shape the sails yourself by trimming them you won't make as much progress as someone who does. Unfortunately in this case there is no substitute for practice.

the genoa because of its critical relationship with the mainsail.

On the subject of proper draft of sails, light air usually requires a fuller sail with the draft located more toward the middle; strong winds need flatter sails with the draft a bit farther forward. I know some racing sails are cut flat for light air as well. But in all cases the leech, particularly the genoa leech, is flat so that the airflow at the exit to the slot parallels the lee side of the mainsail.

When the apparent wind moves aft of the beam, a slightly different situation occurs. While the wind continues to flow across the sails so the slot is still important, you now can afford to have more belly everywhere, even toward the leech.

But a word about twist which will occur when you start to head downwind.

The Barber-Hauler

Ins and Outs of a Genoa Sheeting Device   Rick Grajirena

In the late 1950s two San Diego Lightning sailors invented a gadget that would allow them to increase the sheeting angle of the jib on their boat when they were reaching. Little did the Barber brothers know then that their *gismo* would be found on almost every type of sailing machine in the future.

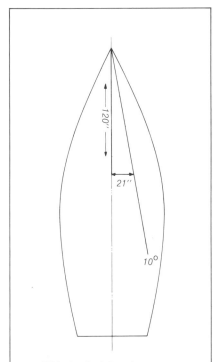

120 inches back from bow and 21 inches from centerline is 10 degrees. Every 2 inches in either direction equals one degree. (For example 17 inches would equal eight degrees)

Figure 1: How to compute jib lead angle from centerline of boat

Although dinghies have been using barber-haulers since the Barber brothers invented the device, the practice wasn't widely accepted in ocean racing until O. J. Young and his team of small boat sailors won the Southern Ocean Racing Conference (SORC) in 1973 with *Munequita.* There were lots of photos taken of *Munequita* going upwind in heavy weather with the genoa barber-hauled outboard and trimmed hard. While this may not have been the first time people used the device on ocean racers, it did draw considerable attention to the technique, and it certainly started a lot more people thinking about what it could do. Because the device still is a relatively new technique to ocean racers who haven't come up through the dinghy ranks, this article is primarily aimed for those who will use the device for the first time on offshore boats.

Barber-haulers are used primarily to increase or decrease the sheeting angle of a genoa or other jib. The device can also be used to pull the jib clew lower, which in effect moves your genoa car forward on the rail. But more about this wrinkle later.

Most modern ocean racers sheet their genoas between seven and eight degrees from the centerline, as shown in Figure 1, when they are going to weather in all but very heavy-air conditions. But in some situations such as large sea conditions or when you've overstood the weather mark slightly, the sheeting angle should be increased. In these cases a barber-hauler should be rigged to the sheet to increase the angle as shown in Photo A. The system here is simply a line that is attached to the clew and run through a snatch block on the rail. Now the sheeting angle can be precisely controlled anywhere from the

Photo A: A barber-hauler system properly set up
to pull clew of jib outboard

original eight degrees to close to 15 degrees at the outboard rail.

Because almost all genoas are cut with low clews, this type of sail does have a tendency to overtwist as you start easing the sheet for reaching. To prevent this you should move the outboard barber-hauler lead slightly farther forward than the original inboard lead. This will pull the clew down, as well as out, and "firm up" the upper leech without over-trimming the bottom of the sail.

You can see in Photo B that this genoa needs some outboard barber-hauling. The top is overtwisting, and about 25 percent of the sail is rendered ineffective. A barber-hauling device that is led outboard and forward would remedy this situation.

Most of the newer boats on the market do have inboard genoa tracks that are properly situated. But some older boats have tracks that lie no closer to the centerline than 10 or 12 degrees. In such cases you can reverse the outhaul procedure by inhauling the genoa clew with an inboard barber-hauler. But when you are doing this be very careful not to overtrim the genoa. A good rule of thumb is to keep the leech of the genoa parallel with the centerline of the boat.

Generally, to check this I sit to leeward halfway between the centerline and the genoa leech and see whether

Photo B: Good example of what genoa looks like when sail is twisted at the top

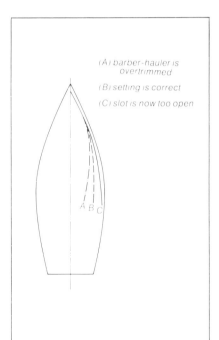

(A) barber-hauler is overtrimmed

(B) setting is correct

(C) slot is now too open

A B C

Figure 2: Best position to observe sail is by looking at sails from directly astern. Clew may be pulled inboard, but leech may appear parallel to centerline when viewed from onboard

the leech of the sail is parallel to the centerline. If you can see part of the leeward side of the genoa, you are overtrimming the sail. Of course, the best position from which to observe this is from another boat, sailing right behind your own boat. Here you can check the slot between jib and main, the jib trim angle, and the trim of the mainsail (Fig. 2).

Now that you know *how* to use barber-haulers, it's important to know *when* to use them. First, let me point out that just because an eight-degree sheeting angle may be correct for your neighbor's new "Superfast 30," that doesn't mean it will work on your "Wasquick 27." But as long as you understand the basic principle, you can experiment with lead locations as you sail. The best lessons are learned by sailing some afternoon against a boat of comparable speed. Then, while he keeps his trim

and settings the same, you try moving your leads in and out and note the speed changes. You'll probably find that you can trim your genoa farther inboard when sailing in smooth water, for example. If the wind velocity and chop increase, it's important to "shift gears" by moving your jib leads outboard and opening up the slot to keep the boat moving.

Now that we've spent some time covering the use of barber-haulers for moving leads in and out, I should mention that they also have another use. Your genoa lead location can also be moved fore and aft with barber-haulers. I've raced in a lot of races where crews are struggling to get a lead jib farther forward under a load. A simple method of easing this problem is to take a second genoa car on a snatch block forward of the one you're using. Then run a line from the clew of the sail through the second block and take it to a free winch. Now by tensioning either sheet you can sheet *anywhere* between the two blocks. Though it is true that you could just move the second block to your desired position and eliminate the original one, the trouble is that you're locked right back into that single lead position problem again (Fig. 3).

If you're the type of sailor who just cleats off the jib and sails by the tell-

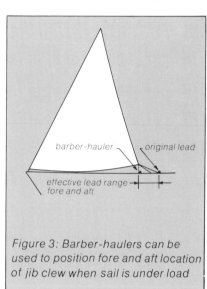

barber-hauler   original lead

effective lead range fore and aft

Figure 3: Barber-haulers can be used to position fore and aft location of jib clew when sail is under load

tales, barber-haulers might not help you all that much. Barber-haulers, after all, are a "fine-tune" adjustment, and they require constant adjustment both with the primary sheet, and the barber-hauling sheets. When they are used cor-rectly, they are a very effective tool for increasing your speed. But like all good things, you've got to spend some time learning how to use them on your own boat.

Let's All Do the Twist

Why and how to shape the mainsail by boom control　　　　　Steve Colgate

Twist can be controlled in the mainsail in part by keeping the boom from rising in the air. When a sailboat is sailing close hauled and the mainsheet is eased, the boom not only goes out, but it rises up. The distance between the end of the boom and the head of the mast becomes shorter and the leech of the sail falls off. This produces the kind of twist as shown in Figure 1.

If twist is allowed to take an exaggerated shape, the top part of the sail becomes parallel to the wind and luffs, while the bottom part still is full of air. Obviously, this isn't efficient sailing for we want the entire sail to luff at the same time. This way it is creating the greatest possible drive when it is not luffing.

If we ease the mainsail, either because the breeze has lightened or because we're changing course to a reach, for efficient sail trim we must hold the boom down. This is where a *traveler* enters the picture. A traveler is a track placed across the deck with a sliding carriage to which the mainsheet is attached. Control lines on either side of the carriage adjust the placement of the carriage along the track. Now, instead of having to ease the mainsheet, which lets the boom rise, we can ease the traveler car out. This eases the boom out which frees the main, but the boom does not rise. There is no twist and the sail still luffs equally its full height.

This method works fine for a close reach as long as the boom doesn't go beyond the end of the traveler. For a broad reach or a run, you have to ease

the mainsail out farther. But if the car has reached the end of the traveler track, the only way to ease the boom out farther is to ease the mainsheet. This will cause an immediate twist as shown in Photo 1, unless you have an additional way to hold a boom down. The answer is a *boom vang*.

There are various types of vangs around though a common type is a simple block and tackle arrangement of the kind shown in Photo 2. The rubber strap permits a certain amount of

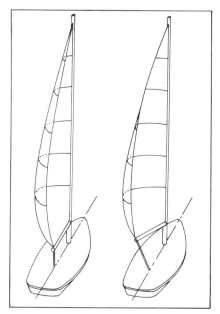

Figure 1: Twist caused when mainsheet is eased

24

Photo 1: When traveler car is at full extension and mainsheet is eased out farther, boom will rise up as shown here unless there is a boom vang to hold boom down

stretch in case the end of the boom dips in the water on the leeward side. Subsequent boom vangs have become more sophisticated and tracks much like traveler tracks can span the deck from side to side. With this arrangement, when a boat gybes the boom vang slides across the deck instead of having to be taken off and reattached again on the new leeward rail. Because many decks are raised in a curve called a crown the track has to be raised so that it is the same distance under the boom at all points. It also must be properly curved so that it follows the identical radius of the vang's point of attachment at the boom.

Hydraulic boom vangs have been appearing recently on many racing and cruising sailboats. Because modern booms are becoming shorter on racing boats, a fixed-position boom vang is more practical than before when booms were longer, forces greater and the danger of dipping in the water more prevalent. Such a hydraulic vang is shown in Photo 3. All these vangs, no matter what kind they may be, do the same thing: control the leech of the sail and the amount of twist allowed in the sail.

A certain amount of twist is desirable. Because of surface friction at the water, wind speed is greater farther up and the apparent wind direction at the top of a

Photo 2: Vang using block and tackle and rubber strap

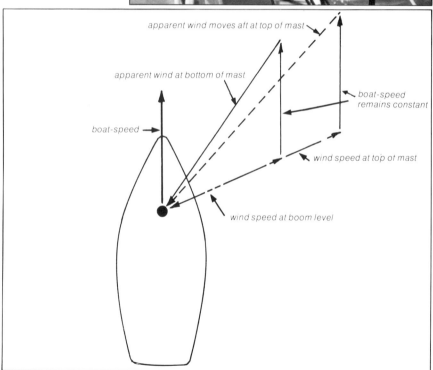

apparent wind moves aft at top of mast

apparent wind at bottom of mast

boat-speed remains constant

boat-speed

wind speed at top of mast

wind speed at boom level

Figure 2: Increased wind velocity at higher levels moves apparent wind direction aft (drawing not to scale)

Photo 3: Hydraulic vang used aboard ocean racer

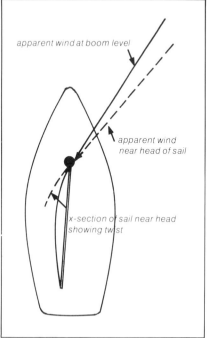

apparent wind at boom level

apparent wind near head of sail

x-section of sail near head showing twist

Figure 3: Because of varying wind speeds, slight amount of twist is necessary

mast is going to be farther aft than it is at the boom level (Fig. 2). Therefore, for the sail to luff equally, a slight amount of twist is necessary (Fig. 3).

If the wind is particularly strong and you want to sail to windward to best advantage, there's a definite limit to how far you should ease the traveler to reduce heeling. The more you ease it, the less you heel. But this inevitably limits the amount of sail force you are able to apply to *point* (go to windward).

If, after the traveler has been eased a bit you are still heeling, you should ease the mainsheet. This will cause the top part of the mainsail to line up with the wind, luff, and become less effective. Because much of the heeling is caused by forces up near the head of the sail, any reduction of pressure there reduces overall heeling by a larger margin than it does farther down.

27

In light wind, a good way to measure the proper amount of twist needed for good sail trim in the mainsail is to sew pieces of wool to each batten pocket. As long as sail trim is correct the wool will flow evenly off the leech of the sail. If there is too much or too little twist, the upper pieces of wool will fly erratically relative to the others. This usually can be corrected by adjusting mainsheet tension. Wool telltales can also be sewn through the mainsail forward of the batten pockets. They can help determine whether the airflow is smooth or turbulent on the lee side of the sail.

To sum up, the mainsheet, traveler, and boom vang all help control mainsail twist and the wool telltales show the proper amount of trim needed. Always remember how important the leech of the mainsail is to getting the whole sail trimmed properly.

Put Your Mainsail Back to Work

Fine-tuning points to achieve maximum power Bob Barton

Harnessing the power of the wind to drive a boat through the water is an old concept that today has become almost commonplace. At the same time, the extremes of sailing technology have become a sophisticated quasi-science. I will try to bridge this apparent gap, and present in words and pictures a basic procedure for making a mainsail work at or near its optimum. Because I want to be both highly specific and quite simple, I am restricting my comments to mainsails for offshore boats. Additionally, I am assuming that you are working with a new sail.

Oddly enough, the place to begin working on your mainsail is with your mast. For an offshore boat, a mast which is straight laterally and has the proper amount of rake and fore-and-aft bend is a must if your mainsail is to do its job properly. To simplify this discussion I will assume that rake and lateral tuning have been properly attended to.

The next important step is to troubleshoot the fit for your sail. Naturally, the most basic aspect of this is that the luff and foot attachment systems on the sail must be compatible with your mast and boom. For example, if you have a tunnel groove in your mast, your mainsail luff must either be a boltrope variety or have round slugs on it that will fit inside the groove.

This is so basic that I almost forget to question it. But most boatbuilders do not specify mast hardware on their plans, and to make things worse, it is not uncommon for mast or boom speci-

fications to be changed by the builder without informing either the sailmaker or the prospective owner. It is always advisable to double check this type of thing before you finalize your sail order.

Beyond the basic hardware, it is important that the tack and clew of the sail sit in their designed locations when the sail is set and trimmed. If, for example, in designing a sail I have planned on the tack's sitting three inches aft of the fair extension of the luff, you would get some distortion in this area if your tack pin held the tack only one or two inches aft. This question of precise tack and clew location (tack and clew *offset,* as it is called) is another one on which the boat- or spar- builder, and sailmaker, must work closely.

If you have a problem in this regard, it will be evident because of strain lines emanating either from the corners (tack and clew) or from the boltrope near the tack or clew. If this type of distortion does occur, you should ask a sailmaker to check the situation out.

The final step in troubleshooting the fit of your sail is to be sure that the sail is the right size in terms of luff, foot, and leech lengths. This may be self-evident if you have black bands on your mast and boom, or if the new sail has replaced another one with which you were very familiar. In any case, be aware that a new sail should be an inch or two undersize in order to allow for future stretching (Fig. 1).

Once the mast is properly tuned and you have successfully checked out the

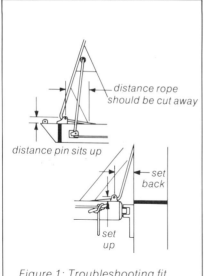

Figure 1: Troubleshooting fit
of mainsail begins by making
sure sail is right size
for fittings on mast and boom

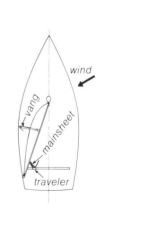

Figure 3: When racing, required
boom angle may be so wide that
mainsheet doesn't exert
enough pull in downward direction
to set leech properly. When
this occurs vang must be used

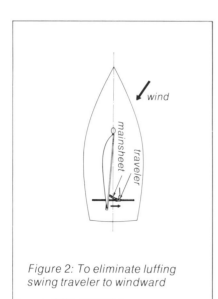

Figure 2: To eliminate luffing
swing traveler to windward

On the other hand, I use *tuning* to refer to all the other variables that contribute to shaping of the mainsail.

Trimming. *Leech tension* is the place to start when trimming the mainsail and this is supplied either by the mainsheet, by the boom vang, or some combination of the two. Using these two devices, optimal leech tension on a main should occur when the second batten down from the top is parallel to the boom. This is judged most easily from just behind the boom where you can see both the line of the boom and the line of the batten. If the batten angles more to leeward than the boom, more sheet tension is needed (Photo A).

On the other hand, if the batten angles to windward (Photo B), ease the sheet a bit. When a main is new, it may be helpful to tension the leech cord in order to help the mainsheet and vang tighten the leech to the point where the *parallel second batten*-situation occurs. Naturally, the leech cord should also be used to remove excess flutter in the leech at any time (Photo C).

The *angle of the boom* to the wind can

fit of the mainsail, you can begin to work on effective tuning and trimming of the sail. *Trimming* refers to the amount of tension applied to the leech and the angle of the boom to the wind.

Photo A: Second batten down from top is too open and more sheet tension is needed to bring batten parallel to boom

Photo C: A fast-looking mainsail. Note smoothness of sail especially at inboard ends of battens. Leech telltales are flowing nicely and second batten down is parallel to boom. Flattening reef has been taken in about half way to achieve proper leech adjustment

Photo B: Leech is far too tight. Second batten down is angling to windward of line created by boom. Remedy is to ease sheet a little or tension luff more

be judged most simply by looking at the luff of the sail. If the sail is luffing, bring the aft end of the boom to windward until the luffing just barely stops (Fig. 2). If you have sailed for a while with no luff in the main, try widening the boom angle until luffing begins, and then narrow it slowly until the luffing just barely stops. The angle of the boom to the wind is best adjusted with a traveler, because adjusting the traveler does not change the tension in the leech.

On the other hand, if you don't have a traveler, or if you have eased the boom out to the point where the traveler is no longer effective, the vang must come into play (Fig. 3). As you ease the sheet to widen the angle, you also must tighten the vang in order to retension the leech and give it the proper setting. If your vang leads from the boom to the mast collar (Fig. 4), the leech tension can be set and constantly maintained by

31

the vang independent of the boom angle.

The close coordination between sheet, vang tension, and traveler position is critical to maximizing the performance of your mainsail. In puffy conditions, constant attention both to leech tension and angle of the boom may be necessary. In puffs, the leech has a tendency to open up, requiring more tension from the sheet or vang. While in the lulls, the leech may be excessively tight as the sail contracts under a reduced load. Obviously, this will require easing the sheet or vang. These adjustments are very small but they are definitely worth making if best performance is desired.

The angle of the boom to the wind is also something that can be continuously adjusted to great advantage. This is particularly true when reaching in a shifting breeze or sailing close-hauled in a puffy wind when the boat may be overpowered or occasionally have excessive weather helm. The boat can be kept on its feet (and helm reduced) by widening the angle of the boom to the wind just as a puff hits. On well-sailed boats in puffy conditions one man almost always has his hand on the traveler control line in order to enable him to broaden the angle quickly and "depower" the mainsail as the puffs strike.

Let's pause for a moment and review. First, the sheet or vang should be tensioned enough to tension the leech properly. Second, boom angle to the wind should be set to just eliminate luffing. The *sequence* of these adjustments is important. Also there is a rough limit on the boom angle. In attempting to eliminate luffing, the boom should not be brought to windward of the centerline of the boat by more than four or five degrees. If luffing persists, there is proper leech tension, and the boom is about on centerline, you need to flatten the sail. Try the techniques I'm going to discuss for tuning the sail. If they don't help, call a sailmaker: your sail is too full or the draft (fullness) is too far forward.

One more thing before you pick up the phone. The luffing of the main may be caused by the genoa. If the genoa

Figure 4: One way to simplify vang arrangement is to rig vang to mast collar

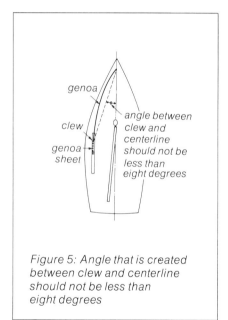

Figure 5: Angle that is created between clew and centerline should not be less than eight degrees

sheeting angle is less than about eight degrees (Fig. 5), a little mainsail backwind is tough to avoid. Similarly, in puffy or heavy air, if you widen the mainsail angle to reduce heel and helm, you may simultaneously induce back-

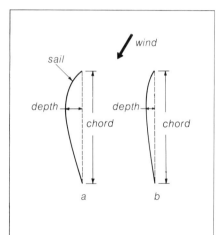

Figure 6: Full sail with lots of depth relative to its chord is good in many conditions but flatter sail would probably be better in heavy winds

winding; again, this is not something to be concerned about.

Tuning. There are many devices and techniques for altering the shape of your mainsail, and I will review them here. First, however, a couple of general comments on sail shape are in order. Up to a point your mainsail will be more powerful and drive your boat faster if it can be made fuller. On the other hand, in heavy breezes the sail frequently will generate too much power and in these conditions you want to make the sail flatter (Figs. 6a and 6b), particularly in the leech area. You also might want to make the sail smaller by reefing.

Battens. You will notice that your battens are quite stiff except for the top one or two which probably will be more flexible and tapered a bit. The thinnest end should be at the forward end of the batten pocket, and the upper batten should be the most flexible. The flexibility of the battens can contribute to a fuller sail shape. Some boats have stiff battens for heavier winds and more flexible ones for lighter winds.

Foot Tension. A more powerful way of altering fullness is to use an adjustable outhaul and/or a *flattening reef* (Fig. 7 and Photo C). Either one allows

variation of the tension in the foot of the sail while under way. The tighter the foot is stretched, the flatter the sail tends to be, and vice versa. For very light air and offwind sailing, the foot should be eased to the point where vertical wrinkles just begin to appear coming out of the tape along the foot of the sail.

As the wind picks up, foot tension should be increased for best windward performance; and in the heaviest conditions there should be a noticeable strain line between the tack and the clew along the foot of the sail. If you don't have a flattening reef and are considering installing one, be sure you locate the fairlead sheave for it aft of the fully outhauled clew by about $3\frac{1}{2}$ inches. This will give the flattening reef pennant the proper angle on the sail when it is tensioned.

Luff Tension. Luff tension can be supplied either by hoisting the halyard more, pulling down on the downhaul, or tightening the cunningham. In all three cases, the objective is to help position the draft in the sail as well as to smooth the material along the luff. As you apply more tension, you tend to draw the fullness in the mainsail forward and generally flatten the sail a little bit. The rule of thumb on a new main is simply to apply just enough luff tension to barely eliminate wrinkles emanating horizontally from the luff tape. With a well cut sail this should also position draft properly. In very light conditions or when sailing downwind, tension can be reduced so much

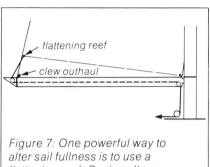

Figure 7: One powerful way to alter sail fullness is to use a flattening reef. Device allows variation of tension in foot of sail while under way

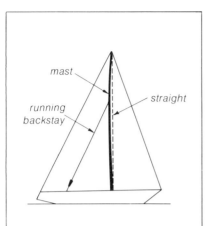

Figure 8: Tightening running backstays or aft lowers induces reverse mast bend and fuller mainsail is result. But be careful about how much bend you put in

mum amount of babystay tension—you might possibly tighten the running backstays if you have them (Fig. 8). To flatten the sail or to eliminate backwind, more bend is required and you should tighten the babystay or forward lowers.

But unless your mast has been designed with this in mind, a good rule of thumb on maximum bend is half the chord depth (one half the fore-and-aft dimension) of your mast. This means that after drawing a straight line between the black bands at the head and the tack, the middle of the mast should not be forward of the line by more than half the chord depth (Fig. 9). Small as it is, this amount of bend can have a significant impact on the shape of the main and it is worth trying to achieve in moderate and heavy upwind conditions especially if you have a full cut mainsail.

Reefing. No matter how much mast bend or foot tension you can achieve, at some point your boat will be overpowered, and it will sail much faster and more comfortably if a reef is put in. Each boat has a different wind strength or set of conditions that will cause it to need a reefed main, but one good indication is an angle of heel greater than 22-26 degrees.

If your main is backwinding badly in

that these wrinkles do appear. And in very heavy upwind conditions it may be necessary to provide additional extra tension in the luff in order to hold the draft forward in the mainsail.

A good way of judging whether this treatment is necessary is to look again at the situation at the second batten from the top. You should be able (simultaneously) to have that batten parallel to the boom and have the upper one third of the mainsail flying firm at the luff (not luffing). If the main is luffing, it may be time for more luff tension. This will open the upper leech, which requires more trimming to reset the leech but it will eliminate luffing.

If a sail has been used in excessive wind strengths for a long period of time, it is possible that the draft in the sail will have moved so far back that the upper leech is impossible to set open enough no matter how much the luff might be tensioned. This situation requires either a recut or a new sail.

Mast Bend. If you can control the amount of fore-and-aft bend in your mast, either with an adjustable babystay or other gear, you have a powerful tool for tuning the shape of your mainsail. To generate more fullness, use a mini-

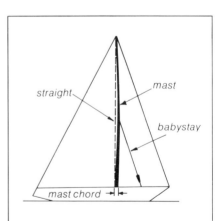

Figure 9: To put in forward mast bend, tighten babystay or forward lowers to flatten mainsail. Bend should be limited to one half of mast chord

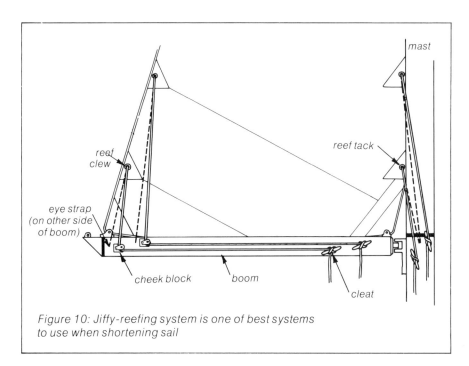

Figure 10: Jiffy-reefing system is one of best systems to use when shortening sail

heavy air, it certainly is time to reef. On the other hand if the sail is flat and drawing well, a smaller headsail may be a better way to reduce heel. This decision has to be made by a skipper whose knowledge of his boat and sail inventory will lead him to the effective method of shortening sail. Incidentally, the system for reefing which I favor is *jiffy* or *slab reefing* (Fig. 10).

On boats that have either slugs or slides on the luff of the mainsail reefing is facilitated by the use of a jackline. This line simply allows the bottom few slides or slugs to "float" away from the luff of the sail when it is being reefed. No special comment is needed about this except that the tension in the jackline should be adjusted so that minimum distortion occurs in the luff area. This usually means quite a bit of ten-

sion in the jackline but it must be judged carefully in each case. Normally, when you reef, there is no need to ease the jackline, but this can vary from case to case. In any event I make my jacklines long enough so that they can be eased if needed.

Mainsail trim on a new main is not that difficult if you know what to look for. And if you can trim your sail properly it will produce more speed, closer windedness, and you will balance the boat's helm so the helmsman can do his job more easily. Take a look at any well-sailed offshore boat and the chances are you will find all the equipment needed to trim and tune the mainsail properly. And you will also find crewmembers who work the mainsail adjustments constantly to get the best out of the sail.

No. 1 Genoa: No. 1 Headsail

Considerations of trim for the workhorse of the foredeck   Ben Hall

Let's assume you have neither a fore-peak full of genoas nor the latest double - triple - swiveling - twin - tri - gem - stay-foil headstay luff-support system. If this is the case your normal run-of-the-mill number 1 genoa is perhaps the most important sail in your racing inventory. And in order to get the most out of this sail over a wide range of conditions, there are a number of critical adjustments you must coordinate to produce the correct sail shape for the existing wind and sea conditions.

If you order an "all-purpose" number 1 genoa from your sailmaker, do not make the mistake of choosing a fabric that will be too light to take an 18- to 20-knot breeze. Generally, for boats 22-40 feet in length the proper fabric weight can range from four ounces to 6.5 ounces. The sail also must be able to survive the abuse of a stubborn skipper (and that means most of us) who refuses to change down to a smaller headsail as the wind pours in on the last weather leg. So, if you are one who likes to use, and perhaps over-use his number 1 genoa, here is a way to get the most out of that valuable sail.

Because almost every adjustment and control of a sail is dependent on the others to achieve optimum sail performance, I will deal with each adjustment in relation to overall sail shape.

Luff Tension

Luff tension determines where the proper draft location is going to be in the sail. By properly using the genoa halyard, or genoa halyard and cunningham combination, you can change the position of the draft to suit the wind and sea conditions. In light air, tensioning the halyard only hand tight often is sufficient to position the draft at the optimum 40-50 percent back from the luff. A common error in light air is to over-tighten the halyard. This both flattens the sail and puts the draft much too far forward in the sail for it to be efficient.

In medium air, the halyard and/or cunningham should be tightened to eliminate any scallops between the hanks (if you have them) in order to keep the entry of the genoa smooth. With this increased tension, the draft position should stay at about 40 percent in the sail. Even more luff tension is required in heavy air to move the draft position forward to 35-40 percent aft of the luff, and to flatten the sail and open the upper leech. Having a stretchy rope luff genoa gives you great flexibility over both shape and draft location, so don't forget to use it.

Sheet Lead Position

Most number 1 genoas today are cross cut with fairly full lower sections and a generous foot roach. The method of sheeting this type of sail is quite different from the older miter genoa with its extremely flat lower sections. The clew height of the newer breed of genoa is slightly higher to allow for a better range of fore-and-aft sheet-lead positions. Generally, the position of the lead for this type of sail is farther forward

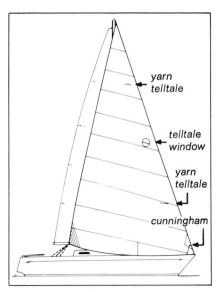

Figure 1: Cross-cut genoa
solid line indicates mean sheet position

labels in figure: yarn telltale; telltale window; yarn telltale; cunningham

than the normal sheeting position for the older type of genoa.

The best way to position your sheet lead accurately is with the help of luff telltales (woolies, ticklers, etc.) on your genoa. You only need to put three sets of telltales on the luff area (9-15 inches back from luff), evenly spaced at $\frac{1}{4}$, $\frac{1}{2}$ and $\frac{3}{4}$ of the length up the luff (Fig. 1). But make sure all three sets are exactly the same distance back from the luff. Begin in light-to-medium air (8-10 knots) and position your lead so all three telltales break (stall) evenly when you head up or fall off. At this point, your leech should be setting up properly and the foot section of the sail should be full and powerful.

As wind strength increases into the medium-heavy range, most number 1 genoas will start to overpower the boat. To compensate for this, move the lead aft. This will put more twist in the upper part of the genoa and also will flatten the lower sections. The effect on the sail is that the upper sections spill the air but the lower sections give you the necessary drive. In these conditions, you should not attempt to keep the telltales breaking evenly. By moving the lead

aft, the top weather telltale should stall much earlier than the lowest yarn.

Don't be concerned with this aerodynamic imbalance in heavier winds because keeping the boat standing up on her feet by reducing the driving power of the genoa will produce much better boat speed than with an overpowered sail with uniform air flow over the luff area.

Sheeting Angle

Once you have determined the correct luff tension, draft location, and sheet-lead position you have to get the proper sheeting angle. There are a number of options you can turn to for adjusting the inboard and outboard sheeting angle of your genoa and they depend on the particular configuration of your boat. The most common method is to sheet to a slider on a rail track or a snatch block attached to an extruded toerail. Unfortunately this system gives you no athwartship adjustment and that is why so many boats have gone to inboard genoa tracks (some as far inboard as 7-8 degrees). With inboard tracks, you can *double sheet* between the inboard and outboard tracks, and thereby achieve almost infinite control between the two points. The problem with this system lies in the fact that it is difficult to readily reproduce exacting adjustments. It also means having an extra "short sheet" and this can slow tacking considerably.

For boats whose layouts do not permit inboard tracks, the only way to have good athwartship control is to use barber haulers. There are two simple ways to do this. The first is simply to take a single part line with a snap hook at one end and attach it to the genoa sheet near the clew. Lead the line across the cockpit to a weather winch and barber haul it as necessary.

A second way is to use a boomvang block and tackle with snap shackles at either end. Attach one end to the genoa sheet and the other end to a convenient padeye on the weather side. With this mechanical advantage, barber hauling becomes relatively easy. The reason you should have athwartship control is to keep the ability to trim the genoa optimally for all points of sail in varying wind and sea conditions. For example, in medium air and smooth water, an upwind sheeting angle of 7-8 degrees usually is best. But as the sea gets lumpy or the wind increases, moving the lead outboard to between 9-12 degrees seems to work well on most boats. Of course when you are reaching, you want to move the lead all the way outboard to the rail.

I am sure most crews have experienced the problems of a long windward leg sailed in shifting air (direction and velocity) and these control methods are fairly primitive. On my Quarter-Tonner *Dark Star* we developed a system that solved the problem of fore-aft as well as inboard-outboard control with one track (Fig. 2). With this system, we could sheet the number 1 between 6½ and 14 degrees and also get a fore-and-aft adjustment of four feet. Because the whole system is ball bearing, movement of the cars under load was no problem. The beauty of such a system is that the lead is positive and can be reproduced at any time. After using it for awhile I do not think I would have anything else on my boat.

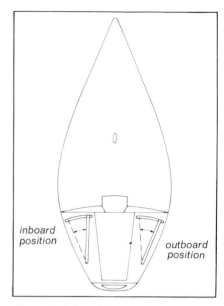

Figure 2: Adjustable genoa track system

Slot and Twist

A direct result of athwartship control of the genoa is the narrowing or widening of the slot between the main and genoa. You must be careful not to close the slot by excessive inboard sheeting for this can create backwinding in the main and cause a severe loss in boat speed. Conversely, if the sheeting angle is too wide, the slot can become too large which causes a reduction in efficiency between main and genoa.

If all the controls of your number 1 genoa are set correctly, the slot between the main and genoa should be uniform and the twist in the genoa and the main will be roughly parallel when the proper slot is achieved. Once the sails are working in harmony, you should be going very fast.

Leechline

The leechline and footline are really not a shape- or speed-producing control in your genoa, but rather are more of a

	Upwind		Reaching	
	Lt. Medium	Med. Heavy	Lt. Medium	Med. Heavy
Luff Tension (halyard & cunningham)	relaxed	taut socko	relaxed	medium taut semi-socko
Draft Location	45-50%	35-40°	50%	40%
Lead Position (relative to mean)	mean	aft	forward	forward
Lead Angle (optimum sheeting)	7-10°	8-12°	outboard (rail track)	outboard (rail track)

Figure 3

nuisance control. If either the leech or foot is fluttering, a slight tug on the corresponding line will eliminate the problem. But just pull it enough to stop the flutter, and no more. Don't expect the sail to be converted from a flat headsail to a super-full drifter just by a three-foot yank on the leechline. It doesn't work.

Telltale Window

Telltale windows are helpful in reading your luff yarns on the genoa. Not only do they allow you to see the leeward telltale when the sun is shining on the weather side of the sail, but they are a must for telltale watching at night with a flashlight.

The diagram chart in Figure 3 is an oversimplification of the most important controls that govern the proper set of your number 1 genoa. The actual numbers will vary from boat to boat, but the way to derive the maximum performance out of the sail is essentially the same.

If you learn how to get the most out of your number 1 genoa, you will find very quickly that it will be the most important sail in your inventory.

Wool Tufts and the Stalled Sail

A physical solution for determining correct wind flow   Eric Twiname

How often do you find on a beat that suddenly every other boat has been lifted and they're all pointing 10 degrees higher than you? Then you poke your nose up into the wind a bit, only to find that you'd been lifted too, but hadn't noticed.

It's the kind of thing that happens when there's a lot of action round you—gusty conditions, other boats crossing and so on. What usually happens is that in concentrating on everything else, the one thing that didn't get noticed was the most important of all, the lift. The reason isn't hard to find. Lifts are much more difficult to spot than headers. In a sudden header, the sails flutter at the luff and you have to bear off to keep moving well. When you're lifted nothing so obvious happens.

So any aid that helps you pick up the lifts as soon as they come your way is worth having—especially when, at its simplest, it consists of nothing more complicated or expensive than half a dozen short lengths of wool.

The positioning of the wool tufts is important if you're to get the best information about the wind flow round your rig. Four tufts should be positioned about 15 cm in from the luff of the jib and roughly equally spaced up the length of the luff. On the mainsail the most important spots are halfway back along the sail, about a quarter of the way up and a position about eight inches forward of the leech at the same height. With a small one-man dinghy there should be a number of tufts down the luff of the sail, but at least 24 inches from the mast to avoid the excessive air disturbance the mast creates.

You fix the wool by making a hole in the sail, thread through an eight-to 10-inch length of black wool to its halfway point and then knot it at each side to stop it from slipping out.

Lighter-weight sails are translucent enough to let you see the woolen streamers through the sail cloth, though there are times when looking into the sun that this is difficult. In offshore classes it is common practice to put in little round windows to view the tufts through the sail.

The principle that wool tufting works on is straight-forward enough. When you've got the boat sailing correctly to windward, the air flow at the luff of the leading sail is fairly smooth over both sides of the cloth, and the wool tufts line up with the flow (Photo 1). As soon as you point too high and the jib luffs, the flow becomes turbulent on both sides of the sail and the tufts flail about, though anyone even half observant should also see the jib lifting here without tufts.

But it's when you fall below your ideal windward course that the tufts really come into their own, even if you've strayed only a few degrees. The smooth flow on the lee side of the sail breaks down and becomes turbulent as the sail stalls. The turbulence whips the lee wool tufts into a frenzy of activity (Photo 2 and Fig. 1).

At the optimum windward sailing

Photo 1: The tufts on both sides of the sail lie along the sail and this indicates smooth air flow even though there is turbulence behind the mast

angle, the tufts don't lie exactly as I've shown them on the Figure. There is a fine point of sailing at which the jib luff is just on the point of lifting without actually doing so. At this point the windward tufts at the luff of the jib tend to point almost vertically upwards, while the ones on the lee side stream back. And this is the optimum windward sailing angle: the jib is giving you as high a pointing angle as it can without losing its ability to provide a lot of forward drive.

The reason for the upward air flow at the luff seems to be that there is an area of higher pressure on the windward side of the sail, so that undisturbed air meeting the aft rake of the jib luff is initially deflected upwards.

When the boat bears off slightly—even by as little as a degree or two—the upward flow on the windward side of the jib luff breaks down and the windward wool tuft streams aft like the leeward one. When this happens the boat is no longer sailing to windward at its optimum speed. So here we have a very sensitive visual aid for windward sailing. It is at least as sensitive as the telltale tremors of the sail cloth itself, and in some conditions appreciably more so. For the less experienced particularly, this visual aid to windward sailing can be extremely useful if it is used properly.

I don't want to go into too much detail about how wool tufts behave in varying conditions and on different boats because their behavior does vary. When a keel boat is being driven hard to windward, for example, she'll be well heeled and there will be an upward air flow over the rig which will be reflected by the tufts. On a single sail boat, the

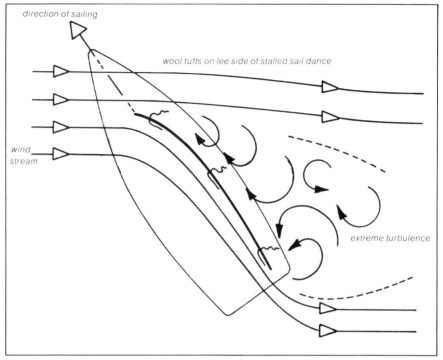

direction of sailing

wool tufts on lee side of stalled sail dance

wind stream

extreme turbulence

Figure 1: Tuft action along both sides of a stalled sail

tufts close to the mast are sometimes unreliable because of the interference to wind flow that the mast causes. Even on different classes of two sail dinghies there are variations in the tuft behavior which are caused by the degree of aft rake of the jib luff and the size of the mainsail/jib slot. But the general principles I have described apply to them all.

What you have to do to get the most out of a sail with tufts is to discover exactly how the tufts align themselves when the boat is making the best possible windward speed. Which isn't too difficult, given a little preparatory work.

When sailing to windward by wool tufts the tufts have, in effect, to be calibrated like any other measuring device. The way to do this is to race as usual with the wool tufts in place, pick a time when you're going particularly well to windward and gaining places, then watch what the wind tufts are doing. In other words, pick a time when you're thinking 'this is just how the boat

should always sail upwind.'

Take a long look at the tufts during that period and remember exactly how they lie, so that in the future you can sail the boat upwind fast in similar wind conditions by getting the tufts to lie in exactly the same attitudes. Remember what I said about the windward tufts on the jib pointing upwards; that may not be ideal on your boat, but many people tend to sail too free by having both windward and leeward tufts streaming aft.

One of the commonest errors in windward work is to bear away too sharply in the lull that follows a gust. Again, this is because there's a lot of action at the time and as the boat heels to windward the natural thing to do is to bear away. Usually this is a mistake; and the mistake will become glaringly obvious when the tufts on the lee side of the jib break out in a wild dance.

The sensitivity of the device can be valuable as well, particularly during a long race, because the tufts are easy to see and you can concentrate on them over long periods of the beats when you're working solely at trying to eke out the maximum boat speed.

Wool tufts can also be very handy downwind. Not only on the jib, but near the leech of the mainsail. Oversheeting is the most common speed killer downwind. The air flow breaks down on the lee side of the sail and becomes highly turbulent. When this happens, forward drive is reduced and the boat slows down. Except in heavy weather it is easy to oversheet without noticing you've done it, particularly when you get tensed up because the boat's not going fast enough. Then it goes slower still.

But if you've got your tufts, you very quickly see that you're oversheeted because those on the lee side of the sail flail about in all directions, while those on the windward side hang down as the air flow over the sail slows. The message that you're oversheeted is otherwise usually conveyed by a nearby boat as it overtakes you.

On a beam reach a small amount of oversheeting is necessary, though, to get the maximum drive from the sail. Take a single sailboat, for example. The maximum drive from the sail comes when the flow is just beginning to break down on the lee side; in fact at the aft part of the sail it may have already broken down (Fig. 2). This optimum mainsail setting is sheeted in as much as 10 degrees closer than the position at which the luff of the sail will begin to lift (Photo 3).

Ideally you want to reach with the sail set at this angle to the apparent wind, but you're in danger of having the sail stall. And this is where your tufts in the middle and by the leech of the sail come in. You can let the tufts near the

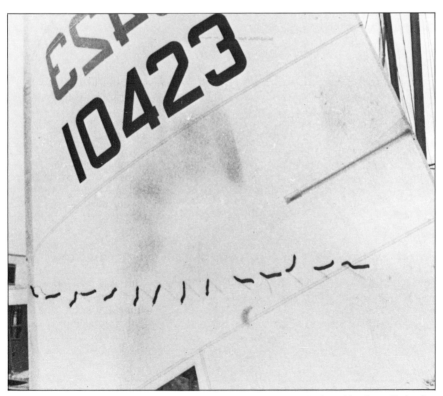

Photo 2. This is a typically haphazard arrangement of tufts on the lee side of a stalled sail

leech begin to leap about, but the tufts on the lee side at the center of the sail should always be streaming more or less horizontally.

As you reach closer to the wind, the optimum sheeting angle for the sail comes closer to the point at which the luff of the sail begins to lift. The reason for this is that the nearer you trim the boom to a right angle to centerline the better the angle of the driving force you provide to power the boat. On a beam reach, sheeting in 10 degrees will hardly affect this. On a close reach changing the angle from 30 degrees to the centerline down to 20 degrees is very detrimental.

Tornados all but stop when their mainsails stall. The drop in speed is so great that a dead run is sailed as a zig-zag, slicing along at about 45 degrees to the dead downwind course with the sole purpose of getting the apparent wind onto the beam to keep the sail providing maximum forward drive.

One other way you can use these little bits of magic wool is in tuning the boat for windward work. Three things above all others determine how efficiently a two-sail rig will power you to windward; the mainsail/jib slot; the mainsail leech; the shape of the jib. All three determine how efficiently the wind is converted into useful forward drive, and all affect the way the wind flows round the rig. And the way the wind flows round the rig is indicated by your wool tufts.

The jib is the most important sail in windward work, and it is vital to get fore and aft sheeting angle right as this

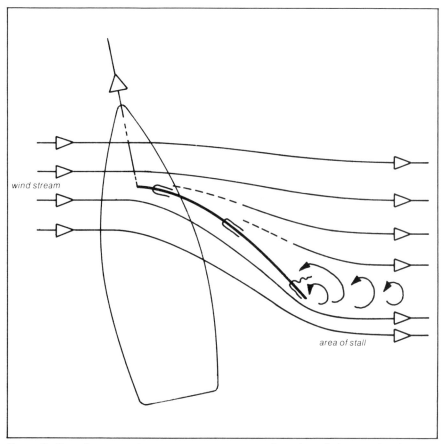

wind stream

area of stall

Figure 2: On a beam reach you can get more power from the sails by oversheeting until the after part of the sail just stalls

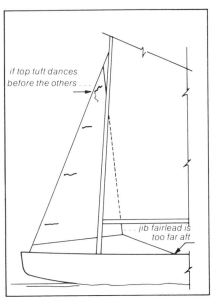

Figure 3: A good way to assess the correct setting of jib lead

Photo 3: Looking toward the mast on a singlehander. The tufts near the leech show the aft part of the sail is stalled while flow farther forward is smooth

affects the slot and the whole aerodynamics of the rig. Usually the position is fixed by eye but it can be more accurately done with tufts. What you do is move the fairlead position fore and aft until you find the place where the tufts at the top, middle and bottom of the sail all react at the same time (Fig. 3). So when you're sailing and have the lower part of the jib at the optimum sailing angle, the top part is correct as well.

The tufts on the aft part of the mainsail can also give you danger signals when sailing to windward. When you either have the mainsail leech too tight

(it is curling back upwind) or your mainsail is sheeted in too hard, the aft part of the main may stall. In both cases the boat loses speed. Again, the leeward tuft close to the leech will flail about if this part of the sail is stalled. The remedy? Usually achieved by easing the mainsheet.

There are many other uses for tufts, including spinnaker trimming. They have so many uses, in fact, that maybe I've made these little bits of wool seem like the panacea for all sailing ills. They're not, of course. But used properly they can be a great help.

Drive Off for Power

Coordinating trim for maximum upwind speed   Paul Schreck

If a windshift threatens to head you off toward a leeward boat and you want to avoid tacking onto an unfavored course, you can retain your advantage as windward boat by easing your sheets just enough to pick up speed and drive over the leeward boat. You should drive off any time you need to stay on top of an opponent. This includes changed positions because of windshifts, overshooting a mark and driving back down to it, or picking up an advantage before the leeward boat gains on you.

You can drive your boat by doing three things: easing the sheets, sailing the boat flat, and eliminating weather helm. All three require close coordination of sail trim and disposition of crew weight.

On an average 30-foot keelboat, the crew will have to ease both the mainsail and the genoa slightly to start driving. By easing the main traveler, you maintain control without increasing the twist

of the main and losing wind from the head of the sail. Once you do this, however, the genoa clew also must be moved out to maintain the slot between the two sails. The genoa block should then be moved forward to maintain good downward tension on the genoa leech. The distance the two clews should move will vary with the particular boat and particular circumstances.

Move the genoa clew forward by repositioning the block on its track; move it out by hooking a *short sheet* (barberhauler) to the clew (Fig. 1). Have the barberhauler attached and ready to go all the time or the harm from having a crewmember over on the lee rail fiddling with lines, sails and winches may negate any advantage you may gain from increased speed. The barberhauler should lead to a secondary winch. If you want the option of trimming it continuously, the sheet must be long enough to reach up to a crewmember on the

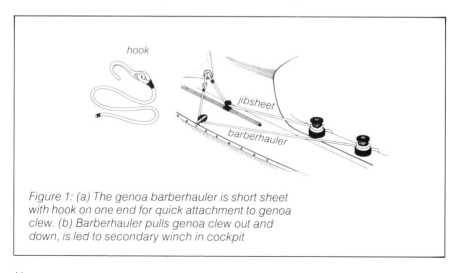

Figure 1: (a) The genoa barberhauler is short sheet with hook on one end for quick attachment to genoa clew. (b) Barberhauler pulls genoa clew out and down, is led to secondary winch in cockpit

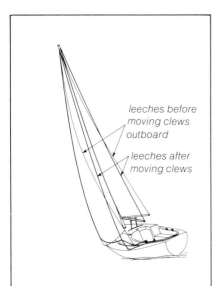

leeches before moving clews outboard

leeches after moving clews

Figure 2: Shaded areas show shape of sails with both clews trimmed outboard. If sails are not allowed to twist to spill wind, sails don't act as rudders, adding to weather helm, or slow boat down by losing too much wind

windward side. In the case of a 30-footer, the sheet would be probably about 15 feet long. Otherwise, 10 feet should be adequate.

Some boats stand up straighter and start driving as soon as the clews are moved out. However, a boat with hard chines or a deep forefoot will probably also require a shift in crew position. In heavier winds, the crew should sit to windward and aft, thereby preventing the bow from digging in. As the wind strength goes down, the crew can move forward and then can shift their weight to leeward as trim requirements dictate.

In addition to keeping the boat flat, a good skipper will not have any lee or weather helm present in the boat. If there is lee helm (the bow tends to fall off when rudder is amidships), the skipper can call for more weight to leeward, and can ease the headsail or trim the main, as circumstances dictate. Weather helm can be corrected by putting more crew weight to weather, by moving the

crew weight aft, by easing the mainsail or by trimming the jib.

Any correction for weather helm must be tempered by considering the condition of the sea. For example, if large seas remain from an earlier high wind, you should probably ease the mainsheet to drive the boat a little more quickly through the fast approaching waves. If you are sailing in flat seas, even in a heavy wind, bringing the headsail clew in will correct the weather helm with less loss to windward. Remember, in general, you don't want to fall off and drive in flat seas because you should use flat seas to gain as much distance upwind as possible.

Contrary to published opinion which states that spilling wind from the head of the sail reduces weather helm, I believe that leeches, both main and jib, should not be allowed to twist very much. If the sails spill a little wind, they will act like airfoils and try to round the boat up into the wind; this actually increases the weather helm. If the sails twist so that they spill enough wind to reduce weather helm, the boat loses so much speed that it can hardly still be considered to be racing.

It's been my experience that if you avoid twist and move the clews of both genoa and mainsail outboard instead (Fig. 2), the boat requires less rudder to keep it sailing in a straight line. In addition, you will spill wind off the lower portions of the sails, thus reducing pressure and providing forward drive. This is particularly important when you are driving for speed and cannot afford to lose time and distance by rounding up into the wind.

To sail your boat correctly requires complete understanding of your boat's characteristics; many boats don't start moving until their owners have had them for awhile. Imagine the nightmares of racing skippers who start out on new boats every season!

To compensate for lack of knowledge you must pay attention to tune and trim. If you want to win, you have to keep your boat going. Work and strive to make the boat go a little more quickly on all points of sail, not just when you want to drive over someone.

You'll be surprised at how you can show up the newest, hottest boat by out-tuning, out-trimming, and out-sailing it over the entire course.

For example, never assume that the genoa blocks should be set at the same place on both sides of the boat. This is possible *only* in smooth water conditions and even then you should trim a little more tightly on starboard tack because of the way the wind comes at you in the Northern Hemisphere. The boat's interaction with waves will vary depending on the tack; since waves bend toward the shore more than the wind does, you will often find that you attack waves at a steeper angle on one tack than on the other (Fig. 3). This is when you must keep your sails loose and driving, otherwise you will stop dead each time you hit a wave head-on. When you are not sailing into but rather at an angle with them, you can hold up tight on the front side of a wave, then drive down the back side to help you get over the next wave.

Other reasons for trimming differently on different tacks include bottom finish, lopsided hull, keel shape, keel finish, rudder and skeg alignment, weight distribution of crew, stores and the skipper. Many skippers steer better with one arm than with the other, or they can play waves better on one tack than on the other.

To maximize this drive you are seeking, you must also minimize drag. Although weather helm indicates drag most clearly, any extreme strain on the tiller indicates drag that you must eliminate. You may have a tremendous force on the tiller, even if the helm remains perfectly straight, when the boat heels over and the bow digs in. As the bow goes down, the stern tries to spin out around the bow. To compensate you should move the crew weight aft to pull the bow up and relieve the strain on the tiller.

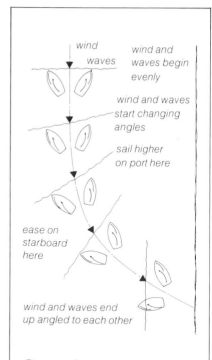

wind
waves

wind and waves begin evenly

wind and waves start changing angles

sail higher on port here

ease on starboard here

wind and waves end up angled to each other

Figure 3: Because wind bends toward shore at different rate from waves, boat on starboard tack must ease sheets enough to drive through each wave, while boat on port tack can trim in more tightly since it attacks waves at greater angle

If you put in some real effort and thought you can learn to sail like the experts. The most important factor in keeping your boat driving is to know the characteristics of your boat. Once you have analyzed your own boat and studied the particular sailing conditions, you will better know how to correct problems as they arise.

The Non-masthead Rig

Principles of sail and mast tuning   Bill Allen

The new generation of non-masthead, under-30-foot boats all use similar methods and strategies to get the best performance. Although by no means all-inclusive, this article summarizes many of the principles for tuning these boats.

Equipment. A few inexpensive items help eliminate problems that can occur on any boat. For boats with horn- or hook-type genoa tack fittings, a shock-cord tied around the headstay and looped over the tack hooks will keep the tack hooked even with the sails on deck (Fig. 1).

Lines woven up and down between the deck and the lifelines are a common safety feature on cruising boats, and are equally useful on racing boats to keep the sails from sliding overboard. Lead the line through deck eyes on the toe rail or through holes drilled right through the teak rail. Space the holes about 18 inches apart. Use shockcord to tie the sails against the lifelines while they are down. Tying a five-foot piece of shockcord at deck level with one end to the bow pulpit and the other to a stanchion near the mast works well. Bring the shockcord under the sail and hook it to the lifeline or the weaving, holding the sail in a large triangular area (Fig. 2).

It's a big help to position a set of spinnaker sheet *twings* or *horses* along the sheet near the clew (Fig. 3). These consist of a block on the sheet that is attached to a line that runs through a fixed block on the end and leads back to the cockpit. When you run it through a camcleat on the cabin top, the twing makes clew height adjustment easy, and, when pulled down on the weather side, makes a much cleaner lead for the afterguy.

You can simplify the foreguy (pole downhaul) by placing a turning block directly in front of the mast and leading the foreguy through it instead of running it forward to the normal lead position on the foredeck. This eliminates having to readjust the foreguy after you move the afterguy. It also helps triangulate the pole during a gybe, so the foredeck crew can just push straight out to get the pole back on the mast after an end-for-end gybe. The outboard end of the pole becomes self-aligning.

Any small boat needs an adjustable and powerful boom vang. I feel it should be double-ended and led to both sides near the cockpit. It is especially

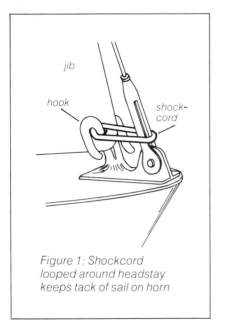

Figure 1: Shockcord looped around headstay keeps tack of sail on horn

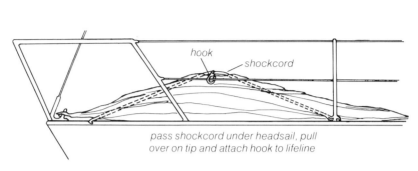

pass shockcord under headsail, pull
over on tip and attach hook to lifeline

Figure 2: Keeping headsails secured on foredeck is easy if
hook and shockcord arrangement are in place

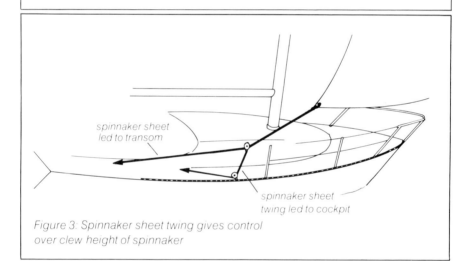

Figure 3: Spinnaker sheet twing gives control
over clew height of spinnaker

helpful in a good breeze, for easing the main for a split second makes the difference between tracking straight or rounding up; the vang has much more de-powering potential than does the mainsheet.

I feel you should add a second genoa halyard, and lead it to the same side as the first. You will need only one cabin top winch for proper halyard tensioning.

Tune. Running backstays, although they are not allowed by some classes and manufacturers, help effectively maintain headstay tension in conditions such as light slop or heavy seas. But be careful not to overbend the spar (put-

ting a big luff curve in the main) while the runners are tight. The opposing forces could easily promote gear failure.

Mast rake will differ with each type boat, and you can usually get an approximate position from the builder or a sailmaker who is familiar with the class. Measure the rake by hanging a weight from the halyard and measuring the distance between the object and the mast at deck level on the cabin top.

After you determine headstay length, and with the lowers and backstay slack, tighten the upper shrouds until there is a small compression bend aft and the mast is in the center of the cabin top hole. Then tighten the lowers to

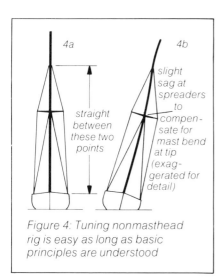

4a

straight between these two points

4b

slight sag at spreaders to compensate for mast bend at tip (exaggerated for detail)

Figure 4: Tuning nonmasthead rig is easy as long as basic principles are understood

straighten the mast (Fig. 4a). When a rig is properly tuned, the leeward shrouds will never have any slack. The boat will point higher for the headstay will not sag off after easing the backstay.

You may have trouble keeping the mast straight when the lowers are let off to take excess luff curve out of the main. While you are under sail, check the lowers again for tune. Make half-turn adjustments with the turnbuckles to align the rig. When you sight up the mast, you should see a slight sag to leeward at spreader height when you are sailing in light-to-medium breezes (Fig. 4b). This will compensate for any bend-off at the mast tip. The spar will straighten out again because of stay stretch and mast bend in heavy air and allow the tip to fall off, opening the slot and de-powering the main.

You should block the mast at deck level in the neutral position, both fore and aft and sideways. To discourage low mast bend, block it farther back, and vice versa. By stopping all movement at deck level, it is much easier to seal off water leakage. Blocking also means you get immediate effects from both mast bend and vang tension.

Mainsail trim. Sail trim is not an exact science. Although every sailor has different ideas, keep in mind three basic concepts.

● The draft of the main moves aft as the wind increases.

● When on the wind, the main should be flattened and the draft brought forward.

● When off the wind, the main should be made fuller and cupped.

Use your leech cord to help set the roach properly in light air, particularly when you are sailing off the wind. Tightening the leech cord will tip the battens to windward, cupping the sail. Always leave the leech cord slack for upwind work, applying only enough tension to remove flutter.

When you are on the wind, sight up past the boom and adjust the trim so the top batten is parallel with the boom. Remember that mainsails require less mast bend in light air than in a blow. Also in light airs, start with a slack outhaul. Pull the wrinkles out in medium air, and put the clew out at the black band in winds above 18 knots or so. This keeps the bottom of the sail flat and moves the draft position down. The mainsail cunningham works the same way: let it completely off in light air; have enough tension to remove the wrinkles in eight-to-10 knots; and increase tension with increased velocity to flatten the sail and pull the draft forward counteracting the effects of mast bend.

Headsail trim. The genoa requires careful shaping of the sail for maximum lift or power. This sail shape also affects the genoa's interaction with the mainsail and the potential to achieve the perfect *slot.* The genoa should maintain a smooth general appearance. Only minor wrinkles should extend from the clew, tack and head. From head to foot, the sail should be uniform, with no bumps.

To determine your correct lead position, watch the telltales breaking along the luff, and adjust the lead so they all flutter at once when you come onto the wind. The leech of the genoa should be flat, not hooked to windward; this allows the sail to release air smoothly. You can accept a very small amount of curl in the leech edge if it's caused by a tight leech cord, but keep it to a minimum.

Never let the maximum draft or camber in the sail move farther than halfway back from the luff. Usually the draft should be between 35 and 45 percent aft; it varies with wind and sea conditions. A tighter halyard moves the draft forward.

The slot between main and genoa is extremely important. A properly trimmed slot (Fig. 5a) shows the leech of the genoa parallel to that of the main. This is optimum configuration for it helps the main increase its power and drive. Too wide a slot (Fig. 5b) creates drag, as the wind backwashes on the mainsail, and a genoa with too narrow a slot (Fig. 5c) causes the main to stall as a large amount of air pushes on the leeward side of the main in its attempt to pass through the narrow opening.

In classes that permit it or in Midget Ocean Racing Club (MORC) competition, use a 170-percent genoa from zero to 10 knots, 12 knots at the most. Always have a slack luff from zero to four knots and increase the tension with the wind velocity to properly position the draft, as on the mainsail. At 12 knots, switch to a 150-percent genoa (though this will vary from class to class) with enough halyard tension to remove wrinkles along the luff. Again, the idea is to increase luff tension with wind velocity.

Watch the space between the tip of the spreader and the leech of the genoa for a useful guide to trim. Keep the sail farther off the spreader in light air and when you are driving for power. Never bring it in closer than four inches from the spreader for maximum flattening and pinching.

As the wind increases and overpowers the boat, change down to an even smaller headsail, probably a 100-percent genoa, before reefing the main. Traveler movement on the main now becomes the key to balance. As the wind continues to increase, it's time to start reefing the main. Start with the flattening reef and, when necessary, add a full reef. Some "touchier" boats may call for mainsail reefing much earlier.

Spinnaker trim. The 0.75-ounce triradial spinnaker is a good all-purpose spinnaker for this kind of boat. If you prefer a one-spinnaker inventory, have

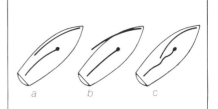

Figure 5: (a) properly trimmed genoa; (b) genoa out too far; (c) genoa in too far, mainsail is backwinded

your sailmaker cut this sail a bit flatter than normal; it's a good compromise between a reacher and a runner. If you prefer two spinnakers, then I suggest either a 0.5-ounce triradial or radial head cut fuller for running and a 1.5-ounce starcut or triradial cut flatter for heavy air conditions. It depends on what conditions you expect most frequently. In either case, modify the 0.75-ounce triradial spinnaker so it becomes fuller or flatter to complement the additional sail.

On a J-24-type boat the spinnaker performs best with the pole cocked up only a few degrees with respect to the horizon. You may want to go up more on heavy-air reaches to de-power the sail and down as far as the bow pulpit in very light winds. When you are reaching in winds above around 12 knots, ease the halyard off about 12 inches to get the head of the sail away from the mast and open up the slot between the leech of the spinnaker and the mainsail. Ideally, the height of the tack and clew should be the same, which may mean pulling the leeward twing tighter as the apparent wind moves aft. While running, pull both twings down tightly. In heavy airs, this greatly increases stability and control.

Mark the topping lift in the up position for easy reference. You can put a telltale yarn on the topping lift about 18 inches above the pole; the crew can read it when they are flying the sail and keep the wind perpendicular to the pole.

What about staysails and bloopers?

They aren't legal under some one-design rules, but are they useful under other rating systems? There has been little proof one way or the other. At no time have I seen a staysail provide extra speed. Therefore, until someone goes screaming by me, I discourage their use.

I have had a similar experience with a blooper. Aboard *Oz*, a J-24, in the MORC Internationals, I saw no one display any increased speed with a blooper. At one point, near the end of the long-distance race, we sailed for 10 miles between two other J-24s who had bloopers and waited to see if the bloopers helped. As it turned out, we had to wait until the finish line to find out, and we actually slid in front of them both. The only time I believe a blooper works is above 15 knots of wind; then it makes an already stable ride even more stable.

Marking sheets and lines. After initial tuning, mark each sheet where it exits the block. As you become more familiar with the boat and sails, you can relate to these marks instead of always looking at the sails. This is especially helpful when you don't want to take someone off the rail. Mark the mainsheet and backstay for the same reasons.

Marking spinnaker sheets helps during reach-to-reach gybes. When a person knows the position of the marks and is setting the new guy, he or she merely eases the sail to the mark without guessing or struggling during the gybe. With a good crew on the pole, this method makes for clean gybes and leaves the spinnaker sheet handler's only concern keeping the sail full.

Also mark all genoa and spinnaker halyards so the hoister knows when the sail is up. This is especially helpful for the spinnaker since it can get very difficult to hoist if it fills on the way up.

Crew weight. Boats of the small, non-masthead rig respond best upwind with crew weight positioned basically amidships. The skipper should move as far forward as possible in the cockpit. But if the wind gets strong enough to make the seas a problem, everyone should move back one position. Downwind,

put the weight well forward in light air. Then, if the boat begins to surf, move aft. When you are reaching, concentrate weight around the middle of the boat, but move it aft as the wind picks up and you begin surfing.

Sail care. Always store your sails dry and folded. If you dry your sails on a lawn, try to keep them from flapping. Never dry spinnakers from the top of a mast except in very light breezes. Fold genoas so the luff tape stacks on top of itself. Then fold the clew toward the tack. When you are sailing and dump the sail on the foredeck, all the luff tape will be next to the headstay, ready to set.

Ultraviolet rays from the sun will eventually destroy sail thread and cloth coating, so store your sails out of the sun. If you leave the mainsail on the boat, flake it over the boom and cover it.

Rinse off dirt and salt regularly. Use a light detergent for the worst spots; simply spread the sails out and gently scrub the surface with a soft brush. Then rinse them well with fresh water and let them dry. Spinnakers should only be rinsed, never with soap. Never use a washing machine or dryer, and never try to iron sails. I do not recommend using any acid, bleach, or other harsh chemicals on your sails.

Even if you have taped every possible cotter pin or obstacle, you still may tear your sails. Look after sail damage immediately. Ripstop tape is great and so is duct tape. Always carry a roll of something.

Carefully check your sails on a regular basis. Check the stitching, D-rings, grommets, batten pockets, leech and foot cords, and all luff tapes. Reinforce all areas that are chafing, and if anything needs repair, fix it before you put it away so you're all ready to go for the next race.

You may not win every race if you follow these suggestions, but you certainly won't lose them. And with just a little work, you should consistently place at the top of the fleet.

An Unusual Telltale Tale

Sailing upwind by constant angle of heel　　　　　　　　John Bertrand

When I'm in fresh wind conditions I use my jib telltales not to tell me if I'm pointed in the right direction when I'm sailing to windward but to tell me whether I have the correct sail shape for windward conditions. My reasoning stems from the following concept:

All boats have an ideal angle of heel when they are sailing hard on the wind. For a light planing dinghy, this is somewhere around five degrees; for a displacement dinghy—a Finn perhaps—it's 10 degrees; and for a keelboat it could be as high as 28 degrees. In any case, no matter what type dinghy or boat you have, your best performance will be achieved if this ideal heel angle is held *absolutely constant* at all times. The boat that is being sailed the steadiest generally is sailing the swiftest (and this is especially true in high-performance dinghies).

I will assume that you have found your boat's optimum heel angle. Now the trick is to adjust your sail shape (and therefore the heeling power) so that when the boat is sailing with its jib telltales streaming, the boat maintains this particular angle of heel.

Let's assume you are sailing in a Soling in 20 knots of wind. I would guess that 15 degrees of heel angle would be pretty good when you are going to windward. If your mainsail happens to be too full, you must feather the boat to windward to stop it from heeling more than 15 degrees. When you are doing this, the weather telltales will lift continuously (Fig. 1). But if you can flatten the main and bend the mast by tightening the backstay and if you can use more boom vang to increase bend down low and open the lower leech area, the mainsail de-powers very effectively. The jib headstay is also tightened because of increased backstay tension; this, in turn,

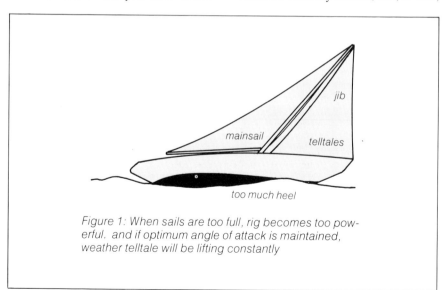

too much heel

Figure 1: When sails are too full, rig becomes too powerful, and if optimum angle of attack is maintained, weather telltale will be lifting constantly

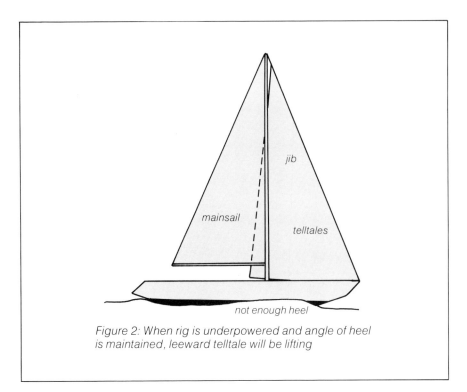

Figure 2: When rig is underpowered and angle of heel is maintained, leeward telltale will be lifting

flattens the jib and further de-powers the rig. But if you de-power too much, you now find that to maintain this 15-degree angle of heel you must sail too low which you will know because the leeward telltales will start lifting on the jib (Fig. 2).

When correct power is obtained in the sails, you will have the ideal condition: the weather telltales are breathing; you have a 15-degree angle of heel; and the whole configuration will be as shown in Figure 3.

So my whole approach to using telltales is based on this angle of heel. In fresh conditions, a helmsman should not be using the telltales to show his course to windward, but he should use them to see whether he needs to de-power or power up his rig. When you are on the wind, your course indicator is actually the heel angle.

When I am on an ocean racer, I never even look at the telltales. Instead, I fix my eyes on the horizon and steer the boat to maintain a constant angle of heel. Then I ask the crew about the jib telltales. If the windward ones have

been lifting continuously, we attempt to flatten the sails. If this is not enough, we then de-power either by reefing the mainsail or by changing down to a smaller headsail.

Conversely, if the leeward telltales are lifting and we are at the desired heel angle then we immediately power up the sails. Remember that it is better to have the weather telltales lift a little.

When this magic combination of heel angle and sail shape is finally achieved, the boat starts to find its own groove and it almost feels as if you are sailing on a set of monorails. The boat's action will become extremely steady with a minimum of rudder action required to keep it sailing high and fast.

Occasionally you see photographs of champions sailing their boats while they are looking over their shoulders at the fleet. Although this is not really a good practice, rest assured that while they have been looking around, their boats have not been sailed either too high or too low. Instead the boats are exactly in the groove at all times because the angle of heel that is transmitted through the

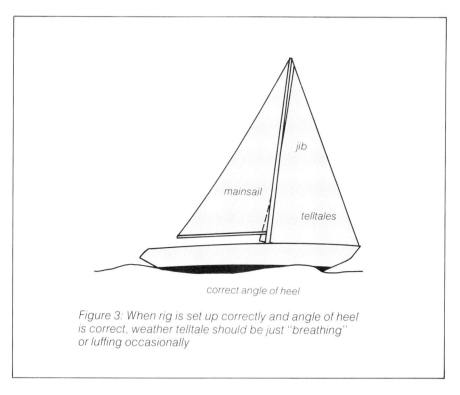

correct angle of heel

Figure 3: When rig is set up correctly and angle of heel
is correct, weather telltale should be just "breathing"
or luffing occasionally

helmsmen's backsides tells them the course they should steer. And when they do look forward, they don't look at the telltales. For them, the indicator is the relative angle of the forestay or mast to the horizon. They have found what that precise angle is from many hours of practice—and they keep the angle constant.

To de-power sails:

• Increase mast bend via backstay or other rigging combination or remove chocks at deck level on small boats;

• Move boom to leeward via traveler;

• Increase cunningham tension to move draft forward and open upper leech.

So there you are. Try to figure out exactly what the ideal angle of heel is for your boat and then try to sail it at that angle in all conditions. If you can think to do that first and then use your telltales to tip you off as to whether your sails are too full and need to be de-powered or if they are too flat and need more draft, you will be well along the road to getting your boat in the best groove.

Crew Work Makes the Difference

Get acquainted with your sails   Philip Marriner

Preparing for an offshore race or cruise requires planning. And proper planning means paying attention to every last detail in advance. I am assuming you have approached the selection of boat and sails by seeking expert advice from manufacturers, dealers, knowledgeable sailors, and sailmakers and you are now at the state where you must learn the capabilities of your boat, gear, sails and crew to assure a safe and fast voyage. Or perhaps you are at the stage where the yearly review of these things is necessary and profitable in terms of race victories and sailing pleasure.

Either to learn or review these capabilities *you must sail.* If you are a racing skipper, racing isn't necessary at this stage, but sailing in your home waters in all kinds of conditions is essential. This, of course, is *practice.* Without practice, you will not know what sails and/or sail combinations work best in a given condition. Without practice, sail setting and trimming become exercises in trial and error that can cost you a race, or can create hazardous circumstances while you are cruising. Without plenty of practice, you will be unsure of the capabilities of your boat and crew.

The best way to prepare is to set up a practice session schedule. For our family-crewed MORC racer/cruiser *Fun* we set a goal each year, before we go racing offshore, of 25 to 40 hours total practice. These hours are broken into equal parts of: (1) light-air practice of zero-six

knots (2) medium-air practice of six-20 knots (3) heavy-air practice of 20-35 knots.

During each session we sail *upwind* two thirds of the time, *reach* and *run* the other one third. Practice sessions are very intensive, well planned and properly recorded. We put in our total hours by sailing evenings and weekends during April and May in whatever the weather eastern Long Island has at that time of the year. Wind is generally abundant but also we manage to get in our light-air practice in early morning or evening.

As part of our race practice (and also helpful for cruising), we make certain all sails and sail combinations are tried and recorded. And we carefully record all trim positions and speeds in varying wind conditions and headings. We also carefully study sail shape, sail condition, rig and hardware layout and we change anything if we find a better, quicker, or safer way of accomplishing a task. We do not curtail our practice because of impending darkness or fog because a good part of our sailing/racing time is done under these conditions, and this is part of being prepared.

Our navigator, my wife Jeanne, has the responsibility of recording everything learned in these sessions so that we have a guide when similar conditions arise. If you do not have a "built in" crew, arrange mutually convenient dates with your crewmembers for practice sessions. Stick to your schedule for you will probably meet with a variety of conditions over a three- or four-weekend period. Set the date, time and place to be on board, make sure you are there promptly, and that you have provisioned properly for the length of time scheduled to sail. A hungry crew is inefficient. To illustrate some typical practice sessions, I've chosen examples from our own logs over the past few years.

For most of our practice sessions, son Blake is on the helm and my wife and I hoist the sails and trim. Daughter Gayle joins us when she can and we fill in with other crews as needed.

Light-Air Practice: If the breeze is under five knots, we hoist the main and a 1.6-ounce light-air headsail using special light sheets. The jib is carefully adjusted for luff tension and lead location. The lead is moved until we have approximate equal tension on both leech and foot. The luff tension is adjusted so that the maximum draft is located about 45 percent of the chord from luff to leech and we use our luff telltales to check that the sail breaks approximately evenly. We mark the halyard; we mark the light-air genoa sheet; we mark the lead position. We carefully note how far the genoa leech is carried off the spreader tip and to help us, the underside of our spreaders are marked with painted stripes two inches apart to judge distance aloft more easily. We set up both jib leads the same, and all this is recorded by my wife, the navigator.

Mainsail adjustment comes next. This requires easing off the outhaul and halyard to the point where no puckers appear and the draft is approximately 50 percent aft of the luff. Then we adjust the traveler to weather of center and trim the mainsheet only hard enough to trim the sail and to keep an open leech aloft. Again, the outhaul, halyard, traveler, and mainsheet are marked and recorded.

We now sail *upwind* and make minor adjustments in sheet and halyard trim and carefully note speed changes, Windex pointing angle changes, and changes in "feel." We know there is a limit for the jib and we discover where

that is as the wind increases, we can no longer control the draft location, and it moves aft.

We record the wind speed carefully and change to the number one 170-percent genoa, repeating the same process of setting and trimming as we did for the first jib.

With the number one genoa set, we practice tacking in light air and assign crew responsibilities for each maneuver. We carefully record who is responsible for what and the composite of our practice session becomes the basis for the *crew assignment list* for the forthcoming racing season.

Our allotted upwind time completed, we go to a *narrow reach*—too narrow to set a spinnaker. We try a tall 110-percent staysail with the genoa, again carefully set and record trim locations, boat speed responses, etc. On the same course, we then set a spinnaker, recording how many degrees on the compass we have to fall off course. We record pole height, and if light or heavier sheets are used, the breeze strength. We check the speed and this exercise tells us whether we can carry a chute more effectively than a double-head-rig combination.

Reaching time completed, we head downwind. In light/medium-air running it is important to discover through practice if it is more advantageous for your particular boat to reach downwind and gybe over *or* to sail dead before the wind with a blooper. We try the blooper and find that it is not effective under five knots of true wind, so we reach downwind and cover more distance in the same time which indicates this is our faster point of sailing in light conditions downwind.

In light air, we are careful to use light sheets when necessary and to properly identify sheet leads for various sails and halyard tensions, you should have marks on the deck, marks on the mast, and halyard reference marks.

With six to 20 knots of true wind we have *medium-air conditions* and in the spring, we are able to get in good practice sessions on the weekends. Once again, we put the boat on all points of sailing. Upwind, we test the mainsail to see when to ease the traveler, when to use the jiffy reef. We also determine limits of the 170-percent genoa and when to switch to our 150-percent full-hoist genoa. Using the same meticulous methods as in our light-air practice, we carefully record heel angle, boat speed, and apparent-wind angle with various sail combinations.

Reaching in medium air, we fly our super star and number one genoa or staysail and carefully note at what angle and wind strength we are overpowered. This determines use and trim of staysail and chute effectiveness.

Running, we use our maximum chute and blooper in the medium-air range. We practice sail trim, wave riding, and we make certain not to oversteer. We also practice gybing the chute, chute sets, and chute takedowns.

In heavy air (20-35 knots) you can get all your practice in one long session but make sure you treat your crew to some refreshments when you're back ashore—they'll need it after a long session of heavy-air practice. Don't skip this session though. You may encounter survival conditions while racing or cruising, and it is imperative you know your boat and crew at this time!

Checking our logs for this article, I discovered that during the past four years we have been out practicing several times in winds over 40 knots. The first time I suggested going out in these conditions I encountered a full-scale crew mutiny. The crew has since admitted that practice in extreme conditions did pay off since we have sailed in these conditions in several long-distance races and have used our heavy-air experience to advantage. We proceed basically in the same manner: by trying sails and recording results.

Upwind, we use the 150-percent genoa and the blast jib, and discover which is the right sail for maximum speed, and when to change. For the main, we study when it is most effective to have in one or two jiffy reefs, and

with what headsail. We have found that it is generally better to sail with more main and someone on the traveler easing out in the puffs, than sailing with too little main and a lee helm.

Reaching, we find we cannot use any spinnaker without overpowering the boat until the breeze is well aft. Therefore, we practice with the staysail and various headsail combinations to get the point of sail until we reach conditions where we can fly our super star.

Running, we again use our maxi-chute until we get into control problems and then we change to the super star. We are not afraid to change chutes by setting the new chute inside the existing chute because we have gone through this drill innumerable times.

The more you sail in heavy air, the more confidence you and your crew will gain. We have found a double-reefed main and a reefed blast jib are extremely effective storm sails up to 50 knots. After that, true storm sails are needed.

To summarize the preparation necessary for fast, safe, offshore racing or cruising: First, spend a total of at least 30 hours beforehand sailing in a variety of combinations and note which combinations increase or decrease speed. And in the case of cruising comfort, make sure all your sails are properly reinforced to avoid excessive stretch or chafe. Finally, mark each sail bag with pertinent notes and type a list to be posted in the cabin.

In addition to recording all sail settings and trimmings you should post your crew assignments. Don't forget to practice man-overboard drills, navigation, and so forth, in an all-out effort to be prepared.

If you have faithfully practiced, when the big race or cruise arrives you will be well acquainted with your boat, your sail inventory, and your crews' capabilities. All that then remains is to get yourself up either to win the race, or to enjoy the cruise.

Balance

Fundamentals of Weather and Lee Helm

Some reasons and cures for excesses   Steve Colgate

Heeling causes *weather helm*, the tendency for a sailboat to round up into the wind when the tiller or wheel is released. The more a sailboat heels the stronger the weather helm becomes. Look at Photo I. The crew is keeping the boat level by hiking out to windward. Now look at Photo II. The crew is inside the boat, the boat is heeling and is not moving through the water very well. But there are other reasons for weather helm.

Sails pull a sailboat forward and sideways when it is going to windward. The hull and keel shape are designed to resist or counteract these side pressures in the sails, allowing the boat to move *forward* through the water with a mini-

mum of resistance. Thus, if the forces that push the boat sideways and those that resist that force are in line, the boat is *balanced* and will sail straight. If the sail area, and therefore the side force, are too far forward compared to the keel location, the bow of the boat will be blown away from the wind; and the result is *lee helm*. Weather helm results from the opposite situation.

To see how this works, Figure 1 shows a masthead fly rigged like a weather vane with a cardboard cutout of a mainsail and jib placed near the fly's center of rotation. In sailing we call this center of rotation the *center of lateral resistance*. This center is the centerpoint of all the underwater surfaces of

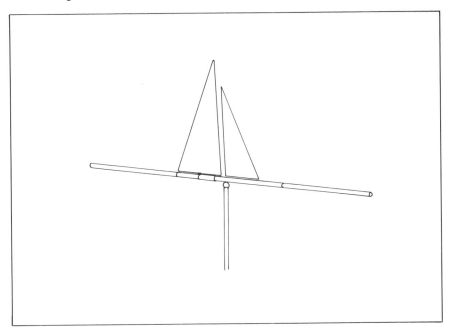

Figure 1: Mainsail and jib are placed at center of rotation

Photo 1: Crew to windward keeps boat sailing level, or flat, which keeps weather helm to minimum

the boat. For years people have found a rough way to find this center by cutting a cardboard profile of the underwater design of the boat. The point where the piece of cardboard is balanced on the head of a pin is the center of lateral resistance (CLR).

If we can find a central point for the underbody surface resisting the water, we must also have a central point for the surfaces resisting the air—the sails. This is called the *center of effort* (CE) and is found by drawing a line from each corner of the sail to the mid-point on the opposite side of the sail. Where the lines intersect is the center of effort of the sail. To find the center of effort of the total sail plan of a sloop, draw a line between the centers of effort of the main and jib. The total center of effort is along that line, a distance proportional to the respective areas of the sails. For example, if the main is twice the size of the jib, then the total center of effort is two thirds of the distance toward the main's center of effort from the jib's center of effort as in Figure 4.

Once you have elevated the center of effort and the center of lateral resistance, you would expect that if the two are in exact alignment, one above the other, the boat would be balanced. Actually, naval architects have found that the center of effort has to be forward of

Photo 2: Crew weight moved inboard allows boat to heel, which increases weather helm

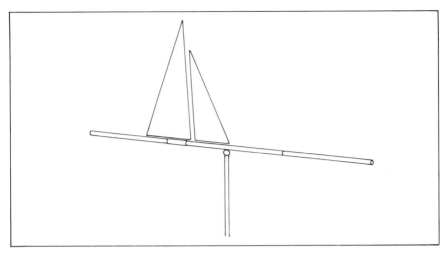

Figure 2: Sails placed well aft of center of rotation

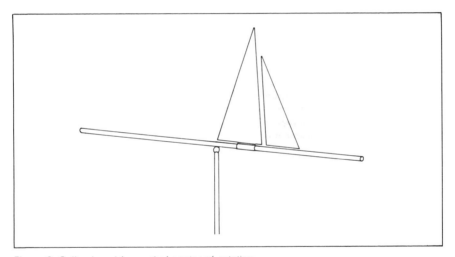

Figure 3: Sails placed forward of center of rotation

the center of lateral resistance a certain distance, called *lead*, for the boat to balance.

Figure 2 shows the sails attached well aft of the center of rotation of the masthead fly. It should seem obvious to you that blowing on this sail will cause the masthead fly to rotate toward the source of the wind. The same thing happens on a sailboat when the center of effort is brought aft by adding extra sail area near the stern. This causes weather helm.

In Figure 3 the sail is well forward of the center of rotation. This simulates a sailboat with a large jib that brings the center of effort forward to the center of lateral resistance. A wind blowing on these sails will tend to rotate the bow to leeward.

So you can see that another reason for weather or lee helm is the position of the sail plan and its center of effort relative to the center of lateral resistance. The center of effort can be fairly easily moved by one or more of the following procedures.

Add more sail area forward or aft on a

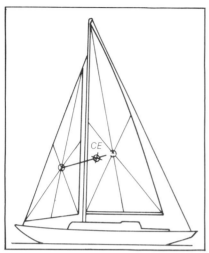

Figure 4: Locate the center of effort of the sails by drawing line from each corner of sail to midpoint on opposite side. Where lines intersect is center of effort. Total center of effort is along line distance proportional to respective areas of sails

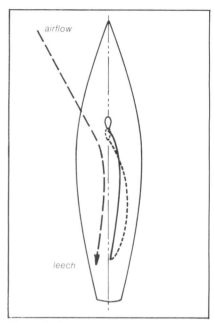

Figure 6: Freeing leech allows air to exit without pushing leech to leeward and this reduces possibility of excess weather helm

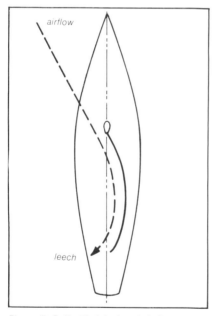

Figure 5: Sail with tight leech deflects air to windward and increases weather helm

permanent basis. A boat with weather helm can add a bowsprit and larger jib. A boat with lee helm might consider in-creasing the length of the main boom, or might consider replacing a mizzen mast with a taller one thereby increasing the size of the mainsail and mizzen.

Change sail area on a temporary basis. Reef the main for a strong weather helm, though you also ought to think about reducing weather helm by reducing the heeling. To reduce lee helm think about setting a smaller jib.

Change the effectiveness of the sails on a temporary basis. Reaching, for example, is a point of sail that often results in increased weather helm. By luffing the main or mizzen it can be greatly reduced.

Free the leech of the sails, particularly the main. Figure 5 shows how the air exits from a main with a tight leech. The reaction from the air that is forced to curve to windward is to force the leech of the sail to leeward and this causes weather helm. By freeing the leech, as in Figure 6, the air exits without having to push the leech to leeward. You can do this by bending the mast—bowing it forward in the middle to flatten the sail as the mast moves forward. The dotted lines in Figure 6 show the original mast and sail location. You can also get a more free leech by easing the mainsheet tension off, though this mainly affects the leech near the head of the sail. Tightening the outhaul will help to free the leech in the lower part of the main.

Move the mast forward or aft. This is an easy task on small boats, but changing the mast position on a cruising boat can be a very expensive, time-consuming task.

Rake the mast. Usually this is a simple operation that involves lengthening the headstay and shortening the backstay. By raking the mast aft, the center of effort moves aft and lower and this helps reduce heeling, for both the main boom and jib foot get closer to the deck at their after ends.

So far we have considered moving the center of effort only in relation to the center of lateral resistance; but the reverse also is possible. The center of lateral resistance also can be moved by exposing more hull, forward or aft or more centerboard area, to the water. By moving crew weight or equipment forward in the boat, the bow submerges farther and the stern lifts out. The center of lateral resistance moves forward relative to the center of effort, and

weather helm is thereby increased. Moving crew weight aft sinks the stern and raises the bow—with the opposite effect. When a centerboard swings down, its tip describes an arc. When halfway down, the tip is angled aft and most of the board area is located aft of where it would be in a vertical position. This means the center of lateral resistance is aft of its location when the board is all the way up or down. If the center of effort of the sails remains in the same spot, weather helm is reduced. On reaches, weather helm is reduced on centerboard boats by raising the board halfway. The more it is raised, the farther aft the center of lateral resistance goes. But a large percentage of board starts to disappear into the centerboard trunk above the halfway mark. The result is more leeway, just what the board is designed to prevent. It then becomes a trade-off between the slower speeds caused by weather helm rudder drag, and the extra distance you have to sail and the hull-crabbing that is caused by leeway.

It can be great fun to learn about, and then fiddle with, ways to balance the helm of your sailboat. When you know enough about it, even thinking about the loss of your rudder shouldn't disturb you much because you'll know how to steer your boat with just your sails.

Steering without a Rudder

Learn to hold course by sails alone

Steve Colgate

Shortly after we had sailed the 58′ yawl *Dyna* 1000 miles after losing the rudder during the 1963 Transatlantic Race a person asked me, "Did you carry a spare?" Though you can have spares of just about everything else, any sailor knows a rudder is one spare item that would be very impractical to carry, in addition to its being almost impossible to replace.

For that reason, unless you have a cruising boat with a trim-tab, you should consider that some day, if you sail enough, you will lose either your steering or your rudder. That is why I think it is so important that everyone learn how to sail without using the rudder. Learning to sail without a rudder gives you a much better understanding of how much the sails really do affect the steering of a sailboat. You will be-

gin to understand that if your steering starts to get difficult, don't fight it, just change your sail trim.

The first thing to understand is balance. If a boat is balanced, she will sail straight ahead when you release the helm. If she turns to windward rather than sailing straight, she has *weather helm,* and if she turns to leeward she has *lee helm* (Fig. 1).

Weather helm is more common, because heeling affects helm. Any heel to leeward helps create weather helm; and heeling to windward helps create lee helm. One reason for this is the shape of the "heeled" hull that is in contact with the water.

Imagine a heeling boat. Now imagine a gigantic saw has cut it right off at the level of the water. The hull of the lee side is large and beamy, but to wind-

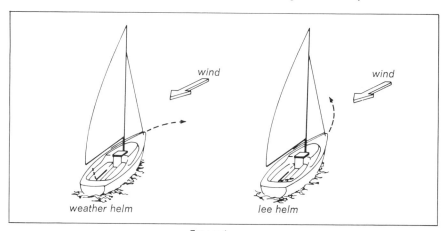

weather helm   lee helm

Figure 1

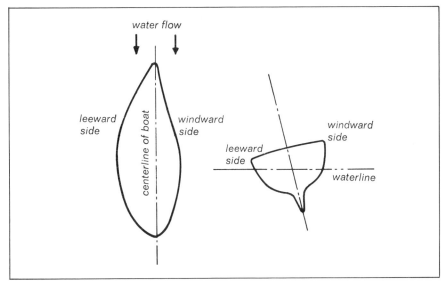

Figure 2

ward of the centerline, the hull will be narrow and the hull area (in cross-section) looks roughly like Figure 2. This shape exposes much more curved area on the lee side and because such an asymmetrical shape can't go straight ahead, it forces the bow to windward.

Another cause of weather helm when a boat is heeled comes from the force on the sails. Because this force is out over the water when the boat is heeling (instead of directly over the hull), it tends to rotate the boat away from the direction of heel.

This can be easily simulated on a small boat in light air. Release the tiller and have the whole crew hike out hard to windward. If the wind is light enough to enable the boat to heel to windward, she should start to turn downwind. Now

Figure 3

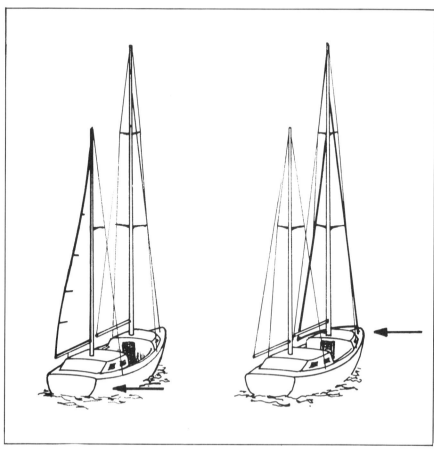

Figure 4: Jib and mizzen, when sheeted in can control direction of bow and stern

do the opposite and place the crew on the lee side; the boat should start to turn toward the wind (Fig. 3).

You can control steering in other ways with crew weight placement. If you all move way forward in the boat and dig the bow more deeply into the water the boat should turn to windward. This occurs because the center of lateral resistance (CLR) of the hull moves forward in relation to the center of effort (CE) of the sails. Of course, the lee side curve in Figure 2 becomes even more pronounced as the bow digs more deeply. Conversely, if you all stand in the stern, this should help turn the boat to leeward.

Certainly the most positive steering control does come from sail trim. On most small sailboats, if you leave the mainsail off and only raise the jib you are going to have a strong lee helm. The bow will be *blown* to leeward because the sail is way forward. The other extreme is to raise only the mizzen on a yawl or ketch. Obviously, this pushes the stern to leeward and causes a strong weather helm (Fig. 4).

Somewhere between these two extremes you can have a balanced boat that will sail straight ahead and here are some more examples.

Take a small boat with both main and jib set. If you luff the main and thereby reduce its effectiveness, the jib will force the bow off (particularly if you trim the jib hard and overflatten it). Conversely, if you luff the jib and trim

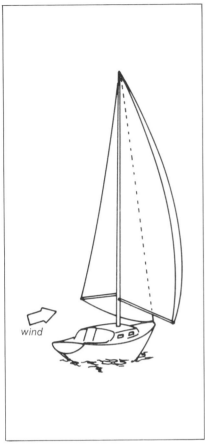

Figure 5: Raise main and jib at same time to keep one from overpowering the other

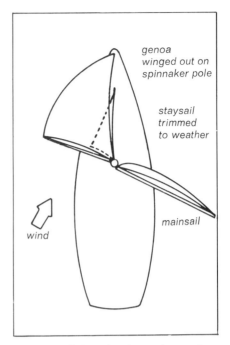

genoa winged out on spinnaker pole

staysail trimmed to weather

mainsail

wind

Figure 6: If boat heads up (to port) staysail backs before the genoa and forces the bow back downwind

the main, you will turn the boat to windward.

Once you know this, you can practice steering without a rudder. Get your boat reasonably well balanced and aim it at some buoy or landmark. Trim the jib quite flat and cleat it. Now try to steer the boat using only the mainsheet. To head up, trim the main. To bear off, ease the main. You'll find it difficult to do at first, but after you get the knack, you'll soon be steering a very straight course. It does take some anticipation, because once the boat starts turning one way or the other, it's much harder to make it stop.

Once you have mastered sailing

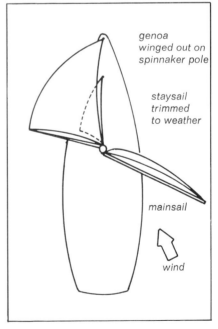

genoa winged out on spinnaker pole

staysail trimmed to weather

mainsail

wind

Figure 7: If boat falls off (to starboard) staysail forces the bow back upwind before main gybes

straight ahead try tacking. Free the jib and trim in the main hard. The boat should round right up into the wind and tack itself. Gybing is a bit more difficult, for just easing the main may not be enough. You may have to back the jib to windward to get the bow moving downwind. You also may have to use some of the other things you've learned that control the boat's direction: hiking all the crew out to windward as far as possible, or moving their weight aft, for example.

On a cruising boat where crew weight has little effect, you must rely totally on sail trim and set. A yawl or ketch is easy to steer on a reach or close hauled when you use only the jib and mizzen. Leave the jib trimmed in one position and ease or trim the mizzen as required to make small course adjustments.

On a really broad reach or on a run, you probably will want more sail area if you hope to get anywhere fast. But when you raise the main, it will give you a strong weather helm and the boat will tend to round up. This can be offset by *winging* the jib out on a spinnaker pole on the other side, but both sails will have to be raised at the same time to keep the boat balanced as the sails are going up (Fig. 5).

Set a staysail, if you have one, amidships. Back it to windward if you want to sail a lower course, or trim it to the middle of the boat if you want to sail a higher one (Fig. 6). This staysail will keep the bow from rounding up, and it also will keep the boat from acciden-

tally gybing (Fig. 7). If you want to gybe on purpose you'll probably have to lower both the main and winged-out jib and use the staysail to alter your course to the other gybe. Then you can raise both main and jib again. The mizzen still can be used for minor course adjustments.

You can steer an excellent course without a rudder even in heavy seas. On *Dyna*, the staysail kept us within 15 degrees of either side of the course, and constant trimming of the mizzen narrowed it down to within 5-10 degrees of course. This was better than we could have done with a helmsman in those seas. Not only were we steering a straight course, we were pegging the knotmeter at 10 knots. It took us 13 days to do the first 2000 miles with a rudder, and six days to do the last 1000 miles without one. In short, we averaged higher speeds without a rudder (in heavier winds).

Practice on your own boat until you have complete control of your boat without touching the helm. This is really so much of what sailing is all about; it's practicing the art of seamanship. From it comes the confidence that you can handle any situation that may arise. But developing that confidence comes from working on exercises like the ones I have described. It is the only way to prepare for the time when a situation like losing your rudder does come up. If you sail long enough, sometime you will need to rely on your sails for steering instead of your rudder.

More Power to You

Efficient sailing with a balanced boat   Philip Marriner

A balanced boat in all conditions is the ultimate goal of any sailor. With a well-balanced helm, your boat's performance, whether racing or cruising, increases tremendously. And with a well performing boat, you get more pleasure out of sailing.

What is boat balance and how is it achieved with sails? Perhaps the quickest way to help you understand the interaction between sails and boat is to suggest you get a small centerboard sloop or centerboard boat such as a Comet, 420, Sunfish or Penguin and sail it without using the rudder. Those of you who have been through this routine know it is one of the most important sailing lessons you can ever take. Those of you who have never tried this delightful exercise have a whole new bag of tricks to uncover.

What does this have to do with getting the best performance out of your offshore racing or cruising boat? Quite a bit. Sailing a small boat without a rudder points out dramatically the interaction between sail trim, weight distribution, and the centerboard.

So borrow a small boat, pick a pleasant light-air day, push off without the rudder attached, and try to reach off on a steady course. You will rapidly discover you need less board and mainsail trim than you thought. You will also find that to stay on course, the boat must be sailed flat.

After you have mastered the boat on a reach, try running. On this point of sail, weight distribution, boat heel, and a raised board keep the boat from rounding up. Once you have both reaching and running under control,

sailing upwind is easy. By trimming sails and distributing your weight properly, you will be surprised at how easily the boat goes to weather.

Does this apply to your 35-foot offshore racing or cruising boat? Yes. By going through this exercise in a small boat you will discover many things. You will learn that sails generally are not eased enough when sailing off the wind. You will learn that by raising the board, you can keep the boat from rounding up. You will also learn that by heeling the boat to windward or leeward, or by placing your weight aft or forward, you can make the boat fall off or round up. You will, in short, have learned a lot about steering a boat with sails and weight distribution instead of using a rudder and tiller.

The next time you go sailing in a breeze, put your boat on the wind. Trim in the genoa and main. Is the tiller up around your neck or is your wheel way over? If so, how can you eliminate this excessive helm and balance your boat? If you can reduce your heel, you will ease the helm, and there are several ways to reduce heel: ease the mainsheet, ease the traveler, reef the main. It is possible to reduce heel by: changing genoa leads, changing genoas, feathering, and sail trim, crew balance and helmsmanship coordination. Other significant factors in achieving boat balance and increasing boat performance involve: mainsail twist, tight leeched main, draft location, adding headsails.

There are even more ways to balance your boat, but that's enough for this article. Let's start sorting them out and see what adjustment is best and when and

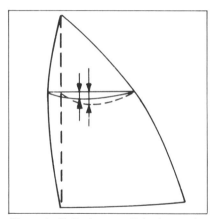

Figure 1: Flattening a sail by increasing mast bend reduces draft

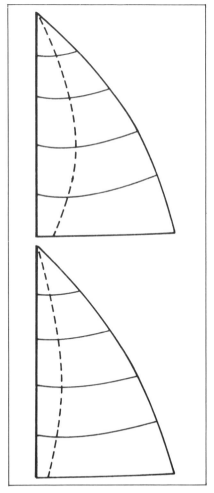

Figure 2: Increasing luff tension moves draft forward

why. At the same time, we'll look at these points not only in relation to sailing on the wind, but reaching and running.

Ease the mainsheet

On the wind one of the most common mistakes is to overtrim the mainsheet. In light air, a full main with a relatively tight leech is desirable. When the breeze comes up and a little backwind starts in

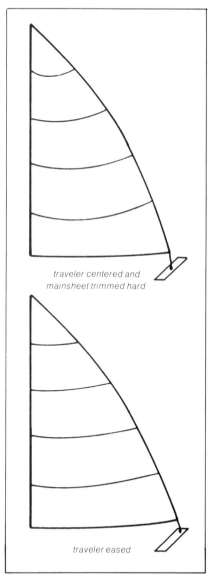

traveler centered and mainsheet trimmed hard

traveler eased

Figure 3: Easing traveler helps flatten main

the mainsail luff area, the tendency is to trim in immediately to stop the back-wind. This makes the boat heel, causing an increase in helm, and your boat is out of balance.

Your first reaction should be to ease the mainsheet. Forget the luff and get your boat on her feet and moving. Then use your adjustments to flatten the main and get the boat back to full power. Some of the adjustments to flatten the sail are: increasing mast bend (Fig. 1), increasing luff tension with a cunning-ham, downhaul, or halyard to move the draft forward and ease the leech section (Fig. 2), easing the traveler (Fig. 3), and reefing the main (Fig. 4).

When reaching you must balance your boat with your sails. How many boats have you seen flying a spinnaker on a reach going from one roundup to another. On this point of sail, it is imperative that you station someone on the mainsheet for quick release every time the boat starts to get out of control. Easing the mainsheet keeps your boat balanced and powered up.

Ease the traveler

On the wind excessive heel slows down your boat by increasing helm and increasing side slippage, so it is essential you do everything you can to reduce side force and get the boat moving forward. By easing the traveler and easing the mainsheet, you also reduce helm and improve speed through the water. The traveler, therefore, is a means of sail trim that must be employed to get the utmost in balancing your boat. Your

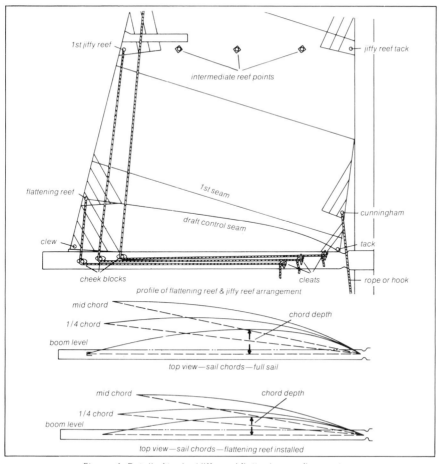

Figure 4: Detail of typical jiffy and flattening reefing systems

traveler should be adjustable to a point where you can trim your boom to the boat's centerline in light air, and to the boat's rail in heavier winds.

Reaching or running when the breeze is up, the main must be out on the traveler, trimmed, and vanged hard to reduce twist and excessive draft aloft.

Reef the main

On the wind, today's modern mainsails use jiffy-reef systems and most racing sails also have a flattening reef (Fig. 4). To balance your boat, reducing mainsail area is necessary if other adjustments do not lead to reduced heel. A flattening reef reduces draft in the lower section and helps lay down the leech. This reduces helm. If you do not have a flattening reef, use your lower reef point. Reducing and flattening the main can put your boat back in balance.

When reaching and your boat is overpowered, leave the reef in, and for maximum speed, reduce only enough sail to make certain you are not carrying so much helm that your rudder acts as a brake (the barn-door effect).

Changing genoa leads

On the wind you can reduce heel by moving your genoa lead aft, which creates twist in the upper leech. Simultaneously, trim the genoa sheet harder, flattening the lower section. If this doesn't reduce helm, then change to a smaller genoa.

When reaching, move the lead forward to keep the leech tighter. This will increase power and lessen helm giving you better balance.

Changing genoas

When the mainsail area is reduced, a genoa that is too large will create a lee-helm condition. This also can happen when the wind increases beyond the capacity of your genoa. Then sail must be replaced or reduced in area (if your genoa has reef points). This is a *major factor* in keeping your boat in balance with sails.

Feathering

Upwind, in relatively smooth water, high wind conditions, the helmsman can help achieve balance by "feathering" carefully up in puffs, coming off slightly in the lulls and maintaining speed. A skilled helmsman can carry more sail than normal for balance and still keep the heel down by feathering. It is something to practice continually.

An increasing breeze causes increased pressure on your sails and results in increased heel. All the adjustments I have mentioned are important in decreasing heel. But it is equally important while reaching or running in a breeze to *keep the boat flat*. This means sails eased when necessary; then trimmed in conjunction with the helm, and crew weight to weather. The helmsman should steer off in hard puffs while running, and come up in the lulls (the reverse of feathering).

So far, I've said that heel affects balance and balance affects speed through the water. The adjustments mentioned so far have all reduced heel and helm. Now let's look at some other factors that help balance a boat and increase its speed.

In a breeze the aim is to reduce heel. But in light air on the wind, your boat probably needs a slight heel to keep the sails on the proper side and to increase the helm to give the boat some *feel*. This should have been one of your discoveries when you learned to sail without a rudder.

If you have read this far, your mind may be boggled. However, if you try each exercise on your boat, then analyze the results, you'll find that your understanding will increase. Then, as you combine these exercises, the pieces will fall in place and you'll be pleased with the increase in your boat's performance and your sailing fun.

Finally, let's examine the rest of the significant factors for achieving boat balance and increasing performance.

Mainsail twist

This is desirable for full power in light air. To get a mainsail to twist, move the traveler to the center line and ease the mainsheet. Twist is essential in order to get a wider apparent-wind angle aloft. In a breeze, air pressure generally produces enough twist so you do not have to overtrim the traveler and ease the sheet. However, in a breeze off the wind, you want reduced twist, and easing the traveler, tightening the vang and mainsheet will accomplish this (Fig. 5).

Tight leech main

A mainsail with a tight leech can increase your helm to a point where it is actually slowing the boat down. The tight leech can be eased by increasing halyard, cunningham, or downhaul tensions and easing mainsheet tension.

Draft location

Draft that is located aft of 50 percent in your sail will increase helm by causing your leech to tighten. Draft located too far forward will flatten the sail too much, causing your boat to lose power. Most modern mainsails are designed to perform with the maximum chord half way between luff and leech and this should be maintained through your adjustments in a wide range of winds. As the breeze increases, draft tends to move aft, and to counteract this, put tension on your luff. As the breeze lightens, draft tends to move forward. If it moves farther forward than 50 percent, ease your luff tension.

Adding headsails

As the breeze lightens, it is necessary to be at full power at all times. Thus, you have to add headsail area. If you are rated to a headsail of a size too small to power your boat properly, you might set a double-head rig and head off slightly to keep your boat moving.

Balancing your boat with sails is not a cut and dried process. It requires time and experimentation and trial and er-

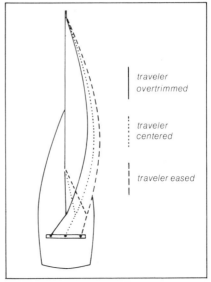

Figure 5: Reducing mainsail twist when reaching involves easing traveler, tightening vang

ror, to find the combination of sails, trimming devices and methods that will produce the ultimate—a balanced boat in all weather and sea conditions on all points of sailing.

There are many combinations of sails that increase—or decrease—speed and balance. But I'd like to close by reemphasizing the importance of that first exercise: sailing a small centerboarder without a rudder. Doing so will help you understand boat balance far better than a hundred diagrams and thousands of words. For once you get that *feel* you have your guideline. Everything else will be more meaningful after you have realized, for yourself, the importance of boat balance.

Maximum Thrust: A Delicate Balance

Trimming headsails in conjunction with the main   Jeremy Howard-Williams

It is pretty well established that the genoa is the vital link in the sailplan when going to windward because it is the leading edge of the combined airfoil that is formed by the jib and main. It follows, therefore, that forestay sag is bad, for it pushes cloth aft into the body of the genoa, which bellies the leech, backwinds the mainsail, and makes the boat less closewinded.

If a mast is allowed to bend forward it almost certainly will ease the tension on the forestay, which then will sag and cause the trouble I have outlined above. Dinghies, Solings, Stars and the like, which have mainsails that are far bigger than their jibs, can use bendy masts with advantage because they can gain more from controlling mainsail shape than they lose because of a slack luff on their small jibs.

However, the average 30-foot sloop does get most of her drive to windward from the genoa, so everything must be directed to the proper setting of that sail.

A hollow mast can work to advantage as a strut in compression, so this is the best way to ensure you have a tight forestay. To achieve this, the forestay should be of such a length that the mast stands with a one- or two-percent rake aft. The backstay then should be tightened until the masthead is bending slightly aft under tension without sails;

the power of the genoa will soon straighten it when the sail is set. A backstay, particularly a hydraulic one, is worth considering in a boat of any real size. Beside the ease of use, it enables a record of tensions to be maintained from the calibration gauge.

Apart from having a slack forestay, the most common fault with mast tune is to have the upper shrouds slacker than the intermediates or lowers. This allows the masthead to sag off to leeward and hampers the efficiency of the airfoil. I won't go into specific tuning practices here because rigs vary widely. However, the results of your static tuning can best be checked by sighting up the mast along the mainsail track. It should not sag off either to port or starboard.

Now take the boat out in smooth water in 10 knots of wind, and continue to check up the track to see that the mast is still straight. If you have running backstays check that they are supporting the mast as they should.

It is hard to generalize about mast rake, for every boat reacts differently. As a rule, however, more rake aft increases weather helm which might help to windward, while an upright spar is said to be best downwind; certainly an upright mast gives you the greatest foretriangle area.

An upright mast also maximizes the

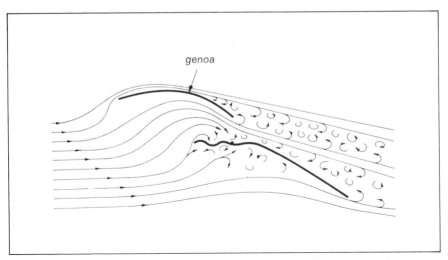

Figure 1: Flow has been pushed aft by the wind. Note how airflow is directed into lee side of mainsail causing turbulence and blockage. A hooked genoa leech would have same effect

separation of the headsail and mainsail, though to be precise there is not a great deal of variation at the small angles we are considering. Only where mast rake becomes excessive do these factors really begin to play an appreciable role. If your boat won't point well, it is more likely to be because of a slack forestay and overly full genoa than a need for more or less mast rake.

If tuning is the semi-permanent arrangement of a boat's rigging to permit optimum setting of sails, sail trim is the minute-to-minute arrangement of the controls that produce those optimum settings. There are two basic points to remember when considering trim: first, the overall smooth flow of air across the airfoil, particularly when going to windward; second the requirement to angle forward the thrust of the airfoils as much as possible and to minimize thrust sideways as much as possible—particularly off the wind.

Smooth Flow. A smooth airflow means having a proper slot, clean entry at the leading edge of the sail, a power point between one third and half way back from the luff, and a flat non-hooking leech. If the leech curls or hooks in, it will divert wind into the lee side of the mainsail and cause turbulence (Fig. 1).

So see that you do have a smooth leech that does not curl in.

Make sure your genoa sheet lead is not led too far inboard or too far forward. There should not be too much tension on the foot, and you can roughly equalize this pull on foot and leech bisecting the angle of the sail at the clew.

Don't let anyone take up permanent residence in the slot between the main and genoa for this will create turbulence.

Forward Thrust. When a boat is sailing closehauled, the helmsman is continually moving the helm, responding to minor windshifts to work the boat to windward. When the boat comes off the wind onto a reaching compass course, those windshifts don't stop happening so it follows that the sails should be constantly trimmed in order to take advantage of any momentary freeing of the wind. I believe it can be said, as a broad generalization anyway, that crews don't ease sails enough when sailing off the wind.

The forces acting on a mainsail and genoa on a close reach can be resolved into heeling moment and forward thrust, in a ratio of about 4:1. If sails can be eased as little as five degrees, and

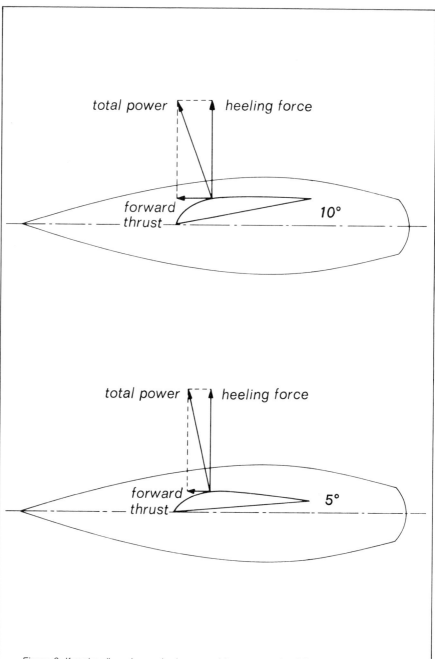

total power   heeling force

forward
thrust   10°

total power   heeling force

forward
thrust   5°

Figure 2: If mainsail angle can be increased from an angle of five degrees to the centerline, to 10 degrees without lifting or altering course, the result is a minor decrease
in heel force and a dramatic in thrust; possibly as much as 50 percent. This assumption does not consider a boat's heading when beating to windward and a closer-
sheeted position may, in fact, be better because of the ability to point higher. This depends largely on wind and sea conditions at the time

still kept full, there will be an improvement in forward thrust by as much as 50 percent, which is accompanied by a small reduction in heeling force (Fig. 2). This is nothing short of dramatic and you should continually be seeking this from both your genoa and mainsail.

Ease off until the sail in question just starts to lift or go "soft," then harden it in slightly. Ease it again as you feel for the point of lift, and keep doing it to both the sails. This is particularly important in light air when any improvement in thrust has a big effect on speed. In brisker winds, the boat probably is already traveling near her maximum speed, so these momentary increases in thrust don't make quite so much difference. But it is still important to make the adjustments.

Spinnaker Trim. Apart from the problems of horizontal and vertical trim (clew height and twist), a conventional spinnaker should be treated just like a large headsail. It does not have the latter's straight luff or flat leech, but the wind still flows across it from luff to leech just as with a headsail, except in a dead run condition, when the wind blows straight into the middle and out of both sides and the foot. The spinnaker, therefore, should be considered in conjunction with the mainsail just as the genoa is.

My remarks about angling an airfoil forward for greater thrust apply with even more force to the spinnaker because it is (relatively) larger and the thrust it exerts is greater. There is also the additional problem of the bellied leech of a spinnaker which can hold a boat back like a brake if it's allowed to pull toward the rear (or stern) on a close reach. This is what makes a spinnaker so rewarding to study. When you get the

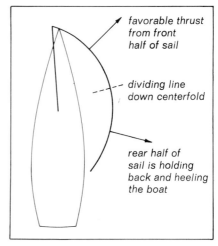

Figure 3: A full spinnaker may well have a bellied leech when sailing on a close reach. The area that is gained over using a genoa will be lost through the after part of the spinnaker which is providing rearward thrust as well as heeling the boat. In such a situation, a genoa or reacher will often be a better sail to use

trim right the results are impressive. But even minor faults in trim can knock a lot of speed off any boat.

One final point, a sailor who is thrashing along on a close reach with his spinnaker pulling and the spray flying, would do well mentally to divide the sail in half down the middle (Fig. 3). Then he should ask himself whether the rear half of the spinnaker is not pulling aft almost as much as the front half is pulling forward. If the answer is yes, a genoa would be a better sail to have up for it will probably heel the boat less— particularly if the wind is blowing above 10-12 knots.

Self-steering by Sails

Some sheet-to-tiller systems   Mike Saunders

Once I was skippering a little 25-foot sloop up the English Channel to London, and the weather was not my only headache. The more serious problem lay in the main bunk, retching and groaning in moving tones. She was the owner of the boat, and had insisted on crewing on the trip to gain experience. Seasickness, unfortunately, had overwhelmed her early on, and it now was clear that, as far as I was concerned, this would be a solo voyage. During the entire trip she uttered only two sentences.

The first, as we crossed the bar, was, "Where is the nearest port?"

I named the nearest convenient port en route (bearing in mind that the boat had no engine), about a third of the way to London.

The second, about 20 hours later, displayed remarkable recall of the previous conversation. "Where," she said, "is the nearest port?"

I sat in the exposed cockpit, shrinking into my oilskins from the wet and the cold like an aging tortoise, concentrating on the course, as far as the unnerving honking of ships in the fog would allow. It was quite obvious that this could not go on for the 36 hours or so it would take to reach port. Apart from anything else, I had to eat and navigate. The boat must be made to steer herself.

First, I tried lashing the helm, but the light little craft was as skittish as a half-broken filly. She wouldn't hold steady for a second. Next, I tried shockcord, but that was no better. Adjusting the sheets helped not at all. The trouble was that we were broad reaching, nearly quartering, and while I had often set up a well balanced boat to sail hard on the wind by herself, this was a most unsteady point of sailing.

Braine Work

Clearly, the mainsheet had to be used to control the tiller somehow. I began fiddling around with the mainsheet and odd lead blocks, but my brain was functioning like congealed pudding.

"Come on brain, you toad!" I exhorted out loud.

Braine! That was the name of the self-steering device used on model yachts, I suddenly remembered. It consists of an aft-pointing tiller quadrant, with the mainsheet tied to one side, and a spring to the other. I set up a similar arrangement, leading the sheet through a block on the windward side, instead of using a quadrant; shock cord was used instead of a spring. The arrangement is shown in Figure 1.

But the boat still wouldn't hold course for more than a few moments, however much I adjusted things. There was only the jibsheet left to try.

By this time night had fallen. I was bone weary, and had lost hope of getting anything to work. I recalled meeting a yacht in Durban which had self-steered across the Indian Ocean, using the staysail sheet on the tiller, and several other long-distance voyagers have used a similar set-up.

In that strength of wind, the pull of the jibsheet was too great a force to go directly to the tiller. So I hitched a line at right angles to the jibsheet and led it to the tiller. Shockcord on the other side of the helm continued to balance the pull of the sheet. The arrangement is shown in Figure 2.

It worked! I waited anxiously for the inevitable luffing up, or bearing away, but the compass held steady. I hurriedly brewed a cup of coffee and darted out again. Still on course! To my astonish-

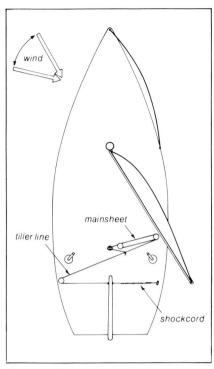

Figure 1: Tiller-sheeting arrangement for use on the wind

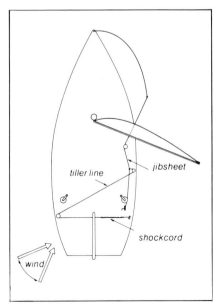

Figure 2: Tiller-sheeting arrangement for use off the wind

ment and relief, the boat held her course right through the night, and through the following day, with only occasional adjustments. The most extraordinary aspect of this self-steering system was that it seemed hardly affected by changes in wind strength. Many of the self-steering gears I had used, even sophisticated production models, tend to alter course with variation in wind strength, as well as wind direction, and frequent adjustment is often required.

But with the sheet-to-tiller arrangement, the pressure of the sails and the helm seems to balance over a wide range of wind speeds. All that night and the next day the wind gradually died away, till we were stealing along at scarcely a knot. Yet the boat held true on her course, even when the jib was slatting about. How this worked, I do not know, but work it certainly did.

Over the following months I experimented with sheet-to-tiller self-steering arrangements, and discovered that, in the main, two systems are required.

1. On the wind, the mainsheet works as in Figure 1.

2. Off the wind, the jibsheet is needed as in Figure 2.

At this point, John Letcher's book, *Self Steering for Sailing Craft* (International Marine Publishers, Co.), became available, and in it a number of things were explained. John Letcher had taken sheet-to-tiller self-steering systems a lot further, and both theory and practice are treated in detail in his excellent book. His system for downwind self-steering, when flying twin headsails, for example, is shown in Figure 3. Instead of fastening the sheets direct to the tiller, which is the usual practice, they are led through tiller blocks, and then to the winches; this makes for rapid and easy adjustment. When quartering, the weather sheet only is used, and balanced by elastic. One is then, in effect, back to system 2.

The most difficult course to steer is on a reach, when the weather helm is most severe. With the tiller hooked up to the mainsheet, the boat tries to insist on sailing a close reach. When the tiller is hooked to the jibsheet, the boat prefers a broad reach. I have found that the best system for reaching is to connect the staysail sheet to the tiller—if you have a staysail. If you haven't, and the boat will not settle down on either system 1 or system 2, then use the system adopted by John Letcher. Here the jib is sheeted to the mainboom, and a tiller line is taken from the mainsheet, as in system 1. In this way, both the headsail and the main control the tiller together.

Incidentally, a two-masted rig presents no problems. The same systems can be used, and a ketch is generally easier to balance—at least on the wind.

Setting It Up

To set up these systems, only the simplest of gear is required: a few odd blocks, preferably with rope tails attached, so that they may be fixed anywhere, and a suitable elastic arrangement, and, of course, enough spare rope.

Adjustment is effected by means of a clove hitch on the tiller but the adjustment on the tiller line is critical; too strong, and she'll bear off, too weak, and she'll luff up. Having a little length adjustment on the elastic allows some variation. The elastic should just be slack when the tiller is a little to leeward. Consequently, the main adjustment to the elastic is its strength, and that is why a system using a number of rubber strands should be able to be used with a clamp; strands may be added or removed as required. Once the adjustments have been made for a particular course, little further attention should be necessary.

System 2 is similar in every way to that which I have described above, except that the tiller line is taken from the jibsheet. Again, the direct pull of the sheet can be too strong, and a tiller line, at an angle to the sheet, is used (Fig. 2). The tiller line may be fixed to the sheet at any convenient point between the clew and the fairlead, or between the fairlead and the winch, provided the latter two are not too close together.

Incidentally, wheel steering does not necessarily rule out sheet steering. I have used sheets tied to the spokes quite successfully, in cases where gearing is not too low, i.e., the movement of the wheel must not be too great, relative to the rudder, or the sheet will lose its horizontal pull. As a rule of thumb, if the boat can be steered satisfactorily on a

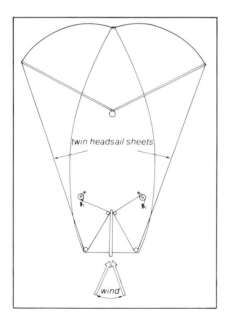

Figure 3: Tiller-sheeting arrangement for use downwind

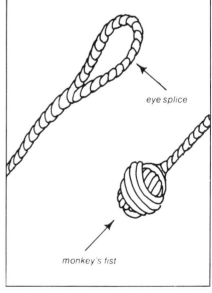

Figure 4: How to make a rope "snap shackle"

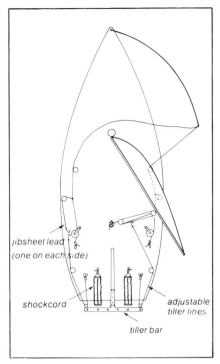

jibsheet lead
(one on each side)

shockcord

adjustable
tiller lines

tiller bar

Figure 5: One possible permanent sheeting arrangement

quarter turn of the wheel, it also can be steered with sheets.

Permanent Sheet to Tiller Steering?

Until recently, I have regarded sheet-to-tiller self-steering as a makeshift measure to be used when sailing short-handed. Recently, however, I have come to think of it more and more as a permanent alternative to vane gear, especially when the owner is penurious, and the boat is small.

What are the advantages and disadvantages of the one system against the other? Much depends, of course, on the layout and geometry of the particular boat, but, in broad terms, the pros and cons can be summarized.

- Sheet-to-tiller systems are cheap and easy. For a few dollars you can buy the gear, and quickly set it up yourself.

- Before installing a permanent system, you can try it out. Many vane gears, on the other hand, do not work par-

ticularly well, for one reason or another, but this is not known until after the expensive installation has been completed. On small boats, and also on ketches, the siting of vane gears is often a problem.

- Sheet-to-tiller arrangements tend to be better helmsmen, in my experience, because they are less affected by wind strength than are vane gears. On the other hand, they are more difficult to set on a particular course often requiring tedious adjustment.

- The most serious drawback with sheet-to-tiller systems, is that they are cumbersome in use. Apart from the fiddling needed every time one tacks or alters course, you are forever tripping over lines that crisscross the boat.

If you are installing a permanent system, however, the last-mentioned drawback can be mitigated, by carefully running tiller lines around, instead of across, the cockpit and side decks. Snap hooks, (for an all-rope snap hook, see Figure 4) for a quick changeover, with Clam cleats or with tiny snub winches for easy adjustment, also contribute to easy use.

One possible permanent installation is suggested in Figure 5. Here, tiller lines are taken from a tiller bar, so there are no ropes trailing across the boat. The tiller lines hook onto the mainsheet, or jibsheet as appropriate, using blocks instead of a rolling hitch. This allows you to adjust the sheets, without adjusting the knots. The length of tiller lines is adjusted on a cleat, after passing round blocks on the tiller bar. And the elastics are also controlled on a cleat.

There are, of course, any number of variations, limited only by the geometry of the particular boat, and by the ingenuity of the inventor. I have no doubt that many will be superior to the one shown in Figure 5. But all, I suspect, will be more cumbersome to use than a vane gear. If you are not prepared to pay this price for reliable simplicity, then sheet self-steering is not for you. If, however, either your budget or boat is small, and your ingenuity large, then you might like to have a go at it.

3

Downwind

Fear of Flying

A novice's guide to overcoming spinnaker apprehension   Steve Colgate

Most beginners try to rationalize away having to use a spinnaker. It's too expensive, they say; or it takes too many crew to handle one. It's only good on runs; it takes too much attention; it rips, wraps, and it throws the boat out of control. And so forth. There are literally hundreds of ways to rationalize what I call *spinnaker avoidance.* Perhaps the best one of all is: if you don't buy a spinnaker or the equipment to fly one, you obviously can't fly one. And if you don't fly a spinnaker you can't get a spinnaker wrap. In short it's my personal belief that many people who are just learning how to sail avoid using a spinnaker because they don't want to look bad in front of everybody.

To me it's a shame because a spinnaker is a beautiful and efficient off-the-wind sail. It presents a far greater projected area to the wind than can a normal jib. A spinnaker can infuse a *zip* into a boat's performance that you didn't know was there. And that is why I think you should learn as much as you can about spinnakers, and learn it as soon as you can.

Let's look first at a spinnaker as a sail and then see how to set it and how to fly it. The basics of spinnaker work are the

same for all boats and only some of the trimming details are the things that can differ widely.

First, though, let's get our terms straight. All triangular sails, including the spinnaker, have a *head, tack* and *clew.* The head of any sail is on the top and this is where the halyard is fastened. The tack is always fixed to something on the boat and the clew is the end that is free. In the case of a jib, the tack is fixed to the boat at the bow and the clew is the free corner of the sail that can move from one side of the boat to another as the boat tacks and it is the one to which the jibsheet is attached.

Similarly, the tack of the spinnaker is also in a fixed position—but it is attached to the end of the spinnaker pole. The free corner of the spinnaker is the clew and it has the spinnaker sheet attached to it. And just as with other sails, the edge of the spinnaker that runs from the tack to the head of the sail is the *luff,* and the edge that goes from the clew to the head is the *leech.* When a spinnaker isn't *set* (hoisted) the two edges are identical so we call them both *leeches*—(and both corners are called *clews.*) This is true until you establish which side is the luff when you put one corner of the sail at the end of the spin-naker pole as you set it.

The spinnaker pole positions, or holds, the tack of the hoisted spinnaker and it is held in place by a number of lines. The *topping lift* is a line that runs from a position about half way up the mast either to the middle or the end of the pole, depending on boat size. Its function is to keep the pole from falling down. The *foreguy* or pole *downhaul* runs from the foredeck up to the pole and it keeps it from rising. The foreguy also prevents the pole from swinging aft toward the stern. The spinnaker *guy* is a line that is attached to the sail, but it runs through a fitting at the end of the pole. The guy prevents the pole from swinging forward toward the bow as the sail fills.

So the outboard end of the pole is ad-justed by lines that can pull it up, down, forward and aft. All however "fix" the position of the pole, and therefore, the tack of the spinnaker but they can do it at any one of an infinite number of po-sitions. Look at Photo 1 to see the names of the various lines that are at-tached to the pole and the spinnaker on a small boat.

Unquestionably, the single biggest obstacle to a problem-free spinnaker *set*—that is what it is called when you hoist it—is making sure the spinnaker goes into its container correctly so that when it is raised, it goes up without any twists and avoids looking like an hour-glass. Overhauling the spinnaker is a critical operation, but once the basic principle is understood and mastered it is simple enough.

To prepare any spinnaker for hoist-ing, you must follow down the two leeches of the sail. The reason is that if two edges of a triangular sail are sorted out, the third edge, the *foot*, has to be clear. To clear the leeches on a small-boat spinnaker start at the head (usually this is the corner with the swivel) and fold the sail back and forth accordian-style until one edge is clear, as in Photo 2. Then fold the other edge the same way and hold onto the three corners and the two edges as in Photo 3. Next stuff the sail into a spinnaker bag, bucket, or other container but leave the

Photo 1: A spinnaker set on a small boat showing lines that are used

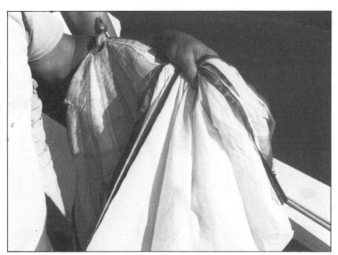

Photo 2: What one side of a spinnaker looks like
after folding one leech back and forth
going from head to clew

three corners on top. Photo 4 shows a spinnaker in a bucket with the three corners doubled under a piece of shock-cord to hold them in place for quick attachment when the sail is needed. I know there are other ways of folding a spinnaker that use elastic bands, yarn, or other devices. But the main point of all the systems is to make sure the two leeches are not twisted and are free from head to clew.

To hoist the spinnaker, the guy, sheet, and halyard all should be led outside the shrouds and sails. I might mention that you always should be heading well downwind in fairly light airs before you try to set the sail for the first few times. Similarly, it will take a bit of practice to

Photo 3: After folding second leech back and forth to
clear it, sail should be in a position where
three corners are together

Photo 4: A good set-up for a small-boat spinnaker. Head of spinnaker is in foreground (with swivel) and two clews are on either side of basket. All three can be attached easily when time comes to put sail up

learn just how far you can use it as you come up toward the wind. But a general rule is that you should always have the spinnaker pole set at 90 degrees to the apparent wind.

To hoist the spinnaker, attach the halyard, sheet, and guy to the appropriate corners of the spinnaker and place the bucket or bag on the leeward side of the boat. Make sure the bucket is tied so it doesn't fall overboard. Next, attach one end of the pole to the mast, attach the other end to the guy, and raise the pole with the topping lift which also should now be attached to the boom. Set the pole to windward, *opposite* the side the mainboom is on. Photo 5 shows a spinnaker that is about to be hoisted. A simple method of setting the spinnaker on a small keel boat like a Soling is to cleat the sheet first, then have one crewmember haul up on the halyard while another pulls briskly on the guy.

The most important part of the spinnaker set on any size boat is to get the tack and clew separated quickly. Doing so spreads the wide base of the spinnaker and reduces the chances of a twist. If a twist does occur, it will be higher up and the swivel on the halyard probably will take care of it.

Unless either the wind or the course of the boat is shifting greatly, once the

Photo 5: A spinnaker that is just about to be hoisted from basket. Note that guy is attached to sail and runs through end of pole that is set and in place. Sheet and halyard also are in place and attached to sail

sail is set and pulling the guy can be cleated and the tack of the spinnaker will therefore be fixed, just like the tack of the jib. By thinking of the spinnaker as just a different type of large jib, the beginner can get a better understanding of how it works. Just as you ease the jib-sheet until the jib luffs (on a reach) and then trim it in to obtain optimum sail efficiency, you also ease the spinnaker sheet until the spinnaker starts to luff. A luff, in the case of a spinnaker, manifests itself as a curl along the leading edge, also called the *luff*. Photo 6 shows a curl developing in the luff as the spinnaker trimmer eases the sheet. Any more easing and the spinnaker may collapse. Any less easing and the spinnaker may be over-trimmed without the crew's knowing it. So the spinnaker trimmer must be constantly easing the sail until the edge curls, and then trimming it in to uncurl it. Ease, trim, ease, trim and so forth, is the way to get the most from a spinnaker.

Once you have flown a spinnaker for awhile, you'll begin to think of it sort of as a contrary child: the moment the

Photo 6: Spinnaker that is not trimmed in quite enough is starting to show curl in luff

Photo 7: Spinnaker is symmetrical sail, and both tack and clew should be level

Photo 8: Different pole heights produce different effects on spinnaker.
Boat in foreground has pole too low; boat in middle has pole too high;
and boats ahead in background have poles set correctly so clews are parallel

trimmer looks away, it gets into trouble (collapses).

As the wind direction goes aft, or if the boat's course becomes more of a run than previously, the pole will also have to be pulled aft to maintain an angle that is perpendicular to the wind. This is called *squaring* the pole. Conversely, as the wind goes forward or the boat comes up to more of a reach, the pole must be eased forward. At a beam reach, the pole is touching the jibstay and is unable to be eased any farther. Nevertheless, if conditions are right you still can keep the spinnaker full by trimming the sheet even when the apparent wind is as much as 35 degrees forward of the beam, but this depends on a lot of things, including the weather conditions and the shape of the spinnaker.

Because the spinnaker is a symmetrical sail, it should look symmetrical as it does in Photo 7 and both the clew and tack should be level. In Photo 8 the boat in the center has set its pole too high and the boat in the foreground has its pole too low. The proper set is shown on the boats to the left in the distance. If the pole needs to be set higher, the entire pole should be raised, not just the outboard end which is controlled by the topping lift. Often there's a spinnaker track on the mast with a sliding device that the inboard end of the pole is attached to, and this allows the entire pole to be adjusted up and down. The reason for this track is to position the tack of the spinnaker as far away from the boat as possible to get it in undisturbed air. Maximum pole length is very strictly regulated on sailboats, so you don't want to lose any of this precious length. When a spinnaker pole is cocked up or down, its effective length is reduced and the tack of the spinnaker is brought that much closer to the sailplan. So keep your pole perpendicular to the mast for greatest effectiveness.

Practice in setting the spinnaker is best achieved by thinking the entire procedure through on "dry runs" before you actually attempt the first hoist. And when you do set it for the first time make sure you don't do it in winds that are very strong. I think you'll find that, before long, the whole procedure will become almost second nature.

Though there is a specific way to take

the spinnaker down, just as there is a way to put one up, if you always remember that the best way to keep the sail under control is to *head off* and let the pole forward until the sail is blanketed behind the mast (i.e., is not filled with wind) you will find that it is relatively easy to lower the sail into the boat as long as you keep hold (on a small boat) of the sheet and guy.

When in Doubt, Let It Out

The basics of proper spinnaker trim   Steve Colgate

The most common mistake the novice spinnaker flyer makes is to overtrim it. The trimmer sees the curl, trims the sheet in to keep the spinnaker from collapsing, but then doesn't ease it back out again to the curl. Before long the chute looks like the one in Photo A: it is starved for air. The sheet badly needs easing to let the spinnaker fill correctly. If you're a trimmer, adhere to the principle: *When in doubt, let it out!*

This works for most sails, but it is particularly true of the spinnaker. Photo B shows a crewmember trying to ease the sheet on a light-air run, but the spinnaker stays collapsed behind the mainsail. There just isn't enough air in the spinnaker to pull it out. The skipper has his hand on the guy and he should pull the pole back to get the spinnaker out into undisturbed air. He should pull the pole back far enough so it could collapse to windward if it stayed out there. Then as the chute fills, he should ease the pole forward again to its proper location. Jerking back on the pole like this brings the spinnaker back against the wind, forces airflow over its surface, and lifts up the troublesome clew.

The crew in Photo B can do a couple of other things to avoid their present problem. They could lower the pole so the luff becomes straighter and doesn't curve to leeward so much. This will keep the luff out from the blanketed area behind the main. They also could heel the boat to windward so the spinnaker falls out by gravity from behind

Photo A: When sheet is trimmed in to stop curl at luff and then not eased out again, result is a starved spinnaker. Rule to remember is, when in doubt let it out

Photo B: To fill spinnaker running in light air, get sail into air not disturbed by mainsail. Helmsman pulls pole back quickly, then, as sail fills, eases pole forward to proper location

Photo C: Spinnaker that has not been fully hoisted. Trimmer on leeward side has obstructed view. Better position is on windward side

Photo D: On close reaches, particularly in fresh breezes, a jib can add extra drive, though it can cause problems in light air

the sail plan. They could use light sheets so the weight of the sheet doesn't pull the clew down in light air.

If the tack and clew location are correct, there's only one other adjustment that can foul up the works: the spinnaker halyard. Photo C shows a halyard that either has slipped, has been eased off too much, or was never pulled up all the way. Again, as in Photos A and B the spinnaker trimmer is in a very awkward position on the leeward side of the boat. He should be sitting to windward where he can see the entire luff of the chute.

An eased halyard is not always bad. On a medium-air reach in 10 knots of wind or so, about a foot of halyard ease will open the slot between the spinnaker and the mainsail, improve the airflow, and reduce backwind in the mainsail. However in heavy winds, halyard ease will tend to accentuate the rolling on runs and broaching on reaches. Neither is desirable. When the halyard is eased on a light-air run the whole spinnaker comes down instead of flying forward away from the wind shadow of the mainsail as you might think it would. And on the light-air reaches, the spinnaker that has been eased can become unstable and difficult to keep full.

The jib is another variable that can

cause problems with the spinnaker. On a sailboat like a Soling, the jib is small and can be carried to advantage in most airs as in Photo D. A jib is particularly helpful on reaches but in light air when the spinnaker collapses, a jib can cause difficulties in getting the spinnaker full again. Airflow over the lee side of the jib creates a suction and what happens is that the collapsed spinnaker is sucked in behind the jib. The cure is to ease the jibsheet until the jib luffs. Then the suction disappears and the spinnaker will refill much more readily.

If the spinnaker continues to collapse fairly regularly, it is best either to lower the jib or to roll it in if that is possible. Some boats, such as the Flying Dutchman, have a jib that is roller-furling so it's a simple matter to roll it up. On other boats if it is too time-consuming to lower the jib, just grab the *middle* of the foot, pull down (for a tight roll) and roll the jib by hand up toward the jibstay. Then take a piece of line and tie the furl tightly. A piece of wire like a single-strand conductor wire with a plastic coating can do the same thing as a "twist-tie." Then, instead of having to go forward and untie the jib when it's needed again, just pull on the jibsheet and break it out.

On runs, particularly those made in light air, the jib is more apt to interfere with the airflow's getting to the spinnaker than it does on other points of sail. In such conditions it's best to get the jib out of the way, using one of the methods I've outlined above.

Some sailors put wool telltales on the spinnaker at various levels a few feet in from the luff and leech. The idea is to keep the leeward ones (on the outside of the sail) on the luff side flowing rather than stalled. It has been my experience that the flowing telltales only show the smooth airflow *before* the sheet has been eased enough to produce a curl in the luff of the spinnaker. If so, the wool telltales are superfluous for they just reinforce what already is known to be proper spinnaker trim.

A spinnaker trimmer on just about any size boat should use either a winch or rachet blocks for the spinnaker sheet. If he holds the sheet in his hand as it comes straight from the spinnaker (though it could go through turning blocks) only his arm absorbs any increased pull that is caused by a gust of wind in the spinnaker. If he wraps the sheet around a winch, this increased pull is transmitted directly to the boat and not dissipated.

This absorption of energy was graphically demonstrated to me during a race on *Dyna,* a 58-foot yawl. In very light air we changed from a regular spin-naker sheet to a lightweight one: 1,000-pound test nylon parachute cord. At that point we were just holding our own with a boat we thought we should be beating. Then we changed sheets again to $\frac{1}{4}$-inch Dacron line: still light but lacking the stretch characteristics of the nylon. We immediately moved away from the other boat. No other item had been moved or changed except the sheet. The stretch in that nylon had been absorbing all the energy we might otherwise have realized from the few small puffs that were getting to our spinnaker.

Always remember that the most important part of spinnaker trimming is *concentration.* The trimmer must give the spinnaker his complete and undivided attention. Whenever there is a change in apparent wind direction there must be a corresponding change in spinnaker trim. If the boat speeds up, by surfing for instance, the apparent wind will go forward, and the guy must be eased and the sheet trimmed. If a gust hits, the apparent wind will come aft and just the reverse is true for trimming. In addition to making the spinnaker sheet and guy adjustments, the skipper should learn to head off in the puffs and the spinnaker trimmer must automatically make additional adjustments for this change in the boat's heading. The best spinnaker trimmers are people who have great powers of concentration.

Gybing the Spinnaker

Contributions of helmsman and crew   Steve Colgate

Spinnaker gybes seem to be a great bug-aboo for most novice crews—and sometimes for good ones too. Though almost any crew can get into trouble, sometimes it is very difficult to analyze why. A gybe often happens fast; all crew-members have tasks to perform; and when you're busy with your own job, sometimes it is hard to notice where things are going wrong. Most of the time the person on the foredeck all wrapped up in spinnaker cloth, lines, etc., takes the brunt of abuse. Actually the fault often lies with the person who is steering.

The skipper who turns the boat too sharply or who gives the crew inadequate time or instructions will almost certainly cause a bad gybe. In heavy air, for example, the helmsman must be sure he counteracts the tendency for the boat to round up into the wind right after a gybe. The reason this happens is that the boom swings over with a great deal of force and when it either reaches the shrouds or comes to the end of the cleated mainsheet, it stops abruptly and the sail creates a wall to the wind. Something has to give until equilibrium is found so the boat heels over and a strong weather helm is the result as the forces in the sail over the water turn the bow of the boat toward the wind. This combination of factors will cause a broach in heavy winds unless the helmsman heads the boat off decisively to meet the anticipated turning moment. When it is done properly the boat, even though it is being steered as though to gybe back again, just sails straight

ahead. Nothing can make a crew look worse than a bad helmsman. But, to be fair about this, some of the worst problems also are caused by the crew handling the spinnaker guy and sheet.

A "reach to reach" gybe is one in which the boat is turned from a reach with the pole on or near the jib stay on one tack to a reach with the pole on or near the jib stay on the opposite tack. It is a difficult type of gybe because the boat is turned approximately 90 degrees. The spinnaker has to get completely around to the other side of the boat and problems occur if this is not done quickly.

Photos 1, 2 and 3 show a situation that often develops. What *should* happen is that as the boat heads down from a starboard-tack reach to gybe, the pole must come aft and the sheet should be eased. After all, the boat is on a dead run at the instant of gybing and the spinnaker must be trimmed properly for that point of sail. Only then should the mainboom and spinnaker pole be gybed and the boat then can head up toward the new port-tack reach with the pole on or close to the jib stay and the sheet trimmed in.

In Photo 2, nothing of the sort has happened. At the point of gybing the bulk of the spinnaker still is on the port side of the boat which is the same side the wind is about to blow over. What happens is that after the gybe the spinnaker starts to blow through between the jib and the main as in Photo 3 (ending with a mess). When this happens, about the only solution is to head back

Photo 1: When sailing on a reach and preparing to gybe
around a mark . . .

. . . spinnaker must be pulled around to new
leeward side before boom swings over (Photo 2)

*Photo 3: If spinnaker is not pulled
around, sail will fill to windward as in this
case, and will blow through between jib and mainsail*

downwind and blow the spinnaker forward again around the jib stay.

On a gybing maneuver the foredeck crew on a small keelboat like a Soling should stand, with shoulder and back braced against the mast, facing forward as in Photo 4. From this position he or she has much more leverage for controlling the pole and getting it off the mast. Also, he can see the spinnaker and help keep it full. On a reach-to-reach gybe, the foredeck crew should take the pole off the mast *first* and then off the old guy. This makes the spinnaker "free-wheeling" and the cockpit crew amidships can pull the spinnaker around in front of the boat without the pole's restricting its movement in any way. The foredeck crew then connects the end of the pole that previously was attached to the mast to the new guy and finally snaps the other end of the pole onto the mast fitting. This is called *end-for-ending* the pole.

If the pole is not taken off the spinnaker completely the foredeck crew has to be extremely quick not to end up in the situation shown in Photo 5. What happened here is that the crew decided to snap the end that came off the mast onto the new guy *before* he unsnapped it from the old guy. Meanwhile the cockpit crew pulled the spinnaker around to the starboard side, but he could not pull it any farther because the leeward side of the pole is against the shrouds. The gybe has been completed and, here again, the spinnaker is starting to blow in between the jib and the main. If the pole were not attached to the sheet on the leeward side the spinnaker could have been pulled all the way around to the starboard side even if the foredeck man was having trouble getting organized.

A gybe that is made when running is much easier. The boat's heading changes only slightly so all you are really doing is changing the pole from one side of the boat to the other while still keeping the spinnaker full. Photo 6 shows a running gybe at the midpoint.

Photo 4: Proper crew position for foredeck
hand prior to gybe. Back and shoulder are against mast, hands
are on pole ready to disconnect from mast fitting

Photo 5: When pole is not disconnected
from old guy before connecting other end to new guy, crew
cannot sheet in spinnaker to leeward and spinnaker gets
caught to windward with results similar to Photo 3

Photo 7: Running gybe at completion stage. Foredeck crew is about to attach pole end to new guy before he attaches interior end to mast

Photo 6: Running gybe just at midpoint with mainboom amidships and foredeck crew just releasing pole from mast

The foredeck crew is in a good position, with his back well braced against the mast and his feet spread apart for balance. In the light winds shown in that photo, the skipper should hold the mainboom in the middle of the boat for a short time to keep the spinnaker full while the pole is being transferred to the other side.

In the case of a running gybe, the pole *may* be left attached to the old guy until the other end is snapped over the new guy. In fact this helps the foredeck crew keep the spinnaker full during the

Photo 8: When taking in spinnaker to windward, first disconnect pole from mast and guy, then pull spinnaker in to windward

Photo 9: After pole is out of way, take spinnaker in to windward

Photo 10: With boats that do not have overlapping jib, spinnaker pole can be left up after rounding mark, can be lowered after boat is steady on new course

gybe. Photo 7 is taken at the point when the gybe is almost completed. The foredeck crew should have the pole on the new guy and should be attaching the other end to the mast. Actually in this case he either is a little behind schedule or the skipper is a little ahead; it depends on your point of view.

The douse, or takedown, usually is the easiest part of spinnaker work. Most small-boat crews take the spinnaker in to windward to avoid getting crew weight to leeward, and, in the case of centerboard boats, causing a probable capsize. Most larger cruising boat crews do take it to leeward of the main and jib in order to blanket the large spinnaker more completely. Soling crews could do it either way; it would depend on which side they want to put the spinnaker the next time they hoist it.

For a windward douse, the crew first eases the sheet and gets rid of the pole (Photo 8). Then they haul it in to windward as the halyard is lowered (Photo 9). Usually the spinnaker will stay full without the pole for a moment after it has been taken off.

The leeward douse is a bit faster. You grab the sheet close to the shrouds on the leeward side, ease the guy off completely and gather the spinnaker in as the halyard is lowered. The pole is left up until last and, in the case of a sailboat without an overlapping jib, it can even be left up even after you have made a tack to windward (Photo 10).

Spinnaker work, when it is done smoothly and well, is one of the most satisfying aspects of sailing, and it is the pride of all those who consider themselves good seamen. Don't miss the fun!

Avoiding Spinnaker Messes

A review of typical foul-ups and how to prevent them   Steve Colgate

There is only one sure way to avoid problems with the spinnaker—don't set one. But if you don't set one you'll also lose much of the pleasure of sailing a boat on a run.

The foredeck crew tangled up in the spinnaker in Photo 1 probably would not agree with me about the pleasure of sailing at that moment. But in the long run it is true. Besides, there are certain procedures you can use that can avoid or at least reduce the problems. And there are others that will solve them more quickly.

For example, in Photo 1 the crew would have been able to get their spinnaker "sea anchor" aboard far more

easily if the skipper had turned the boat right into the wind. The boat then would have stopped and the water pressure that was filling the spinnaker would have disappeared. Then by concentrating on pulling on *just one* corner of the spinnaker it could be brought aboard quite easily even with the water resistance.

Here are some other common problems—and the easiest way to solve them.

Tangled spinnaker halyard. Photo 2 shows what happens when nobody checks to see whether the halyard is clear all the way up before hoisting. In this case it is led up on the wrong side of the spinnaker pole topping lift and it

Photo 1: Though spinnakers provide that extra bit of pleasure to sailing, they have to be handled properly or trouble will develop in very short order

Photo 2: When no one checks to make sure spinnaker halyard is clear, result is bound to be a fouled sail

Photo 3: With midpoint spinnaker wrap, best way is to blanket sail behind mainsail; shake it; and pull down on leeches

happened when the topping lift was attached to the spinnaker pole. The way out of the mess is either to lower the halyard and untangle it, or to disconnect the topping lift from the pole, let it go and grab it again after the spinnaker has filled. So always make a last-second check *before* you hoist to see that the halyard is clear all the way up.

Spinnaker Wraps. This problem plays no favorites. Even large boats get spinnaker wraps. The problem comes up when the spinnaker collapses for one reason or another and then starts to rotate around itself. Wraps can also occur during the hoist if the lower corners of the spinnaker are not pulled apart quickly enough or if the stowage bag has been inadvertently rotated before the set. If the wrap is down very low in the spinnaker it probably should be lowered and sorted out. *Never* pull the pole back or head the boat up in order to fill the spinnaker on the assumption that the wrap will unwind if the spinnaker is full. This never works and, in fact, the wrap gets tighter. It's better to get the spinnaker in the dead air behind the main and jib and *blanket* it. Then either shake it by hand or pull down on the leeches. The wrap shown in Photo 3 should come out with this method. If the wrap is high up in the sail, releasing the halyard a few feet should allow the swivel, which may be jammed in the block, to rotate and unwind the spinnaker.

A very bad type wrap to get is one that winds around the jibstay. If it gets tight, it can be next to impossible to un-

Photo 4: When spinnaker is wrapped this badly, best solution is to lower and start over again

Photo 5: Dramatic illustration of what happens when sheet or guy is released prematurely. Problems like this tend to occur more often in heavy weather

wrap without cutting the spinnaker away. The problem is that a wire jibstay has strands that are twisted around each other. As the spinnaker is pulled down (assuming a crew member can reach the foot of the sail and pull it), it tends to be rotated by the strands and gets tighter and tighter. A rod jibstay sometimes found on cruising and racing boats is smooth and a wrapped spinnaker can slide down it more easily.

But in either case, once this type wrap occurs there are only a couple of things that can be done: (1) send a man up in a bosun's chair to untangle it (if the boat is large enough); or (2) gybe the main-

Photo 6: Early release of spinnaker halyard can result in sail's either filling with water or being run over by boat. Once cloth hits water, trouble is not far behind

Photo 7: If crewmember lowering spinnaker releases halyard before crew can gather it in, sail will tumble into water, be difficult to recover

boom over so that the airflow off the mainsail is in the opposite direction. Instead of wrapping more and getting tighter, the spinnaker will start rotating in the opposite direction and unwrap itself.

I had heard of this method for many years, but never had to resort to it myself. Recently, however, one of our teaching boats wrapped a spinnaker tightly around the jib while running in a 25-knot wind. Nothing seemed to work, so I suggested (from a chase boat) that the crew gybe the mainsail. Within minutes this "impossible' wrap unwound.

The type wrap shown in Photo 4 which is down low in the spinnaker and obviously includes some extraneous lines for good measure is probably incurable without lowering the spinnaker and starting all over again.

Losing the guy and sheet. Often either the guy or the sheet or both get free inadvertently. It sometimes happens during a gybe when one person is holding onto both, and the spinnaker suddenly fills with a gust of wind. More often, it happens on the lowering maneuver. The guy is released before someone has hold of the sheet behind the mainsail on the leeward side and the sail goes flying out as in Photo 5.

One solution is to turn the boat dead downwind. In all but the heaviest winds, the spinnaker will come down within reach and can be gathered in. Another way out is to pull on either the guy or the sheet, and let the other trail free. As the corner gets close, ease the halyard. Premature easing of the halyard, however, greatly increases the risk of having the spinnaker fill with air way out beyond the boat. When this happens the problem becomes serious. The boat may be pulled over so far she fills with water and the heeling makes it impossible to turn the boat downwind toward the spinnaker. Freeing the halyard completely may become necessary.

Losing the halyard. Releasing the spinnaker halyard before another crewmember is prepared to gather the sail in or inadequate cleating of the halyard after the spinnaker is raised can cause the problem shown in Photo 6. If this halyard isn't caught and immediately brought back up, the spinnaker either will fill with water or be run over by the bow of the boat.

Finally, easing the halyard on the takedown more quickly than it can be gathered in leads to the problems of the crew in Photo 7. The head of the chute is about to fill with water, and the weight inevitably will wrench the rest of the spinnaker from the grip of the crew.

All this could have been avoided if the person easing off the halyard had watched the gatherer(s) and tried not to get ahead of him (them).

I guess the most important thing to remember about spinnakers is that regardless of the type of problem you encounter, rest assured that someone else has been there before. Don't feel upset or stupid about it. Just try to analyze first what caused the problem and then attempt to avoid it next time.

Spinnaker Launchers

Making a neat job of setting and dousing   Jack Knights

The sailing world is divided into two, very unequal parts. Those, the enlightened, the elect, who know about spinnaker launchers and those, the barbarians, the philistines, the great unwashed who toil in darkness because they know not.

The enlightened are few, for they worship high-performance dinghies and not even all of them. And they remain few because they entirely lack the evangelizing, crusading spirit which led early Christians to drop everything and to devote their lives to saving or killing pagans. This is why the only time you see spinnaker launchers used in craft larger than racing dinghies is when such boats are owned by former dinghy sailors.

As with the blinding flash of light which we are told comes suddenly to chosen pagans and sets them forevermore on the paths of righteousness, so it is with spinnaker launchers. Only those who have witnessed the special miracle they perform and re-perform can see the light, the *truth*. The rest have no comprehension.

Before we proceed further, for the completely unenlightened we will say that a spinnaker launcher is basically a mouth at the front of the boat which swallows and regurgitates the spinnaker. Boats thus fitted no longer handle the sail by hand.

Many claim to have invented the device. I saw one first in the earlyish 1960s on a Flying Dutchman raced by the Canadian Green brothers. They sailed quickly, the Greens, with brother Roger at the helm, and they sometimes argued as quickly as they sailed, but one thing they agreed about was the efficacy of their spinnaker system. Other Dutchman sailors were soon agreeing too, and today no self-respecting FD is without one launcher. Many have two, one for the running kite and the other for the reacher, each with its own halyard and sheets.

Soon the 505 was following the lead of the Dutchman. This wasn't easy. The FD has a long hull with plenty of deck ahead of the forestay where a suitably-sized mouth could be excavated. The original sail plan of the 505 has the forestay ending close to the stemhead. But those who had seen the light were not to be discouraged by a little obstacle like that. Faith moves mountains and these people moved back their forestays, which meant moving back their masts, which led to moving their mast steps. And then, to retain the right balance, they had to move their centerboards and that, of course, meant moving their centerboard trunks. The fact is, they had to redesign and rebuild their boats from scratch just to find room for the launchers. But they didn't complain and today all top 505s have launchers and all good 505 crews are of the elect. Billy Graham might well envy (if envy were not unchristian), the conversion ratio. Today, too, the FDs and 505s are quickly going over to automated spinnaker pole handling, but that is another story.

The launcher next spread to one or two of the smaller keelboat classes to which aging dinghy sailors are inclined to drift. The Dragon was one such. Here, too, there were special problems, foundering being one of them. The Dragon is scant of freeboard and its heavy construction and iron keel make it wet. It ploughs its low bow easily and if that bow should have an open mouth, then the spinnakers wouldn't be all it would swallow. The answer here was to contrive a small sliding door which ran on rails from one side of the bow past the forestay (Fig. 1). Luckily the spoon

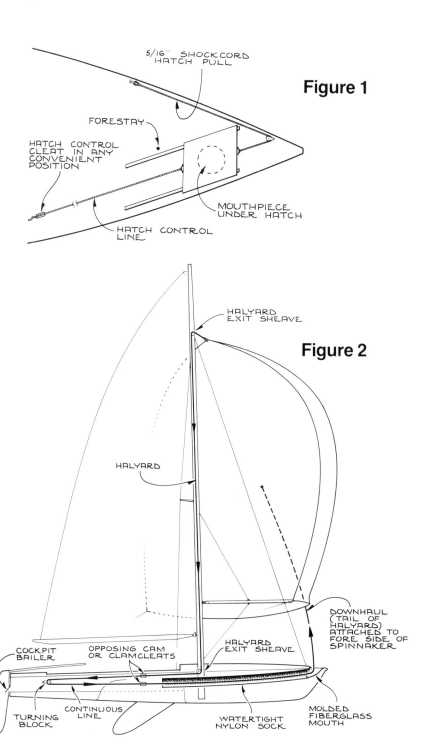

Figure 1

5/16" SHOCKCORD HATCH PULL

FORESTAY

HATCH CONTROL CLEAT IN ANY CONVENIENT POSITION

MOUTHPIECE UNDER HATCH

HATCH CONTROL LINE

Figure 2

HALYARD EXIT SHEAVE

HALYARD

DOWNHAUL (TAIL OF HALYARD) ATTACHED TO FORE SIDE OF SPINNAKER

COCKPIT BAILER

OPPOSING CAM OR CLAMCLEATS

HALYARD EXIT SHEAVE

TURNING BLOCK

CONTINUOUS LINE

WATERTIGHT NYLON SOCK

MOLDED FIBERGLASS MOUTH

shape of the Dragon bow makes for considerable width on deck forward. The door is actuated by lines and shock-cord, and it can lead to embarrassment since crews, to keep water out, will keep on closing the door after the spinnaker is hoisted and then will forget to open it again before they try to lower the spinnaker.

One Class, the Tempest, has tried spinnaker launchers and, by and large, has rejected them. But then one could say that many have tried the Tempest and have rejected it. Moreover, the Class rules prevented a mouthpiece of suitably large dimensions. Further, most of those who crew Tempests appear to have quit dinghies before the launcher really caught on. They never got to see the light. Yet even the Tempest is trying harder, with new rules intended to bring about a second coming for the launcher.

Some classes have resisted all attempts at conversion. Those who govern Solings, mindful of how easily they sink, have ruled against further breaching of the watertight integrity of the bow compartment. The fathers of the 470 have the mistaken idea that a launcher would add cost and complexity.

In the offshore classes there are no such restrictions. Yet, so far, only a small minority have explored the possibilities. They who have done so have not kept quiet about the advantages thus gained. You might argue that since offshore crews are big and strong, there is no need for such labor-saving devices as a launcher. In the biggest yachts this is true, yet the size yacht in which crew weight forward of the mast is dangerous when overdriven offwind steadily increases. The trend is toward taller rigs, lighter displacements and finer bows, all factors tending toward uncontrollable broaching when the bow is allowed to dig, under the press of a spinnaker.

Without a launcher, at least one man must always go all the way to the bow to trip the guy out of the pole end which has been eased forward to him before the sail is taken down. Again and again a boat will survive the fiercest squalls on a downwind leg only to succumb to a wild broach as it approaches the lee mark and its crew go forward to take down the spinnaker.

One of the greatest advantages of the launcher is actually in the dropping, not the hoisting. You can rid yourself of the kite without anybody moving an inch. There was a major FD series in the Bay of Naples. It may have been the Worlds; it may have been the Europeans ... at all events, Britain's double-gold medalist, Rodney Pattisson, and his favorite crew, Iain Macdonald-Smith, were lying second on the third leg of the opening triangle. It was a shy spinnaker reach with Macdonald-Smith extended to the end of his trapeze wire and the wind drawing too far ahead for comfort. With the pair in the lead looking nervously over their shoulders, Pattisson and Macdonald-Smith unrolled their genoa and doused their kite into its funnel. They did this without losing a yard of ground, the pole remaining in place. Seeing that the famous aces had seemingly decided the wind was too far ahead for spinnakers, the leaders gratefully dropped their kite too. Lacking a launcher, there was a fair amount of flogging and flapping and the gap diminished noticeably.

Then it vanished completely because, while the leaders were dropping their kite, Pattisson and Macdonald-Smith were deftly hoisting theirs anew, out of its launcher. Within seconds, under spinnaker once more, they had driven straight through the others' lee. Soon after, ahead now and slightly down to leeward, they doused their kite in earnest and jib-reached up for the mark and the lead.

That's the great advantage of a launcher—it enables you to risk a kite when it would otherwise be rash. If the wind does freshen or head, you can always rid yourselves of the sail before it gets to be an embarrassment and this applies just as much on Quarter-, Half- and even today's One-Tonners as it does on dinghies.

Another factor favoring the greater use of launchers aboard offshore racers is that foretriangles are getting smaller and lower. Giant masthead spinnakers would demand bigger launching

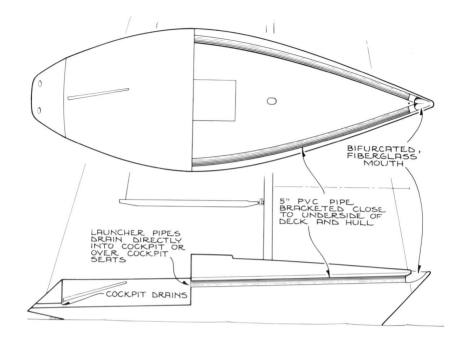

BIFURCATED,
FIBERGLASS
MOUTH

5" PVC PIPE
BRACKETED CLOSE
TO UNDERSIDE OF
DECK AND HULL

LAUNCHER PIPES
DRAIN DIRECTLY
INTO COCKPIT OR
OVER COCKPIT
SEATS

COCKPIT DRAINS

Figure 3

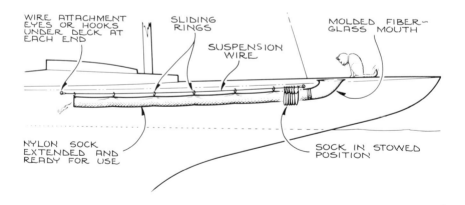

WIRE ATTACHMENT
EYES OR HOOKS
UNDER DECK AT
EACH END

SLIDING
RINGS

SUSPENSION
WIRE

MOLDED FIBER-
GLASS MOUTH

NYLON SOCK
EXTENDED AND
READY FOR USE

SOCK IN STOWED
POSITION

Figure 4

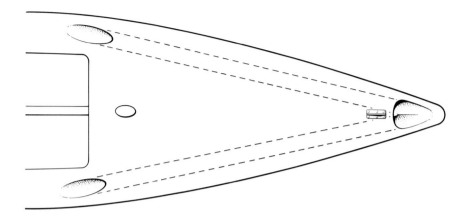

Figure 5

mouths and there needs to be stowage within the boat for slightly more than half the spinnaker hoist. The shorter the hoist and the narrower the width, the better.

The normal dinghy arrangement (Fig. 2) is for the mouth of the launcher to consist of a thinly-molded fiberglass laminate. This connects to a more-or-less watertight fabric sock which contains the lowered sail and which, as said above, needs to be half as long as the sail itself. When I fitted double-spinnaker launchers to my Quarter-Tonner *Odd Job* in 1973, I ensured that the complete device would be watertight by having the fiberglass mouthpiece bifurcate into two five-inch plastic sewer pipes, one leading aft on each side, straight through the interior (in the corner formed by the deck and topsides), out through the after cabin bulkhead and so into the wide self-draining cockpit (Fig. 3). Any water that washed into the mouth drained straight through, into and out of the cockpit (and once or twice washed the sail out, too).

One year in the Mini-Tonner *Minnehaha,* I dispensed with the pipes altogether and the watertightness, too, since I reckoned it would be simpler, cheaper

and lighter to positively seal off the launcher in bad weather. We simply pulled the spinnaker back aft into the interior. If you don't like the idea of a wet, dripping sail lying the length of your accommodation—and there is no reason, apart from rain, why the sail should be dripping—you can borrow an idea from the Dragons. They rig a light taut wire from above the mouth, close under the deckhead, aft in the direction of the pull on the downhaul line: A nylon sock is suspended from this wire on light metal rings so that it can be drawn aft for use and afterwards can be pulled forward, out of the way like a curtain (Fig. 4).

Paul Whiting, the successful, young New Zealand designer and perpetrator of some of the most nervous of the new wave of light, fine-bowed centerboarders, fits small-bore watertight tubes direct from the mouth, under the deck, to emerge out on deck amidships, one each side (Fig. 5). They take advantage of the steep camber of his flush decks. This way they are very seaworthy though the downhaul may be more difficult to get at and to pull.

If the system is not essentially watertight in one of these ways, then it is vital that there should be both a watertrap in the mouthpiece and a method of positive sealing. The watertrap is simply arranged and will also serve as an excellent exhaust ventilator (the airflow inside a boat is always, surprisingly, from aft forward, contrary to the outside airflow, so the mouthpiece teams up with an air inlet near the transom). A partial bulkhead just aft of the mouthpiece will stiffen the boat at an important point and will simplify the fitting of a watertight door (Fig. 6). Last fall, a Stephen Jones-designed Quarter-Tonner, sailing from the Channel Islands to England in order to race, foundered because of water flooding in via the launcher.

In *Odd Job* we went to some trouble to fit the pulpit aft of the launcher mouth thinking this would reduce friction. Now I believe that a normal, smoothly-shaped pulpit ahead of the mouth will actually help by holding the sail higher above the water. This way it also enhances appearance and, to an extent, safety.

Some designers, David Thomas is one, have a special circular hole fashioned in the pulpit through which the sail is drawn on its way to the launcher mouth which, in this case, is fitted in the foredeck aft of the forestay. This seems to add expense and weight with no real gain. With the mouth in the foredeck, it

is necessary to have folding "bomb doors." These may not be strong enough to walk on (Fig. 7).

The controlling part of the mouth should always be ahead of the forestay whether it be part of the pulpit or some other device. Only in this way will it be possible to hoist and lower the kite while on either tack, with the wind square aft or on the beam.

What the non-launcher crews tend to overlook is that the spinnaker which is being doused into a launcher collapses more quickly and remains more amenable than the hand-lowered one. This is because it is being pulled in from its center so it is immediately snuffed. This explains why, although it often seems about to fall under the forefoot, it somehow never does. It is usually possible for one man to cast off the halyard and to let it run out, then to reach for the downhaul and to pull in fast. On larger boats, it is better to have one man on the halyard and another on the downhaul.

The lovely feature is that the sail is already folded to half its length as it comes into the mouth. When fully stowed, the three corners will be uppermost and if hauled home to the correct distance, these three corners will be easily accessible at the top of the launcher mouth. Thus it will be easy to

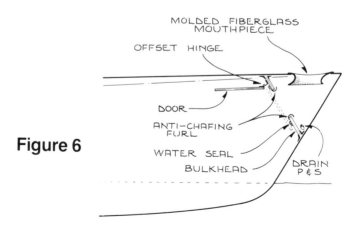

Figure 6

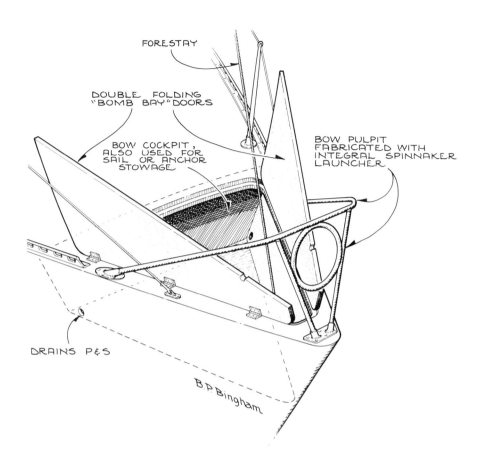

FORESTAY

DOUBLE FOLDING
"BOMB BAY" DOORS

BOW COCKPIT,
ALSO USED FOR
SAIL OR ANCHOR
STOWAGE

BOW PULPIT
FABRICATED WITH
INTEGRAL SPINNAKER
LAUNCHER

DRAINS P&S

B.P. Bingham

Figure 7

switch halyards and sheets. This is why it is practical to operate double chutes, with a reacher in one and a runner in the other, with only a single halyard and set of sheets and guys. If you must have a third or a fourth kite, then these will certainly be a lightweight floater and an extra-heavy, small storm kite. These will best be handled in the old-fashioned way, by hand.

Paul Elvstrom is, of course, one of the elect, a confirmed launcher-user. But he has his own individual way of doing it. He fastens the downhaul to the tack of the kite, then has one man haul down the kite while another eases away on the weather guy. According to the gospel of

St. Paul, this method simplifies spinnaker switching but you end up with a greater length of sail inside the boat and the need for teamwork is greater.

Always make sure the downhaul line is led forward of the sail. This way it helps gather in the sail as it comes down and helps keep it out of the water. Remember that, in the simple system, the attachment point must be equidistant from the three corners of the sail, which is not quite the same thing as saying that the point must be at the sail's center (Fig. 8). The attachment point must be strongly reinforced but do this with strips that radiate outwards rather than with concentric, circular discs of extra

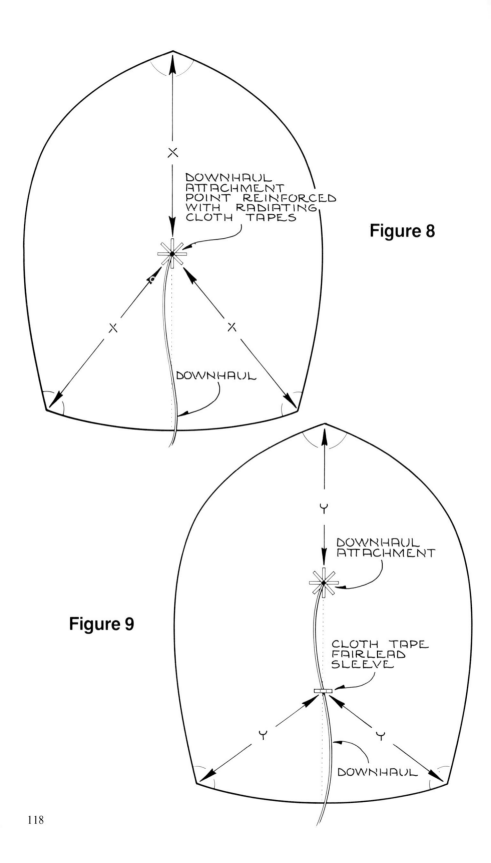

DOWNHAUL ATTACHMENT POINT REINFORCED WITH RADIATING CLOTH TAPES

Figure 8

DOWNHAUL

Figure 9

DOWNHAUL ATTACHMENT

CLOTH TAPE FAIRLEAD SLEEVE

DOWNHAUL

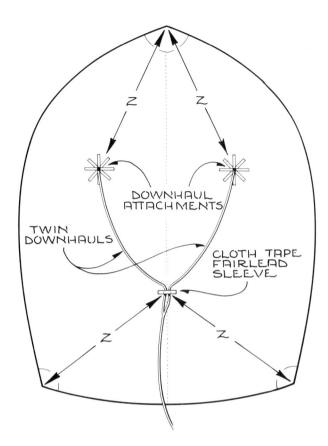

Figure 10

cloth. The strips will be more flexible and less bulky. This point is the part of the sail that first enters the mouth and which causes most friction.

To speed dousing, some people first pass the downhaul line through a short sleeve toward the bottom of the sail before leading it up to the attachment point which, this way, may be closer to the top (the distance from the sleeve to the clews can be the same as the distance from the attachment point to the head) (Fig. 9). The disadvantage is that you will now have a larger "wodge" of sail to force through the launcher mouth. For the largest spinnakers, the system might be further modified as in Figure 10, although I have no personal knowledge of such an idea.

Two words of caution: launchers do give the spinnaker fabric a pretty heavy going over. Dynac, in particular, does not appear to relish the treatment, particularly when it is wet and clammy. For this reason you hardly ever see Dynac used for the spinnakers of FDs and 505s. This is also why we suggest the floater should be set in the old style, labor-intensive way. But much may be done by careful mouthpiece design. It should be shaped as if to conduct high-speed fluids rather than nylon and, of course, all nearby protuberances, lifeline bottlescrews, split pins, mooring cleats, navigation lights and such, must be removed to a safe distance or taped over. Some people shake baby powder or dance floor chalk into the sail.

In extreme weather, gybes may be facilitated by lowering the kite into its chute, gybing main and pole, and then rehoisting on the new tack. Before hoisting, always over-run the downhaul line. Otherwise it will often snag and impede the kite on its upward journey. Hoisters and lowerers should be prepared to haul lustily. With even the best system, there is considerable friction. Those minding sheets and guys must check away early, otherwise the sail will be further impeded as it comes down. Conversely, they can help by pulling as the halyard is hoisted.

The technology of spinnaker launchers has now reached the point where the device deserves its place on all Mini-Tonners and Quarter-Tonners and similarly-sized boats which are used in winds of any force. You would also expect to see them being generally adopted in all modern-style Half-Tonners with smallish foretriangles. And you would like to see them being played with on boats of One-Ton size and even larger. From all accounts the latest One-Tonners are so skittish that the weight transference and change of trim when two men move forward of the mast and the pole is pivoted forward for lowering, may often be the last straw that leads to the spin-out broach. As a true believer, I would rather be restricted to everyday use of only two spinnakers (only one in the case of a Mini-Tonner and Quarter-Tonner), as a trade-off against the manifold advantages conferred by a properly-arranged and fully-exploited launching system.

Taming the Blooper

Optimum trim of an effective downwind tool   Rick Grajirena

Contrary to the popular belief that the blooper is a very modern weapon in the ocean racing arsenal, actually it had its beginnings in the early 60s. At that time the venerable designer Joe Byars from Tampa, Florida, was dazzling the opposition with what he called his *Tampa Bay Skysail.* Joe was flying what looked like an upside-down genoa to leeward of the spinnaker when he was broad-reaching and running. The Cruising Club of America, then firmly in command of ocean racing, quickly put a halt to his use of the skysail.

It wasn't until the early 70s that the skysail, now renamed *blooper,* surfaced again—this time in force in the United States. The International Offshore Rule put restrictions on the measuring of genoas which in turn put restrictions on blooper design. But for the modern ocean racer the blooper is a potent weapon and it will be around for some time to come.

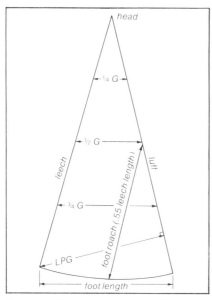

Figure 1: Measurement points of a genoa jib

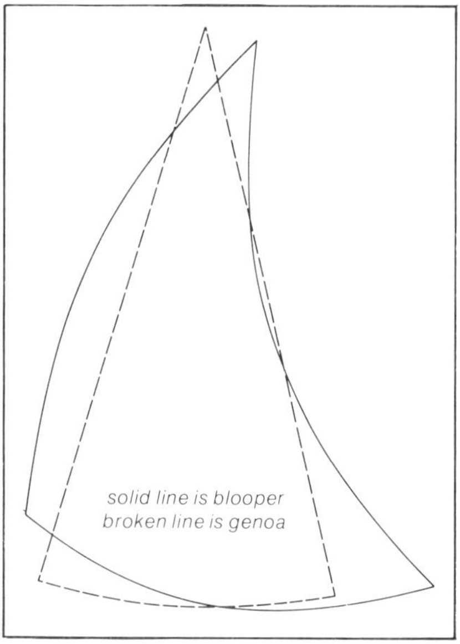

Figure 2: A blooper and a genoa may measure the same, but there is a world of difference between the two sails

Because the blooper is measured as a genoa, let's first cover the measurement restrictions governing genoas. Genoa size is limited by the LP (luff perpendicular), three girth measurements, and a foot roach measurement.

The LP is the distance from the clew to a point that is perpendicular to it on the luff. The three girths are functions of the foot length; at the top ¼ girth, the sail cannot exceed .25 of the foot length; the middle cannot exceed .50 of the foot; and the lower quarter cannot be greater than .75 of the foot. Although it's difficult to exceed these girths when building a genoa, a blooper is designed to the maximum at each girth station. The foot roach limit, which was imposed to prevent high-clewed genoas with excessive foot round, is limited to .55 of the leech length and is measured from the half luff to the middle of the foot (Fig. 1).

Although it is measured as a genoa, the blooper looks like anything *but* a genoa. This sail is maximum in every dimension except the luff length. The rule says that the blooper, when hoisted tight on the halyard, must be tight on the luff. The luff of the sail, therefore, is cut with a large amount of "hollow" to help keep the sail away from the spinnaker and project more area to leeward of the mainsail. With this hollow, of course, the girths can be made quite large and the leech of the sail now has a positive round to it. Figure 2 shows a blooper that measures the same as the genoa it is superimposed over.

The total effect is a sail with more area than a genoa and, when it is designed properly, it becomes a very effective half-spinnaker.

Usually bloopers are constructed from ¾-ounce nylon. However, on some small boats ½-ounce is more effective. Conversely, in boats over 45 feet, two bloopers are needed because of the wind velocities. A boat this size could easily have a ¾-ounce and a 1.2- or 1.5-ounce blooper.

The blooper becomes most effective when the apparent wind angle is from 130 to 180 degrees. In very light air, however, it is sometimes better to forget about a blooper and concentrate on the spinnaker. The spinnaker is the primary sail and the skipper always should sail

Figure 3: To operate at its best, blooper should be set as far to leeward as possible to get maximum projected area outside mainsail

70

the boat with this in mind. And he should steer the fastest course and leave the flying of the sail to the halyard and sheet trimmer.

Setting the blooper is no big deal. The tack is placed at the same spot as the genoa is tacked; *it is illegal* to tack it farther aft than this if it is maximum on the LP. Here it's a good idea to lead the tack outside the pulpit. Attach the head of the sail to the genoa halyard led *outside* the spinnaker sheet and hoist away. The blooper sheet should be trimmed as far as possible, for this helps the sail

Figure 4: To achieve optimum trim, halyard should be eased so foot of sail is just out of water

project its maximum out to leeward. A common mistake I see made is to trim the sheet through a lead on the mainboom. This restricts the sail from moving to leeward and the key is getting the sail as far to leeward as possible. This allows for maximum separation between it and the spinnaker and gives more projected area outside the main (Fig. 3).

When you are trimming the blooper, teamwork between the trimmer and another person on the halyard is all-important. The trimmer keeps the sail full and drawing, and the halyard trimmer is responsible for getting the sail away from the boat as much as possible. As the sail fills, the halyard should be eased so that the foot of the sail is just out of the water. If the sail collapses, the halyard must be trimmed to keep the sail out of the water (Fig. 4).

If you are having difficulty flying the blooper in light to medium air, try overtrimming the main slightly or even putting in the first reef. The vast difference in size between a main and a blooper dictates which sail is more important.

When you are dropping the blooper, the easiest way to do it is to release the tack and pull the sheet in, very much as you do with a spinnaker douse.

The blooper is truly an effective weapon for downwind racing. But for the best results it must be constantly tended, and this can be a very fine art indeed.

Heavy Air

Dinghy Speed vs. Dinghy Survival

Procedures for staying up straight while others go over   Eric Twiname

If you find yourself sailing in survival conditions (and if you race long enough you are going to), the basic ingredient for success is to get yourself around the course without capsizing. When the wind is blowing 20-to-25 knots that is going to be quite an achievement. If you can be successful in staying upright in such extreme conditions you will automatically finish well up in the fleet. But to stay upright in that kind of wind you first have to know what makes you capsize, so let's look at the most "popular" ways of tipping over.

When beating in very heavy gusts, the knockdown is probably the most widely favored type capsize among middle-and back-of-the-fleet sailors. A helmsman and crew may believe that survival in a sudden 20-knot gust is impossible and that nothing they could do would save them from capsizing. They're wrong. Any properly sailed centerboard dinghy will survive such a gust on a beat. Most boats can survive a 25-knot gust; some will even stand up to more. It all depends on how the boat is handled.

Knockdown capsizes on a beat usually happen because the jib is cleated in very flat and the helmsman spills wind by completely letting go the mainsheet. In moderate winds you won't capsize this way, but given enough wind this is a sure way to go over. The jib pushes the bow off and, with no mainsail to balance the helm, the boat develops excessive lee helm. Nothing you do with the rudder will bring her back up to a close-hauled course. The result is that the boat is forced beam on to the wind; forward way is lost because the jib

stalls; and the whole mainsail flogs uselessly. With a jib cleated square to the wind and the enormous drag of a flogging mainsail, the capsizing moment of the rig becomes greater than any righting moment that the fully extended weight of helmsman and crew can provide.

This type capsize can easily be avoided. First, if you keep the boat approximately on a close-hauled course and do not allow it to lose way and fall beam on to the wind, excessive capsizing forces cannot develop. By sailing with the jib eased so that both jib and mainsail spill wind, lee helm will not develop, nor will the full area of a stalled jib be presented to the wind if the boat does fall much below a close-hauled course. Not only will the boat survive the gust with the jib eased but it'll also be surviving with even greater speed than before the gust.

By spilling wind on the jib and main together it is possible to stay upright until the wind becomes so strong that, with both mainsail and jib flogging, the heeling moment of the rig finally exceeds the righting moment of the fully extended weight of the helmsman and crew. For most dinghies, this only happens in winds of 30 knots or more.

When the wind is so strong that you have to ease the jib, it still pays to sail to windward pinching with the jib lifting several inches back from the luff. You should ease the mainsail too, so that the first third or so is backwinding. Then the boat is balanced on the helm and you can feather it to windward in such a way that the heeling moment of the rig always balances the crew weight. In the heaviest winds you can feather the boat higher on the wind so that you are back-winding even half the jib and half the mainsail; in less extreme wind you can drive the boat off with the whole jib and most of the mainsail drawing. Heavy-weather sailing is a balancing act—the art is to use your sense of balance and feel to keep the heeling forces of the rig and the righting moment of the crew weight in equilibrium.

Since the big gusts are what cause the trouble, you can usually avoid a capsize by spotting the gusts before they arrive. Fortunately you can't mistake the darker and more threatening-looking patches of water that gusts send out as calling cards. All you need do to predict their arrival is to glance upwind every 20 seconds at the surface of the water. With practice you should be able to read the water well enough to predict *to the second* the moment the full force of the gust will strike. This will enable you to ease the jib and to sit out fully *before* the gust strikes. Then the first impact of the gust drives the boat forward rather than sideways or, worst of all, horizontally.

Your aim when sailing a dinghy to windward in heavy weather should be to always keep the boat level. Get maximum crew weight over the side to achieve that; otherwise you will need to sacrifice extra sail power to compensate for the lack of sitting-out power. But once you have your crew and yourself sitting out to the limit, you must then sail the boat level doing whatever it takes to achieve that. This includes spilling wind from most of the mainsail and most of the jib. Keep your boat level and you'll have more control, more speed and a higher finishing position.

Lifting the centerboard a third of the way up will make most dinghies easier to hold up on a beat in the heaviest weather, even though you increase leeway. By sailing with two-thirds board, you decrease the heeling moment of the boat because the lateral resistance of the hull is brought closer to the sideways (heeling) forces of the rig. This brings a significant reduction in the heeling tendency of the boat so you need to spill less wind. The risk of being blown flat is further reduced because, as the boat heels, even more of the centerboard comes out of the water and the hull slides off to leeward rather than capsizing. Some classes actually sail more quickly to windward in very heavy weather with the board partially raised.

There is a temptation to relax and sit in as soon as the boat becomes level. Don't—that's just the time your sitting out provides the biggest righting moment. I always try to sail upwind heeled slightly to windward and fail by just enough to leave the boat perfectly upright most of the time.

As long as you and your crew are sitting out hard and spilling and feathering up to windward as much as is necessary to keep the boat upright, good windward speed is an automatic result. You will also have an easier and faster ride when a gust strikes even if you don't spot it coming. With the boat sailing level and crew weight well over the side, the wind has much more to do to heel the boat; it has to lift you and your crew several feet into the air. As this begins to happen you have time to ease the mainsheet and to pinch up before the boat heels way over.

If you and your crew are not sitting out hard or are not holding the boat level before the gust, first, you must get your collective weight properly over the side. While you are attempting to do this, the boat may heel too far and the moment will be lost for playing the mainsheet and helm for maximum boat speed. Instead you may flounder sideways at reduced speed until control is regained, or swim! It is a mistake to sit out hard *only* when things are going wrong.

Many people have the idea that spilling wind is bad because it's sacrificing power. In fact much more power is lost in a dinghy by allowing the boat to heel. Spilling wind in the mainsail and, when conditions get really heavy, in the jib, gets rid of excessive and unmanageable heeling and leeward forces in the rig, yet retains the essential forward driving forces. The result: good forward speed without excessive heeling or leeway.

One technique works really well for holding the boat flat as a gust first strikes without sacrificing unnecessary power. At the moment of the gust's initial impact, let go an arm's length of sheet and *immediately* pull most of it back in again, while at the same time, push the helm to leeward to keep the boat pointing up. If the boat still wants to heel, let out an arm's length of sheet again, then sheet back in. You may have to pump the mainsail this way two or three times before the boat is properly under control, pointing fairly high on a close-hauled course and moving quickly.

The purpose of mainsail pumping is two-fold. By letting out the mainsail as the gust strikes, the initial blast passes without causing the boat to heel unduly. Then immediately hauling in most of the released sheet fills the aft part of the mainsail and it acts like an airborne rudder holding the boat on a close-hauled course. Two or three repeated pumps of the mainsheet allow you to hold the boat level and on a high close-hauled course until the main impact of the gust has passed. The technique is particularly useful in a sudden lifting gust.

Usually it is better to over-prepare for an imminent gust than to be caught unaware. If you ease the jib too much it can easily be sheeted in right away with little lost. Near a windward shore in gusty weather the gusts tend to be more vicious, more variable in direction and shorter lived. In these conditions it usually pays in survival weather to sail with the jib uncleated, or at least freed off a few inches.

At the back end of a gust you can get an extra kick of speed by sitting out hard a moment longer than you think you should while at the same time sheeting the mainsail back in to its usual, more central, close-hauled position. This gives an extra two-or-three feet of gain after the gust has gone. Repeated after each gust, these small gains become boat lengths and, finally, places picked up by the end of the windward leg.

A gusty wind always has one devas-

Charles Mason

For speed and survival in heavy weather, first priority is to sail boat flat, spill wind and feather to windward as much as necessary

tating trump card up its sleeve: the slam header—the sharp gust that attacks you suddenly from ahead, backing the jib and tipping you over to windward. Everyone knows that this can happen, but the middle- and back-of-the-fleet helmsmen and crews tend to sail gusty heavy-weather beats as though it's always going to happen.

They shouldn't be so worried. A slam header that is violent enough to make a capsize certain is extremely rare. I can remember only one in all my racing and that was when beating in a lee of a mountain in an unusually fluky 20-knot breeze. The fear of the slam header has a far more devastating effect on your attitude toward heavy-weather windward sailing than the event itself has.

Curiously, helmsmen and crews who don't sit out hard when they are beating in a gusty wind make themselves *more* vulnerable, not less, to the sudden violent header. All dinghies have one thing in common with bicycles: they tend to be more easily controlled and kept upright when they are traveling quickly. If you fail to drive your boat hard upwind it goes more slowly and does not respond as positively to rudder move-

ments. When you work hard, the boat is more responsive and will bear off more sharply as the header strikes.

The state of extra alertness and agility that helmsmen and crews enter into when sailing hard means that their own responses to a slam header are faster, more definite, and therefore more effective. An alert crew can be sitting out hard one moment, then be diving for the lee side of the boat with jib already uncleated. A crew whose sitting-out efforts are tentative in the first place tends to react tentatively to a slam header. A keenly aware helmsman working his boat to windward for all he's worth will bear off more quickly and more positively than someone who is sailing very cautiously.

As I have already mentioned, a really perceptive helmsman and crew will know that a slam header is coming *before* it arrives; it will not catch them unaware. If they scrutinize the water upwind, they will know not only when a gust is about to arrive, but also the direction of the wind in that gust.

In shifty wind a top-flight helmsman will be taking a continual read-out of the water immediately upwind so that

A capsize is almost always your own fault, rarely that of the wind

he not only adjusts his mainsheet but also alters his boat direction to anticipate the gust. This naturally helps his survival on a gusty beat, and enables him to sail more confidently and more quickly than those whose only clues to wind strength and direction are their wind indicator and sails. Boats that are ahead are also excellent wind-direction indicators. Many a windward capsize has been a warning to the helmsmen behind to prepare themselves for a slam header.

One of the all-time favorite ways of capsizing, and it is as widely used today as it was when the jam cleat was invented, is the backed-jib tack. The crew fails to uncleat the jib during the tack so that once past head-to-wind, the boat is flipped over by the backed jib. In survival conditions even uncleating the jib requires a determined effort.

The heaviest gusts even make tacking hazardous. The enormous drag of the flogging sails as the boat goes head-to-wind may be powerful enough to stop the boat dead in the water and to throw it rapidly into reverse and into irons. So always look for lulls to tack in, and always go into a tack with good boat speed and a determination to get around onto the new tack. It's the tentative or half-hearted attempt that puts a boat into irons.

Also try to attack heavy-weather beats with determination and to drive the boat hard. Not only does this make staying upright more likely, but it's also the right attitude to have to get to the weather mark first. When you do capsize, work out why. Except in the most extreme heavy weather, a capsize is always going to be your own fault—never the wind's.

Reaching to Leeward

Proper courses for planing hulls in increasing winds　　　　　Frank Bethwaite

How should you handle a boat so that you can sail it at its best across the wind? This is where the fun begins because a skilled small-boat crew can enjoy a wonderfully rich variety of techniques as they coax a boat to achieve and to maintain the highest speed possible. On no other point of sail are the differences between the experienced and the inexperienced sailor so obvious. And on no other point of sail does skill in achieving the highest performance possible contribute so much to excitement and to pleasure.

Think about reaching as a blend of two facts: the wind is never steady; and a performance sailboat capable of planing can, when properly handled, produce tremendous bursts of speed and can quickly outdistance its competitors. There are numerous opportunities to shift into a planing mode and to keep the boat in that range for considerable periods of time. In fluctuating winds these opportunities are repeated continuously.

The art of sailing well on a reach lies in anticipating, identifying and exploiting these fluctuations as they occur. Crews of high-performance boats experience special excitement in stronger winds, for two more elements can then be woven into the technique. The following suggestions are valid for all boats, but will apply to some more than others.

In very light winds (less than three knots), laminar separation occurs on the sails and they lose power; this action accounts for very low light-air boat speeds. In stronger winds and on those points of sail where the crew are hiking their farthest and easing sheets to keep the boat upright, I am assuming that only the lull wind strength can be used for forward drive and speed.

Farther off the wind, a point occurs at which the boat can be held upright while the crew drive it at its hardest. At this point, the drive force and speed increase abruptly, and show on a polar curve as humps (Fig. 1). Farther off-wind, the highest attainable speeds decrease rapidly as the speed of the apparent wind becomes smaller. It is interesting to see how these humps appear in a calculation, and they are certainly there in practice.

In moderate air, sailboats begin to divide into their performance categories: some can plane and some cannot. We will look at not only how to plane for more of the time on any reaching leg, but also how to use the wind's fluctuations to advantage in a non-planing boat such as a catamaran.

Four factors dominate in the wind-speed range from about six-to-12 knots. First, the speed advantage from planing *is always decisive.* Second, the point of sail on which a light boat will plane soonest in an increasing wind is always about a beam reach or directly across the wind.

Third, once a boat has started planing, it can then vary its course quite widely and still maintain the plane. Fourth, (unlike the one-or-two-knot light-air regime) a boat will sail most quickly in lighter winds when it is close reaching and in all stronger winds when it is broad reaching. This is clear from the figure.

The technique that puts all this together is beautifully simple. Assume that the wind is fluctuating every 10 seconds between, say, seven knots and 11 knots, and your boat will just plane on a beam reach in a wind of about eight-to-nine knots. The heading to the next mark is close to a broad reach.

With two different helmsmen, one will always steer directly for the mark. In the seven-knot lulls, he or she will sail at about 5½ knots. In the 11-knot puffs, he can plane cleanly at speeds less than about eight knots so usually he will spend most of the 10-second period of the puff at a speed from six-to-seven knots. Only after some fortunate peak in the wind puff has pushed the boat over the eight-knot hump in the drag curve can it achieve, then stabilize, at its potential speed of nine knots. The average speed, if the boat is handled this way, is likely to be about six or 6½ knots because the boat won't be sailing at nine knots for much of the time.

However, the second helmsman sails just a little high in the lulls, and goes at six knots. He watches the puffs approaching him across the water and, as the leading edge of each puff reaches him, he luffs up smoothly about 20 degrees, leans mightily to hold the boat absolutely upright, pumps his mainsail, and flicks his boat cleanly onto the plane, achieving about 10-to-11 knots very quickly. The total force developed by the sails of a Tasar in 10½ knots of wind is 180 pounds. The extra force obtained from pumping is drive force available to accelerate a boat of less than 500 pounds total weight. So, the acceleration from six knots to 11 knots is very fast—about one second. Sails should be set for the greatest possible drive during this second or so.

Immediately after the boat is up and planing hard, this second helmsman bears away smoothly until he is sailing a little low of the mark to get down to the rhumb line. At the very least, he will average his full nine knots during the puff, and will probably average more if he bears away farther in the maximum of

the puff and then starts to come up gently as the puff dies. Sailing this way, he might sustain a plane at eight knots or better for one or two seconds into the lull. His average speed can be about 7½-to-eight knots, or 25 percent faster than his less enterprising competitor.

The whole technique calls for close observation of approaching puffs, anticipation, coordination, and smooth and powerful handling to exploit each puff.

If the heading to the next mark is a close reach, exactly the same principles are applied but in the reverse direction. In the lulls, the helmsman should steer a little high. In any case, this will be the heading on which he sails most quickly in a lull. As soon as the puff arrives, he should bear away to a beam reach; flick his boat onto a plane; then immediately luff to a heading that is a little lower than the rhumb line; and thereafter adjust heading and sail trim as necessary during the puff to maintain the highest planing speed possible for as long as the puff lasts.

For a lightweight boat rigged with a spinnaker, exactly the same principles and techniques apply, but the angle of sail is always a little farther off the wind.

The fastest technique for a non-planing boat is completely different. Given a typical performance curve for a non-planing boat, there can never be any advantage in heading in any direction *other than directly toward the mark*. This will always be the fastest technique for these boats.

In stronger winds, reaching is the point of sail on which full-range performance boats are unique because of the way their handling characteristics enable them to match and to exploit the wind fluctuations.

Four factors dominate when reaching in winds stronger than about 12 knots: to keep the boat upright, ease sheets on all close reaches; in any wind, if a helmsman bears away onto a progressively broader reach, there will be a point at which the boat can be held upright without your easing the sails; as the wind becomes stronger, the point at which the boat can just be held upright will occur farther and farther offwind;

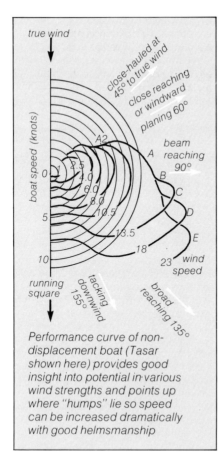

true wind

boat speed (knots)

close-hauled at 45° to true wind

close reaching or windward planing 60°

beam reaching 90°

A2

A

B

C

D

E

0

2.5

4.0

6.0

8.0

10.5

13.5

18

5

10

23 wind speed

running square

tacking downwind 155°

broad reaching 135°

Performance curve of non-displacement boat (Tasar shown here) provides good insight into potential in various wind strengths and points up where "humps" lie so speed can be increased dramatically with good helmsmanship

sail must be set progressively fuller as the headings approach B.

Throughout this exercise, the boat should be close reaching at about 20 feet per second and the apparent wind (across the deck) will be about 25-to-30 feet per second, so the boat will encounter the natural fluctuations of the wind more quickly than when at rest (exactly as you encounter waves more quickly when you sail toward them).

A fluctuation every three-to-five seconds would be about normal. As each puff occurs, the apparent wind will increase from 17 knots to 20 knots, and the heeling force on the boat will increase by about 40 percent. To correct for this, the helmsman must take some action: he has four choices.

He can sail with a slack sheet, and move in and out of the boat as the wind fluctuates. This is the technique used by most beginners, and it is woefully slow. He can lean hard, set the sheet or traveler at some intermediate position, and then luff in the puffs, and bear away in the lulls. This, while better, is also very slow because at high speed when the heeling boat is luffed, it will tend to roll to leeward; that is, it will tend to heel even farther by its own turning action.

The result of this is that there will be less righting force left to oppose the wind. Acceptable sail force and, hence, speed is proportional to this righting force, so a boat that is luffed in the puffs will sail slowly and generally it will be heeled. The sail will be far too full when the boat is luffed. This looks exciting, and gives a lot of people a lot of pleasure, but it wins no races, and it isn't very safe.

He can aim the boat straight, and play sheet or traveler to keep the boat absolutely upright through the puffs and lulls. This is much faster and much safer. But the boat can be sailed more quickly yet.

He can bear away a little as each puff occurs and at the same time ease the sheet or traveler just enough to keep the boat upright. This is the fastest and safest technique of all. It increases the boat's righting moment and keeps the boat absolutely upright exactly when the wind is strongest. And, equally im-

and if you are steering a boat for balance in a strong and fluctuating wind, the direction and amount you should turn it to keep it upright is almost exactly the same as the direction and amount you should turn it to maintain the highest speed possible in that wind.

To see how all this goes together, look closely at the stronger wind curves of the figure. To achieve point A, a skilled crew will have to lean or trapeze to their limit; and to hold the boat upright, the sails must be well eased and quite flat. If they are too deeply curved, they will merely backwind, and only some lesser speed (A2) will be possible. As the helmsman bears away onto headings that are progressively closer to a beam reach, the crew will still be leaning at their maximum, and the sails must still be eased, even in the lulls. But to attain the speeds indicated, the main-

portant, it continually adjusts the wind angle so that the same sail fullness is correct throughout the *puff-lull* sequence. The boat is luffed up and the sheet or traveler is recovered at the end of each puff.

This is a brief description of how a planing boat should be handled at any point of sail from A to B in the figure. The real excitement, however, is still to come. When a helmsman heads off to a point of sail at C, he will suddenly find that it is no longer necessary to ease the sheet or traveler as he bears away in the puffs. Now the sail force is directed sufficiently forward, rather than sideways, so that a four percent added heeling force of a puff can be compensated for entirely by slightly turning the boat to leeward as the helmsman steers for balance. So from here on, as the wind increases in a good gust—from, say, 14 knots to 18 knots—all that happens is

that the helmsman can bear away a little to steer for balance, and can adopt heading D or E in the stronger gusts, and C in the lulls. And he can do so and never increase the set of the sails. The increase in speed is dramatic; clearly, the heart of this technique is to *steer for balance.*

With spinnaker-rigged boats, the technique will remain basically unchanged, but everything occurs when sailing farther off the wind.

As the desired point of sail progressively shifts toward a broad reach, the apparent wind will quickly become less strong, and the power of the sails and the subsequent boat speed will decrease rapidly.

The fastest technique on any point of sail that is greater than E in the figure is to set the sails up properly and then steer for balance as the puffs and lulls pass by.

The Heavy-air Run

Enhancing your chances for survival

Eric Twiname

The secret of successful heavy-weather racing is fearlessness. Get rid of fear or excessive anxiety and you automatically start thinking about getting around the course as quickly as possible. But if you sail tense, fearing a capsize, gear failure or heavy weather in general, your whole approach becomes half-hearted and tentative.

Heavy-weather panic is by no means rare; it can afflict anyone. It doesn't seem to be related to courage in other fields, either. Three years ago I was talking to a keen Laser sailor who had taken up the sport six months earlier. The club race was due to start and the wind was blowing at 10 knots, maybe just touching 12. Yet this helmsman didn't seem at all keen to go out, which was extraordinary, so I asked whether he was racing. He wasn't because he had lost his confidence the week before when he had capsized often on heavy-weather downwind runs.

"Come on," I urged him, "it's hardly more than 10 knots out there."

"I know," he replied, "but last week I really scared myself. In my previous sport I never got that scared."

"What sport was that?" I inquired innocently.

"Motor racing."

In time, he regained his confidence—that is, he was able to remove some of his heavy-weather fear. But I didn't manage to persuade him to go out that afternoon.

Evidently, his worst problems had overtaken him when he went onto a dead run. The boat took control and he became little more than a helpless and alarmed passenger. Most of his capsizes happened when the boat sheered off suddenly to leeward and the rig fell smartly to windward. He retired from the race after failing to find any way to prevent these windward capsizes.

Running in heavy weather takes courage. Once you're pointing dead downwind you move quickly, whether you want to or not. And unlike a beam reach, which allows you to ease off the mainsail and spill wind, a run provides no safety valve which will slow you down or get you out of trouble. With the boat powering off on a fast plane and a 20-knot wind dead astern, your concern is survival. Speed, maybe more of it than you'd like, is inevitable; survival is not.

So what can you do to be sure of staying upright in heavy weather on a dead run? First, learn what causes capsizes. Then you will know what danger signs to look out for so you can avoid doing anything that might make you capsize.

The most likely problem with the Laser sailor was that he was letting the mainsail out too far. A Laser, like a Finn, has no shrouds to prevent the sail from going out beyond a right angle to the boat's centerline. When the sail is let out too far, the direction of the air flow over it reverses: the flow tends to be from the mast toward the leech rather than from leech to luff as it would be with the boom sheeted farther in.

This reversal of flow reverses the direction of the rig's heeling forces. Instead of there being a leeward heeling force, the reverse flow generates a windward heeling force (Fig. 1). With the helmsman already on the windward side, the windward heeling force in the rig makes a quick death roll to windward inevitable. This can be avoided by keeping the mainsail farther in. Then the windward heeling moment created by the helmsman sitting to windward can be counterbalanced by the leeward heeling moment of the rig (Fig. 2).

Another more precarious way to prevent a windward capsize is for the helmsman to sit to leeward with the boom sheeted just forward of a 90-degree angle, and to run by the lee. In some singlehanded boats—the Laser among them—a little extra power is available from the rig when doing this. However, the boat is then more difficult to keep upright so this is not something

you should try in survival conditions. One Laser sailor discovered this technique by accident. He bore off to gybe at the start of a heavy-weather run, moved his weight over before the boom came across, but failed to gybe. Afraid of doing anything drastic to induce the gybe, he remained sitting on the "wrong" side of the boat for the rest of the run, running precariously by the lee at enormous speed. The gains he had inadvertently made were enough to encourage him to sail his runs that way deliberately, when conditions were right.

One sure way to make any boat without a spinnaker uncontrollable on a heavy-weather run is to sail with too loose a vang or kicking strap. To control the boat on the run, you must have the kicker tight enough to prevent the top of the sail from twisting off forward

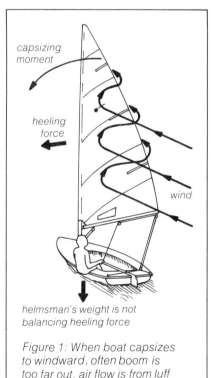

Figure 1: When boat capsizes to windward, often boom is too far out, air flow is from luff to leech. This creates windward heeling moment. With helmsman to windward capsize is almost inevitable

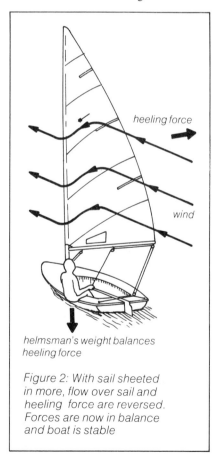

Figure 2: With sail sheeted in more, flow over sail and heeling force are reversed. Forces are now in balance and boat is stable

137

when either a gust strikes or the boat buries its bow into the back of a wave.

With a half-tightened kicker, the first impact of a gust twists the sail so the top third is pushed forward of that 90-degree angle. The wind flow reverses over this top part of the sail and again we have windward heeling forces of the sort shown in Figure 1. The boat reacts with a sudden lurch to windward which is usually violent enough to put the boat out of the helmsman's control and into a permanent roll to windward.

A spinnaker can make staying upright on the run easier. Set fairly high, the sail creates a downdraft. This produces a lifting force in the sail which lifts the bow over the backs of waves so the hull is more easily driven, especially in the gusts (photo). The other big benefit of the spinnaker is that it makes the boat plane more quickly, which reduces the apparent wind and heeling forces in the rig, making the boat more stable.

Although a dead run turns into a relatively secure ride with a spinnaker up, the risk of capsize increases dramatically when you are hoisting and lowering the sail. A cool helmsman and a sure-footed, fast-moving crew can nevertheless set spinnakers safely.

During the hoist, the helmsman should move all the way aft to counterbalance the crew who is moving forward to fix the spinnaker pole. The boat should be kept on a dead run for most capsizes during the hoist happen because the boat is allowed to head up and to broach. Even with the spinnaker up and drawing well it is still possible to broach, usually because the helmsman is too slow on the helm to counter the broach. A broach starts as a fairly small luff. Catch the luff in time and get the boat bearing off back onto a dead run; then there's no broach and no capsize.

Windward capsizes under spinnaker take place because both the guy and the pole are hauled too far aft while the sheet is eased too much. Instead of being presented square on to the wind, inducing a vertical downdraft, the sail is now angled so that the wind also flows horizontally: from the luff of the spinnaker to the leech. This horizontal flow generates a heeling force acting to windward, which in moderate wind may not appear to matter (although the spinnaker will be less efficient). But when a gust arrives, the heeling force will increase sharply.

Without a spinnaker, a running boat is more stable with the jib goose-winged than with it left to look after itself in the lee of the mainsail. A goose-winged jib balances the rig and, like the spinnaker, gives that extra lift and forward drive which helps prevent the bow from burying itself in the biggest gusts.

For both survival and speed on heavy-weather runs it is vital to get helmsman and crew weight back as far as possible, one on each side of the boat. Without a spinnaker the boat becomes hydrodynamically unstable in the heaviest gusts because the mainsail presses the bow down, tilting the hull forward onto the narrower forward sections and lifting the wider and flatter aft part of the hull off the water. If you get the hull riding on these flatter aft sections by moving weight back, the boat will have greater stability and will move more quickly.

Keeping crew weight well aft also reduces the chances of getting into the familiar downwind roll—a rhythmic and ever-increasing roll from side to side which usually ends with a splash. The way to stop the roll from ever happening is to sheet in the mainsheet several feet so the boom is 15 or 20 degrees back of a right angle to the centerline.

Once the roll has begun it becomes self-perpetuating because, as the rig sways from side to side, the air flow over the surface of the mainsail reverses with each oscillation. When the rig rocks to windward, the air flow over the mainsail is to leeward and it reverses as the rig rocks back to leeward. But by sheeting in the mainsail so the boom is a foot or two off the lee shroud, the flow over the sail is always from leech to luff, never from luff to leech. The boat will then have greater stability and any roll which begins will be dampened rather than amplified by the rig.

So the most secure way to sail a survival run without spinnaker is for the helmsman to sit firmly on the windward side of the deck with the crew wedged just to leeward of the centerline, both well aft. With the mainsail sheeted in slightly from the square angle, the rig's heeling moment is counterbalanced by the combined weight of helmsman and crew to windward. Any tendency to heel can then be counteracted entirely by rudder movements. The boat will be moving quickly, and quick jabs of the rudder are very effective for killing any tendency to heel or for dampening a rhythmic roll.

It's important for helmsman and crew to stay firmly rooted by their backsides to the boat; they then become part of the boat, doubling its moment of inertia and greatly slowing down any rolling there may be. The certain way to turn a rhythmic roll into a quick capsize is for both helmsman and crew to get onto their feet and attempt a corrective dance. Only when the boat heels more than about 25 degrees on a dead run should anyone move his position. The movement should be small and the one who should move is the crew.

With practice, a dead run need be no more scary than any other point of heavy-weather sailing. You know you've got it right when, with weight all the way aft, the boat can find no other way to put you in except by cartwheeling forward. Rare as this is, it happened once to a friend of mine in a Fireball on a day race. As he hit the water, he cut his face on the masthead wind indicator. That is the kind of wound you can be proud of!

139

Oscillation and Rolling

Fundamentals of Broach Prevention   Steve Colgate

No matter what size boat you sail, if you set a spinnaker in heavy airs, you probably will broach at some point. Fifteen-footers broach and 80-footers broach: size makes no difference. The difficulties experienced in the last Transpac Race, when masts went over the side, were caused almost entirely by this broaching phenomenon.

A mild form of broaching is shown in Photo 1. Essentially it is an overpowering weather helm that is caused by a number of factors. When the weather helm—the tendency for the boat to round up into the wind—becomes so strong the helmsman is unable to counteract it by using the rudder, the boat will broach. Most of the time this means

the boat will wallow broadside to the wind until steering control is regained and the boat can once again be headed back downwind.

A major factor that causes a broach is excessive heeling. When a boat is upright in the water, the hull is symmetrical, splits the water evenly and is not pushed in one direction more than the other. However when the boat heels, the bow wave on the lee side becomes quite large and pushes against the curve of the hull as it works aft. The helmsman has to apply a good bit of rudder (steering as though to head off) to keep sailing straight.

Contributing to even more weather helm is the fact that when the boat heels

Photo 1: A boat under spinnaker just about to go into classic broach. Understanding why is the first step to learning positive control

the force of the sails moves well to leeward. Let's use our imagination for a moment. Imagine that in Photo 1 we have tied one end of a line around the mast just above the spreaders and run it ashore where we've tied the other end to the back of a car. Now we drive the car away, going faster than the hull of the boat allows it to go. By looking at the photo and using your imagination, it should be clear to you that the boat first will rotate until the hull becomes parallel to the shore, and then the whole mess will be dragged sideways by the mast through the water toward the shore.

With a spinnaker flying out over the water, the total wind force affects the boat in precisely the same way as that imaginary line. The more the boat heels, the more it wants to rotate into the wind. The more the boat rotates into the wind, the more it heels until what you have is a full-fledged broach on your hands.

In a broach the rudder becomes next to worthless. The boat is lying on its side so the rudder is near the surface where it can't get a good bite on the water. Because the rudder now is more parallel to the surface than it is perpendicular, any attempt to steer to leeward has about the same effect as horizontal elevators on the tail of an airplane. The stern and keel will lift rather than turn. So the more the boat heels, the less effective the rudder becomes when you try to turn it back downwind to reduce the heel. In fact after a certain angle of heel is reached the rudder will start to increase the heel.

If you, as a helmsman, are able to turn the boat in the early stages so the hull parallels the direction of pull, the hull creates less resistance, has a better chance of keeping up with the sails, and the tendency to broach will be reduced. So broaches can be controlled, and there are certain precautions both a skipper and crew can take to catch a broach before it occurs.

Because excessive heeling encourages broaching, on a small boat the crew and skipper must hike out hard using their weight to counteract any heeling force developed during gusts of wind that could overpower the boat. The crew in Photo 1 have not placed their weight correctly and are about to pay for it.

Another way to reduce heeling is to luff the sails but leave the spinnaker until last for it gives the boat a great deal of drive. First luff the mainsail. Remember, if your boom vang is set up tight—as it should be on reaches and runs—the boom is going to be held down. When the main is eased, but the boat heels, the end of the boom goes into the water and is pushed even closer to the hull by the water flow. This makes the sail more close-hauled which causes even more heeling. It's a vicious cycle and inevitably it ends in a broach. So obviously the boom vang must be eased first. In fact, racers who sail Solings disregard the mainsheet to avoid a broach and play only the boom vang. The boom lifts as the vang is eased and the top part of the sail up near the head luffs first. Because this is the part that causes most of the heeling, the effect is to reduce heeling without detracting much from the general drive of the sail. Of course, on those boats without boom vangs, the mainsheet is the only adjustment you can use to spill air from the mainsail.

The next sail you should ease is the jib, if you use one while flying the spinnaker. If you believe that trimming a jib will reduce weather helm by blowing the bow to leeward you are mistaken. Whatever lee helm might develop by this method is going to be nullified by the additional heeling force caused when the jib is trimmed in tight. The inevitable result is more weather helm.

When it becomes obvious that truly drastic measures are needed to avoid a broach, the spinnaker can be collapsed quickly by easing the sheet a couple of feet. The helmsman, however, has to anticipate this need and give the command to the spinnaker trimmer to *break* the spinnaker. When the boat has been headed back downwind and is under control and straightened up, the spinnaker can be trimmed in again and filled for maximum performance.

A few other factors can also contribute to broaching. If the spinnaker halyard has stretched or is not all the way

Photo 2: Running under spinnaker can cause rolling and oscillation problems that can only be countered by proper sail control and knowledge of what can go wrong

Steve Colgate

up at the *two-blocked* position (with the swivel at the head of the sail right at the block on the mast) the pull, or center of effort of the spinnaker, will be farther out over the water and will aggravate the turning moment.

The tack of a spinnaker always should be right out at the end of the spinnaker pole for the same reason. If the pole is too high as it is in Photo 1, the luff will have a large curve to leeward, which also causes the drive to be further out over the water. And if the leech of the spinnaker is cupped, as it is in Photo 1, rather than being flat and free, the trapped air will also cause more heeling.

On reaches, crew weight is a big factor in boat control and it should be placed aft for two reasons. First, the forward force on the sails that is pushing against the resistance of the hull has a natural tendency to bury the bow and lift the stern. This is vividly demonstrated by many catamarans which, on a reach, tend to bury the bow of the lee

hull and sometimes actually trip over it and capsize. To counteract this, a catamaran crew has to move way back near the stern of the weather hull. The same effect takes place with a monohull. A second reason for putting weight aft on reaches is to keep the rudder deeper in the water and increase its effectiveness.

Photo 2 shows another problem that can occur when a spinnaker is up: rolling or oscillating when running downwind. In this photo the boat is rolling to windward and shortly will roll back in the opposite direction. In heavy seas this can become wildly exciting, with the boat practically gybing as the mast rolls to windward then nearly broaching as it heels to leeward.

Much of the problem is caused by giving the spinnaker too much freedom. In Photo 2, the clew has been eased way out to or beyond the jibstay (it is hidden from view) and the result is that the spinnaker has been able to get completely around to the starboard side of the boat. This pulls the mast over in that direction. As the boat heels, the starboard bow wave is going to increase and as we have already seen, that shoves the bow to port toward a gybe. The helmsman may steer hard in the opposite direction (to starboard) but the spinnaker is now going to oscillate over to the port side of the boat causing heeling to that side. A strong weather helm is the result. The helmsman counteracts again and the rolling starts again.

An eased spinnaker halyard also increases rolling as does a loose boom vang. Though the vang in Photo 2 appears to be fairly tight, you can see by the mainsail that the top part of the sail is well forward of the bottom. This looseness allows the forces near the head of the sail to push the top of the mast to windward.

If rolling conditions exist, think first about trimming your jib in flat. It will help keep the bow downwind and will also dampen the rolling by acting like a baffle. Make sure the boom vang is tight so the top part of the mainsail is not greater than a right angle to the centerline of the boat. If it is, as is the case in Photo 2, trim the mainsail in a little and alter course up to more of a reach. Also make sure the spinnaker halyard is all the way up, and try lowering the pole and trimming the spinnaker sheet.

Get your crew weight on opposite sides of the boat. Just as children can see-saw faster if they're spaced close together on the board instead of being at the very ends, a boat will roll less if crew weight is out on either side. And finally, change helmsman if it appears the person who is steering doesn't quite have the timing or ability to anticipate enough to counteract the rolling.

Broaches and rolling can, and do, happen to everyone. But a good sailor will know how to reduce these problems to manageable terms: ones that he or she can control with relative ease.

Beating and Reaching in Larger Boats

Considerations of helm and sails when the going gets tough   Chris Bouzaid

Whenever anyone talks about heavy-weather sailing I immediately think about balance. The rudder on a yacht is supposed to be there purely for the purpose of turning the boat when you want to make a major change in direction. However, how often have you heard someone say "the rudder isn't large enough on my new boat and I have trouble steering her." The rudder on a modern-displacement One-Tonner is nearly twice the size it was 10 years ago. Why? Because the rigs of the boats are larger. But let's face it, they are not twice as large as they were 10 years ago, so why are the rudders twice as big?

I believe the reason is simple. Because the rigs on today's boats are larger, it is more difficult to keep the boat in balance at all times. On a modern ocean-racing yacht, the difference between the size of the spinnaker and the size of the mainsail when you are sailing downwind is something on the order of five to one! And unless you keep your boat balanced, especially when you are going downwind, it is a little bit like trying to walk a tight rope with a 50-foot pole for balance and holding the pole 10 feet from one end. The chances of getting to the other end without falling off on numerous occa-

When beating to windward, maintaining correct angle of
heel and proper balance on helm are
critical elements in getting top performance

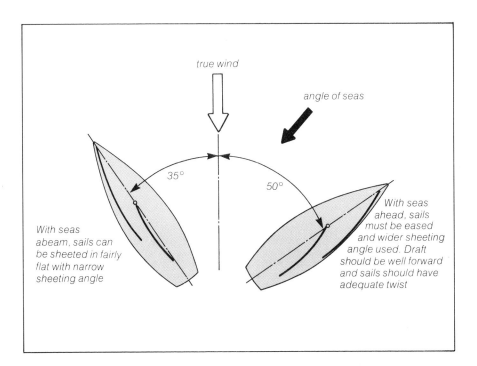

true wind

angle of seas

35°

50°

With seas abeam, sails can be sheeted in fairly flat with narrow sheeting angle

With seas ahead, sails must be eased and wider sheeting angle used. Draft should be well forward and sails should have adequate twist

sions would be fairly slim.

But to talk about heavy-weather sailing, you really need to look at the different angles of sailing.

Going to windward: Apparent wind 25° to 40°. On most offshore boats, one of the most important elements of sailing to windward is rigging your boat for the conditions. The angle of heel is critical at all times. On older, narrower boats, the angle of heel that was acceptable was often as much as 35 degrees. But on the more modern lighter-displacement boats with flatter sections, the angle of heel has to be kept around 20-25 degrees. When you are sailing to windward, don't overpower the boat, and be sure to keep her in balance. You should never need more than five degrees of helm at any time to keep your boat on track. I find that the most convenient way of sailing a boat to windward in heavy conditions is to concentrate predominantly on the angle of heel and if I find that I have too much angle of heel to keep the boat moving, then either I have too much sail or the sails should be sheeted differently.

Another thing that is very important when you are beating in heavy condi-

tions is to be extremely aware of sea conditions. Quite often, on one tack the sea conditions are different from the other tack. If you are sailing with the seas on the beam, generally you can carry more sail, can point higher, and are able to keep the boat moving at all times. However, when you tack, you will be going straight into the seas. If this is the case, the sails should be sheeted farther outboard with more twist and should not be sheeted in quite so hard. Usually you need to point a little lower—in some cases as much as 10 degrees. Sometimes it will pay to carry less sail when you are going into the seas than you would when you have them on the beam. Quite often I have found that when I am going into the seas the boat will sail much better with a double-reefed mainsail. But with the seas on the beam the boat can easily handle just a single reef. Obviously, on a short race, be aware of the situation and adjust the sails each time you tack (Fig. 1).

Selecting sails for heavy-weather sailing conditions varies from boat to boat. On my old One-Tonner, the S&S designed *Rainbow II*, I always found that

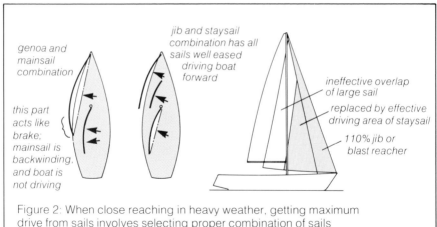

genoa and mainsail combination

jib and staysail combination has all sails well eased driving boat forward

this part acts like brake; mainsail is backwinding, and boat is not driving

ineffective overlap of large sail

replaced by effective driving area of staysail

110% jib or blast reacher

Figure 2: When close reaching in heavy weather, getting maximum drive from sails involves selecting proper combination of sails

she sailed best with a full mainsail. In fact, during three years of racing and over 30,000 miles of sailing we never once reefed the mainsail, and that included a 45-knot gale in the 1967 Sydney-Hobart Race which we won. However, when I was sailing *Mareva II*, a new Holland Swan 39, off Newport last year, I found that a double-reefed mainsail and a #3 headsail was the most efficient way by far to get maximum boat speed in a breeze. In one race we wound up sailing with the class that started 10 minutes before we did. Nearly all the other boats were sailing with more mainsail and less headsail than we were. But at the end of the day we won our class by such a large margin that we finished in the middle of that class ahead of us. The reason we did was simply because of our upwind speed.

The shape of the sails must also be correct. A lot of people believe that heavy-weather sails should be cut flat. I have always believed that heavy-weather sails should have plenty of drive and they should be kept well forward at all times. How often have you been sailing along with your heavy #1 genoa and been overpowered? Then you changed down to your #2 and you went even slower. This is because many sailmakers make their heavy-weather sails flat, and it really isn't because the #2 genoa is too small. In fact, it is

probably the right size but the sail is too flat, and with a fine leading edge, it is not forgiving and tends to create too much sideways thrust with not enough forward drive.

Remember that heavy winds shift the same as light airs. The trouble is the wind shifts are nowhere near so great because of the velocity of the wind, and therefore they are harder to detect, particularly in round-the-buoys racing. But by working these wind shifts you can gain significant time over the boats that do not. My golden rules for going to windward are *don't overcanvas the boat*, and, *beware of all the changing wind and sea situations.*

Close reaching: Apparent wind 40° to 70°. This is an area where you can get a tremendous amount of speed advantage over other boats. I am looking only at close reaching without spinnakers for it is a rare occasion when you can carry a spinnaker within this wind angle. Unlike going to windward when a headsail overlap is a significant advantage, to my way of thinking, an overlap when you are reaching does not help (Fig. 2). I have found that when I am reaching, any part of a sail that turns back into the boat tends to create a sideways motion and very little forward motion.

In last year's Bermuda Race, we had a close reach in 30-35 knots of wind. We were sailing alongside two larger boats, and we were carrying a high-clewed #3

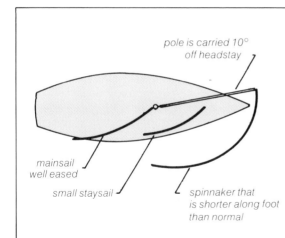

pole is carried 10° off headstay

mainsail well eased

small staysail

spinnaker that is shorter along foot than normal

Figure 3: In heavy winds where spinnaker can be carried, best combination is small spinnaker and small staysail that is carried inside chute. Crew must be alert and balance boat by use of sails rather than helm.

genoa which had no overlap at all. Our storm jib was set inside the genoa as a staysail, and we had a single-reefed mainsail. The boat felt alive, and every time we picked up a sea or got an extra burst of wind the boat accelerated way above any of our expectations. The two bigger boats we were sailing with were carrying #2 genoas and were laboring under them. Theoretically, anyway, they were both faster boats. However they were not reaching their potential because too much of their headsails were overlapped. This caused the mainsail to backwind and made the boats stumble to windward rather than drive forward.

When you are close reaching, a small, overlapping headsail and staysail is the best combination by far. You do need to carry a lot of twist in all three sails so that when any of the sails backwind, the tops must backwind first. A lot of people carry far too much boom-vang tension and also sheet their headsails too far forward when they are reaching. These are definitely mistakes although it does make the sails look better, it does not make the boat go faster. If your boat is trimmed properly when you are reaching, she should be delightful to sail, should carry very little helm and should really want to jump ahead. If the boat is not rigged correctly you are probably carrying a lot of mainsail backwind, and the boat has the feeling that she is burying herself in the water

at all times. My golden rule for close reaching is simply *make the boat feel alive!*

Reaching: Apparent wind 70° to 100°. In this range we are reaching with a spinnaker. In heavy conditions a spinnaker is a tremendous asset. However, to be effective, the spinnaker needs to be very small and needs to carry very little overlap. If it is used correctly, it can be flown with a #3 or #4 genoa or a spinnaker staysail. These two sails will work far better together than either will individually. I always carry a very small spinnaker on all my boats, and I find that although it does not get used very often, when you can use the sail, it is a real race winner (Fig. 3).

The small spinnaker I carry is usually between 90 and 92 percent of maximum luff length and is not much longer along the foot than the genoa. It is a small, flat-cut sail that virtually never overlaps the mast when it is set properly. By using this rig and by having a person work the spinnaker sheet, the staysail or headsail *and* the mainsail, you can get tremendous boat speed with the wind on the beam. In the puffs you merely ease all the sails a little. Remember that in puffy conditions, whenever the wind strength increases, the apparent wind moves aft and therefore you should always ease the sails more than you would normally expect. On *Rainbow II* we always had a standard rule that whenever we got a puff of wind, we al-

147

ways eased the spinnaker sheet three feet, the jibsheet 18 inches, and the mainsheet 18 inches. My crew always used to nickname this "flow and go"; you ease the sheets and you can feel the boat come alive and get moving rather than stumbling along because the sails are overtrimmed for the stronger wind conditions.

If the wind strength gets too great, you can always ease either the headsail or the spinnaker and let one of these sails flog momentarily. In doing so, you lose no boat speed and you are able to maintain course at all times. If you find you are flogging your mainsail too much, reef it, for a flogging mainsail tends to upset the trim of the boat. Once again, the angle of heel is all important here. Sometimes you can wind up sailing on a very fine line with this rig, and if this is the case, it pays to keep a little low on course at times to keep your boat speed up.

When you are reaching in heavy weather, trimming all the sails is of major importance. But the advantage that you can gain over your opposition in these conditions is very clear. Remember, never overtrim your sheets and always keep the boat moving. If you can't lay your course, sail a little low, douse the spinnaker early, and come back up to the mark.

Finally, the people who are trimming the sails must realize that they are also steering the boat; they are responsible for keeping her in balance. If the boat heels too much, they must ease the sails. If the boat begins to have too much weather helm, the trimmer on the mainsail must ease the mainsail to avoid that excessive helm which slows the boat down. So my golden rules for close reaching with a spinnaker are *flow and go*, and *steer with your sails*.

Downwind in a Breeze

Achieving the critical balance on a broad reach and run   Chris Bouzaid

I have talked about how you should handle a boat when the wind is blowing hard and there is a good sea running. I mentioned that when you are going to windward in such conditions you have to be constantly aware of the angle the seas are making with the boat and adjust both your sheeting angle and your sails to compensate for it. When you are going into the seas, you increase those sheeting angles and have your sail draft well forward for power. The situation changes when you are going across the seas. In these conditions you can sheet the sails in a good deal closer.

I also mentioned that it is important that you not set large headsails that will hook in toward the boat at the leech and backwind the main. This situation usually occurs when you are close reaching in a breeze. Here, a large headsail can act like a brake when it hooks in at the leech. In such conditions it is far better to use a smaller jib such as a #3 genoa which has no overlap, then set a staysail inside that jib.

Now I'll talk about what you should do in broad reaching and running conditions in a good breeze. But before I go into that I would like to re-emphasize that maintaining good balance with your sails is absolutely critical, for the rudder you have is not going to be all that effective against the forces created by the large modern racing rigs. If you keep this in mind, you will be a long way ahead of those who are constantly

fighting their sails by trying to use their rudder to compensate. Doing this can really slow you down, and in many cases you can't apply enough force to make all that much difference anyway. So always keep your boat balanced by using the sails.

Apparent wind 100°-150°. Here you are broad reaching and sailing with the wind abaft the beam. The one thing you have to remember is that now the wind is pushing you along, not pulling you. Any spinnaker you use under these conditions must be very free in the leeches, for big shoulders and wide head angles are not necessary to be efficient.

When you are in this range of apparent wind, you should not need much boom vang tension, and in really strong conditions it doesn't hurt to have a reef in the mainsail as well, rather than letting it flog. You should also think about using a spinnaker staysail underneath the spinnaker to help balance the boat. But if the spinnaker staysail is having a bad influence on the spinnaker, take it down. Large spinnaker staysails do tend to choke the spinnaker as the pole becomes more squared aft. For this reason make sure that the staysail is never overtrimmed. It can even pay, on certain occasions, to let the spinnaker staysail sheet go entirely to make sure that it is not slowing the boat.

For anyone who is tending the spinnaker he or she must ease off the sheet

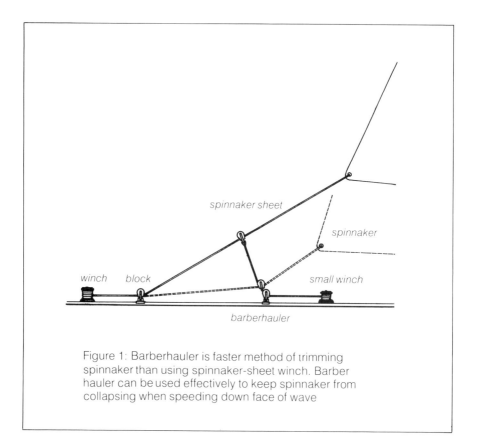

spinnaker sheet

spinnaker

winch block small winch

barberhauler

Figure 1: Barberhauler is faster method of trimming
spinnaker than using spinnaker-sheet winch. Barber
hauler can be used effectively to keep spinnaker from
collapsing when speeding down face of wave

in the puffs to avoid rounding up. Crew weight should be well aft at all times and all the weight should be up on the rail. When all is in place you should be able to start using the seas to give you better control as well as greater speed. By squaring away on the tops of the seas and by running down their backs, then coming back up in the trough, you should be able to maintain a good course without losing any distance to windward and still produce increased speed.

When you are running in these conditions, have a barberhauler on the spinnaker sheet (Fig. 1). A barberhauler is an important item and requires the attention of one person who should be able to adjust it immediately at all times. Whoever is working the barberhauler during this maneuver must be very quick. If the barberhauler is eased, the effect is very much like easing the spinnaker sheet: it opens up the head and allows any captured air to escape at the rear or overlapped portion of the spinnaker. When the barberhauler is pulled in, it will keep the spinnaker from collapsing when you start to run down a sea and increase speed. Using a barberhauler is a much faster and more efficient method than trying to grind in on the spinnaker sheet itself. This is especially true on large boats. Generally speaking, on boats up to 50 feet in length you can work a barberhauler by hand with a snubbing winch and you do not need a separate grinder to help you.

You must keep the boat moving at all times, and if a broach is imminent, both the spinnaker trimmer and the mainsail trimmer must ease the sheets *quickly* so that you can keep the boat on track rather than round up and lose boat speed. Sheets should never be cleated, and in extreme conditions keep the spinnaker pole as far aft as possible. One of the mistakes that many people make both reaching and broad reaching is to keep the spinnaker too far forward. It is essential that the pole be kept well off the forestay even when you are close reaching. In hard conditions, I never ever let the pole go closer than 18 inches to the forestay.

I remember in a One-Ton Cup off Marseilles, France, when I was sailing on a Farr-designed boat called *Jiminy Cricket,* we were the only boat to carry a spinnaker on a close-reaching leg into the finish during one of the short triangular races. Other boats tried and they just kept rounding up. The reason we could do it when the others couldn't was not because our boat was more stable but because we did not have our spinnaker pole on the forestay. The spinnaker we used was the right size for the conditions, and on many occasions we carried the front quarter or third of it luffing to keep us moving through the puffs. We were not overpowered. The golden rule when you are broad reaching with a spinnaker is: it is not how *big* the sails are, it is *how well you use them.*

Running, apparent wind 150°-175°. Running in these conditions with up to 30 knots of apparent wind you can generally carry full sail in the form of a full mainsail, and a maximum-sized spinnaker. The only compromise to this is that large shoulders on a spinnaker do tend to cause problems in these conditions. Here a few things become very important. Not only are they important, but also they must be done in haste when you are sailing with a spinnaker downwind. If they are not, control problems will take over before you have time to get going.

First, when you are trying to settle the spinnaker down, understand that the size of the spinnaker out to one side, as opposed to the size of the mainsail out on the other, is on the order of a 5:1 differential. Therefore when you first set the spinnaker, do not move the spinnaker pole aft more than 45-50 degrees from the centerline and keep the spinnaker well overtrimmed so that at least a third of it and possibly even more is on the leeward side of the forestay. In

this way you keep the boat *under* the sails, which is really the principle of all downwind sailing. You must keep the boat under the sail at all times, and if you do so, the sails will just pull the boat along. If you let the boat get out to one side and the sails out on the other side, control problems start immediately. This is basically what happens when a boat starts to roll going downwind. The boat rolls out one way, the spinnaker rolls the other, and this sets up a pendulum effect with the boat following the sails all over the ocean.

To overcome this problem, sheet the spinnaker in and get the boat back underneath the spinnaker. After the spinnaker is up and oversheeted, you then can set the blooper (shooter). I was primarily responsible for designing this sail, and the reasons for it are obvious. Without a blooper it is almost impossible to sail a modern International Offshore Rule boat downwind effectively. The blooper adds a lot of pull to the leeward side of the boat and tends to make the boat more in balance. Once the sail is up and set you will find that it is quite easy to start moving the spinnaker pole back and easing the spinnaker sheet out at the same time (Fig. 2).

At this point the spinnaker should lead to a block located well forward; on some boats it can be as far forward as the chainplates. Now you can ease the spinnaker sheet and move the spinnaker pole back at the same time, although the amount that you can do this is dictated to you by the helmsman. You just keep moving the pole back until the boat is in perfect balance for going downwind.

However, as we all know, certain things can happen at this stage and all are caused by the problems of balance. The spinnaker can take charge, the blooper can collapse and the boat can either start to charge up into the wind or square away and gybe. When any of these situations occur, start winding the spinnaker sheet in really quickly. I have found that I can carry a lot of sail dead downwind in really strong conditions just by having a really good man on the winch who is working his heart out

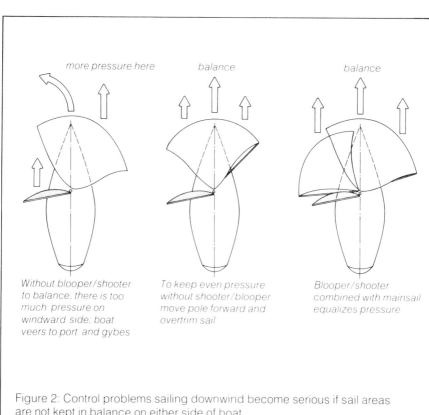

more pressure here — balance — balance

Without blooper/shooter to balance, there is too much pressure on windward side; boat veers to port and gybes

To keep even pressure without shooter/blooper move pole forward and overtrim sail

Blooper/shooter combined with mainsail equalizes pressure

Figure 2: Control problems sailing downwind become serious if sail areas are not kept in balance on either side of boat

trimming the spinnaker. As soon as the boat starts to roll, starts to lose control, or the blooper collapses, he immediately starts winding the spinnaker in frantically. In doing so he brings the boat back into balance, gets the sails balanced over the boat, and the boat will then proceed again in a seamanlike manner in the right direction.

I have found in moderate surfing conditions it often pays to sail around 165-175 degrees apparent wind rather than sailing dead downwind. In doing so I can take advantage of the blooper and the surfing conditions. However, if conditions get really strong and you can surf at all times when you are running square, it definitely pays to run as close to 180 degrees as possible. When doing this, use a smaller spinnaker as well for this is a very dangerous time as far as control is concerned.

In a windy Newport race week series last year on *Mareva*, a Swan 39, we sailed a downwind leg with a full-sized flanker instead of using a maximum-sized triradial spinnaker. Though the flanker had less area and reduced shoulders, we were able to sail straight to the leeward mark on the square run, whereas all the other boats with larger spinnakers went running way out to one side of the course, and then gybed and came back in again. Because everyone was sailing at maximum hull speed we got to the leeward mark a considerable distance ahead of all of those other boats. So the golden rule for running square in heavy conditions is *concentration*, and keep the boat under the sails.

Gybing is always a very touchy issue in strong wind conditions. I tend to be extremely cautious when I gybe a modern boat for I know a large amount of

When shooter/blooper is not set to counteract force of spinnaker, mainsail alone is not sufficient and boat will broach to leeward and gybe. which is what has happened here in heavy-weather running conditions

time can be lost if I execute a bad gybe. If you have good crew who know the boat you should be able to gybe in almost any conditions. But if you have crew who are unskilled or who do not know the boat as well as they should, a careful move would be to hoist the headsail, drop the spinnaker, gybe the boat and then reset the spinnaker. You do not lose all that much time if everything is done quickly. However, if you do want to gybe in heavy going and you do have crew who are up to it, here are a few pointers that might make your gybing experience a little smoother.

First, put the spinnaker back in the position it was before you hoisted the blooper. Move the spinnaker pole forward and overtrim the spinnaker. Once you get this done, lower the blooper as quickly as possible and get ready to gybe the spinnaker. If you are doing a dip-pole gybe don't forget to hoist the inner end of the pole high enough up on the mast so the outer end can easily pass inside the forestay.

Now comes the real test, the actual gybing of the spinnaker. The helmsman plays a vitally important role here but very few people realize how much he can help. First, have the spinnaker fly free of the spinnaker pole and move out to windward. This makes the clew of the spinnaker come in toward the man at the bow so he can put the new spinnaker pole afterguy into the pole. A good helmsman can make this happen.

The second test is to swing the spinnaker out to leeward of the boat to make it easy for the crew stationed aft to pop the spinnaker pole back up and to square it aft. Again, the helmsman can play a crucial role. When this is completed, gybe the mainsail (Fig. 3).

These procedures apply to all conditions, but in heavy weather they must be done very quickly to avoid any mishaps. Remember that after the gybe, the spinnaker must be set up the same way it was before the gybe. The pole should not be too far aft and the spinnaker should remain well overtrimmed until the blooper is reset on the new gybe.

These are just a few things you should keep in mind when you are running in any heavy-weather conditions. There is really no substitute for going out and trying these maneuvers ahead of time when the wind is blowing hard for only then can you see how the boat and the sails actually behave. And whatever you do, don't forget that the rudder on any boat that is sailing in heavy weather is not all that effective when it comes to steering. So even though it is there for that purpose, do

153

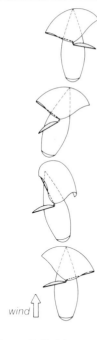

4. Gybe completed. Keep spinnaker overtrimmed until blooper/shooter has been reset. Then square pole

3. Swing bow back to starboard to move sail to port. Pull pole back and gybe mainsail

2. Trip pole and swing it forward. Helmsman turns to port, sail moves to starboard. Fasten new afterguy to pole

1. Before gybe, drop blooper/shooter and overtrim spinnaker to keep boat in balance

wind

Figure 3: Gybing sequence in heavy winds is very critical, must be performed quickly

not depend on it to slow the boat down.

In short, if you are going to enjoy your heavy-weather sailing and you are going to do it effectively, remember the most important rules of all: keep the boat in balance, and balance her with your sails!

Design

Fault-finding Afloat

Help your sailmaker understand your problems　　　Jeremy Howard-Williams

It is not always possible for a sailmaker to go sailing on a boat that has sail faults that need to be corrected. He may have neither the personnel nor the time to spare, especially as everyone seems to clamor for attention during the busy time of year. Alternatively, the boat may not be afloat, or the sailmaker may be too far away to arrange a mutually convenient time and date for a sail check.

An indoor or outdoor sail test rig is a useful addition to a sailmaker's armory in his fight against creases and badly shaped sails. It cannot, however, always reproduce the conditions found afloat and it works best in conjunction with actual observation of an offending sail set under sailing conditions.

Let's see how you can best help your sailmaker by using photographs, drawings and notes of faults, when you take a sail to him and complain of a poor set.

But before you reach for your camera and sketch pad, it is worth noting how the sailmaker goes about the job.

Tune and Trim

A surprising number of sail creases can be traced to faulty tune or trim. It should go without saying that the mast must be straight on *both* tacks, and the rigging set up properly. Sight up the luff on the mainsail to check on both lateral and fore-and-aft alignment. Naturally, a mainsail made for a bendy mast should not be expected to set properly on a straight one and, more important, vice versa (Fig. 1).

Check to see that all drawstrings and leechlines are completely slack even though they may have been steadied to quiet a gentle drumming. If they are not slack you may get a false impression. Now make sure the sail in question has been properly bent on. This includes

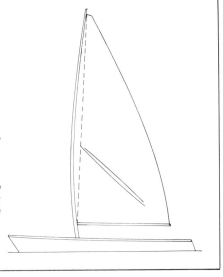

Figure 1: A crease from the clew is caused by the mast bending too much for the cut of the sail. If a mast which bends is used with a sail that hasn't enough cloth built into the luff to allow full movement, mast bend will be restricted. The mast will remove all flow from the sail as it tries to bend fully, and a crease will run from the clew to a point on the luff where the shortage of cloth is most acute. The cure is not to let the mast bend so much (by tightening the aft lower shrouds) or to tell your sailmaker more about its characteristics next time you order a new mainsail

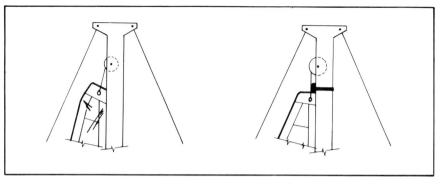

Figure 2: If the Headboard is pulled over and you cannot fit a larger sheave, a hard metal stop can be added to the aft face of the mast to force the halyard away from the mast so that it arrives at the headboard with a fair lead

the following points:

Mainsail Luff Rope. The sail should lead fairly to the tack pin. If it isn't back from the mast to accommodate a roller-reefing gear, the sail must be cut accordingly or creases will show. Similarly, the halyard should lead straight down to its attachment point at the headboard, and it should not pull over toward the mast when the sail is fully hoisted (Fig. 2).

Mainsail Slides. All slides should be at an even distance from the rope or tape. If an odd-sized shackle or a slacker or tighter seizing is used, the luff will be out of alignment and creases will run from the offending point.

Mainsail Clew. The clew should be in a straight horizontal line with the rest of the foot rope. If it is allowed to rise, either because there is no slide at the clew eye, or because there is no lashing round the boom at the clew, bad creases will result (Fig. 3).

Battens. Battens should be the correct length (you wouldn't smile if you had seen as many as I have that were a quarter of an inch too long) and be sufficiently flexible; particularly the top one.

Main Halyard. A mainsail that is not hoisted hard enough will show a slack leech precisely because the length is slack. Haul the sail up properly and greater tension will be put on both luff *and* leech.

Jib Luff. The luff should be in a straight line. Usually, the most comes at the tack; either the tack itself is set back too far from the forestay, or there is no

hank near the tack. This allows the luff to fall aft up to the first hank, particularly if the sail is set on a tack pendant (Fig. 4).

Jib Sag. If the forestay sags to leeward, the jib will become too full. There will not be creases necessarily, but you will find yourself complaining rather vaguely that the boat will not point as well as your rivals.

Jib Hanks. The things to watch for with hanks are somewhat similar to those regarding mainsail slides. A jib will suffer most, however, from hanks that are seized and not screwed to the sail. These may have been lashed too tightly compressing the eyelet and the cloth hard against the luff wire or rope. This results in local creases that radiate from the seizing, and there is a tendency to have a big one running at right angles to the luff.

Principal Faults and Their Cures

Slack Leech. If the sail is a mainsail (or, if you are dealing with a rope-luff jib), first check that the halyard is up tight enough. Now try the leechline to see what effect it has on the slackness, and *write down your findings*. In all probability a seam or seams will have to be tightened, so you should note the vertical and horizontal extent of the slackness. Also check to see whether the tabling on the leech is slack, or whether it returns to tightness to form a *question mark* or cup when you view it from above or below.

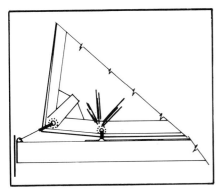

Figure 3: Mainsail will crease if clew is not lashed down. If you don't have a positive metal clew slide that holds the sail firmly down on the boom, take a lashing round the boom. This should also be done with a sail that runs in a groove because strong winds and high sheet loading can cause the sail to pull out of the groove at the clew

Tight Leech. This is worse than a slack leech because it means the wind is not escaping from the sail properly. Double check the leechline then sight up the leech to see the extent of the tightness: does it extend into the sail, or come purely from a tight leech tabling? Remember that an *appearance* of this fault can emanate from extreme fullness in a sail. It also can be caused in a jib by past misuse of the sail in winds too strong for the cloth weight in question. This is a problem most ghosters and light-weather genoas suffer from at one time or another when an owner is reluctant to change to a heavier sail as the wind increases. As the cloth overstretches, the flow is blown aft. A tight leech can be helped either by easing one or two seams and/or the tabling itself, or by stretching a jib harder on its luff wire to draw flow forward again.

Clew Creases. It is not possible in this short article to list all sail creases and possible cures and I shall deal here with the most frequently met creases. Multiple creases radiating from the clew probably come from tight sewing of the clew eye, coupled with the large stresses set up in a sail by modern winches and outhauls. Such creases are hard to re-

move but sometimes they can be helped by a piece of stiffer cloth placed under the clew reinforcement (if the rules allow it).

One single crease running from a mainsail clew to the inner end of the lowest batten can result from a bad batten, a slack leech, a tight leech, too much roach, too much foot round (or fullness) at the clew or overstretched cloth resulting from badly laid panels, or from using sailcloth that's too light or of poor quality. You can see that this is a difficult fault to diagnose, and photographs are essential. Even then I do not hold out too much hope of a sailmaker's being able to pronounce a verdict with any real confidence.

Rope Creases. Small creases running at an angle from the bolt rope of a mainsail or jib indicate either that the sail needs hauling up or out more, or that it is ropebound; too little rope has been put onto the sail, and it therefore cannot be stretched properly because of the limitation on the length of rope. If it can be done, try pulling the sail out beyond the black band to see the effect, then measure the amount that needs to be cut off. If the sail will not pull out,

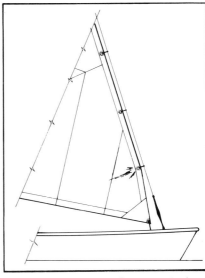

Figure 4: Headsail tack creases. In this particular case, the cure is obvious. See that the tack is nearer to the forestay

you will have to assess the extra amount it may need to be stretched; this is not a job for the inexperienced.

Batten Creases. A crease along the inner ends of the battens may mean there is too much roach to be properly supported by the battens; about one third of the batten length can be safely set outside a straight line from head to clew. Roach can be measured and the excess trimmed off. This problem also could result from a generally slack leech. Here, double check that the main halyard is hard up. If it is and the headboard can rise no higher, pull down on the lowest slide eye and also pull at the outer end of the boom at the same time, to simulate a tighter halyard. Then take action as described above under *Slack Leech.*

Headboard Creases. These may stem from the stitching around the headboard's being too tight. Alternatively, the halyard may be pulling the board over toward the mast when the sail is right up, either because the lead is not vertical from the sheave, or because there should be another slide near the top of the headboard. It possibly could be a combination of both.

Sail Too Full. Before deciding that a mainsail is too full, check the jib leech to see that it is not curling and backwinding the mainsail, giving it the impression of fullness. If a sail is genuinely too full, it is easy to flatten it along the luff by pleating. But a sailmaker will want to know how far up the luff to continue the pleat, and roughly how much fullness should be taken out. If it is later decided that the correction was wrong, it is equally easy to rip out the stitching and restore the sail to its original condition, except for two rows of stitch holes that will cause no harm.

Sail Too Flat. A mainsail that is too flat will need major surgery and will *have* to be seen by the sailmaker when it is set on spars. A jib, however, can easily be set up in a sail loft without a special test rig. It is possible that a cure may lie in pulling harder on the wire, in order to induce more flow at the luff. But it may be that the luff of a jib has moved on the wire so that part of the luff is too full, and part is too flat.

This type of movement will manifest itself first by small girts running from the hanks at an acute angle to the wire. The acute angle helps to distinguish this fault from hanks that are too tightly seized. Those are revealed by radial creases at right angles, the small girts will later show as localized flat and full spots if the fault is not corrected. A cure can be effected by regulating the sail on the wire by pushing and pulling the canvas along it. When it is properly stretched out again, it should be firmly seized at intervals along the wire to prevent a recurrence. If the relatively minor changes are not effective, the sail needs major recutting.

Sail Too Small. Major recutting is needed to make a sail larger. It often happens that a sail looks undersized because it is kept from reaching its proper dimensions by the rope or wire when it is laid out on the floor or a lawn. Remember that a sail should be pulled until all wrinkles disappear, and normally this is not easy except on a spare. A jib should be pulled on its luff until the wire is straight or until the wrinkles at the luff rope disappear. Measure the amount a sail is genuinely short *when it is set on the spars* under full halyard and outhaul tension and tell your sailmaker the figure you find.

Sail Too Large. Once again check actual distances on the spars. Reducing a sail is easy, but the lay of the cloth has to be checked if the threadline angle is going to change by more than a degree or so. A sailmaker would far rather be told to cut an exact amount off the foot, than be asked to reduce the foot to stretched sizes of a certain distance. The reason is that he will not know exactly how hard you are pulling the sail nor how much to allow for the tack fitting, which may or may not be a few inches aft of the mast.

Documentation. You can help your sailmaker by taking plenty of notes and measurements while you are sailing. Never rely on your memory to write it all up afterward. You can even mark the sail itself (in pencil) to help identify creases, etc. Count seams or other reference points out of reach of your pencil

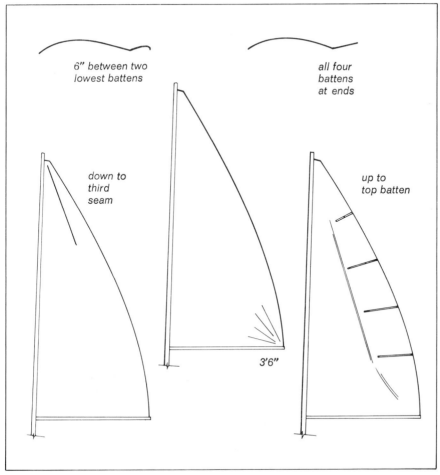

Figure 5: Some typical sketches of sail faults that you can make aboard your boat to show to your sailmaker. Anything written down while actually sailing is likely to be more accurate than your memory later. Mark the sail itself with a pencil to supplement your sketches

and write it all down as you note the distance.

Take photographs from the leeward side if possible as well as from the cockpit. Try getting onto another boat, or even ashore, for an effective general shot. Get as close as possible in order to reveal detail; background doesn't help you any. Make maximum use of shadows to highlight creases and write down your shots as you take them, for you will be surprised how hard it will be to identify a particular sail if you have a real close-up shot. Make sketches, with measurements and list fully all the faults you find. Then take all your documentation to the sailmaker for discussion while it is still fresh in your memory. And to help him, (and yourself) do it early in the season.

Mainsail Shape to Windward

Available options to produce manageable sails　　　　Robert Bainbridge

Much has been written about how to set a sail to obtain maximum speed and efficiency from the aerofoil shape designed and built into that sail by the sailmaker. However, despite all the devices and techniques a sailor uses to tune his rig and sails, the aerofoil shape determines the potential performance of a sail. Understanding what options a sailmaker has when he makes a sail may help a sailor better understand how to set that sail.

A totally flat sail with no draft would not propel a boat satisfactorily as there would be little of the pressure differential created by a sail with a foil shape. Yet sails as foils can take many different shapes just as bird wings can vary from the long, thin foil of the albatross to the shorter, deeper draft of a pigeon wing.

Thus the draft in a sail can range from full to flat, or it can have a combination of the two. One sailmaker may design a sail that is full down low and flat up top, while another may make a sail that is full aloft and flat near the boom for the same class boat. Still another sail may be built to the theory that the ratio of chord length to chord depth should be constant from the boom to the headboard. To complicate the matter, all three of these sails may provide the same potential performance although the sailors using them may adjust them in wholly different ways.

The differences in the shape of mainsails are evident in any fleet of racing boats with sails from different sail lofts. However, the variations are most conspicuous in high performance craft such as 470s, 505s, Flying Dutchmen, Fireballs, and Finns, to name a few. These are one-design classes, and there are virtually no permitted variables in hull shape and sail area, and only minor variations in rigs, so boat speed differences because of sail shape are much more detectable than in offshore boats where such factors are not so constant. In fact, in big boats there is so much attention given to different hull designs that it is often hard to determine the merits of the sails.

In high-performance dinghies only the human factor—he skill of the skipper and crew—makes a more significant impact on boat speed than sail shape. However, in top level competition even the best of crews would find it difficult, if not impossible, to get performance out of mediocre sails just as the best of sails will not assure a poor crew winning boat speed.

The fact is, though, that good crews simply do not use poor sails; they know what well-shaped sails look like and how to set them to get the performance the sailmaker built into them.

In high-performance dinghies mainsail shape is crucial to performance. For this reason many good sailmakers have learned to build shape into a sail by designing small-boat sails and continue their research and development of sail shapes by working with such sails. For the same reason it is no accident that many successful "big boat" sailors have come from the ranks of sailors of small performance boats where they learned to recognize good sails and to tune their rig and trim those sails for maximum effectiveness.

The fore-and-aft location of maximum draft in a mainsail is a basic determinant of sail shape. The current practice in high-performance jib-headed dinghies is to place the point of maximum draft nearly midway between the luff and the leech of the sail.

In contrast, a boat with only a mainsail may have the greatest draft somewhat farther forward. However, a sailmaker designing such a mainsail does not have to take the effect of the jib into consideration.

The presence of a jib forces alteration in the shape of the mainsail. One reason for this is because of the air this jib redirects close to the leeward side of the mainsail. If the maximum draft of a mainsail is forward, the slot between the mainsail and jib becomes restricted and the jib tends to backwind the mainsail. The problem of keeping this slot open is important in any jib-headed rig but it is especially critical in a high-performance boat where the jib is often sheeted quite far inboard.

Another reason for the aft location of maximum draft is to delay separation. Once the wind hits the draft point, it becomes increasingly difficult to keep the flow attached to the foil. The moving air tends to take a direction tangent to the mainsail curve at that point. When the flow follows that tangent and breaks away from the surface, eddies result and the pressure differential and hence the efficiency of the foil is diminished.

The farther back the draft is, the greater the chord section the wind will follow before reaching the tangent point and the greater will be the drive of the sail.

In many sail designs the draft is proportional to the chord length from the headboard to the foot in a constant ratio. No section of the mainsail is any fuller or flatter than any other and when properly set and vanged the sail presents the same relative curve throughout its height (Fig. 1).

Some sailmakers believe in fullness at every level. They carry fullness all the way to the top to get maximum power out of the top of the sail. The theory behind this shape is that, as a result of surface gradients, the wind is blowing faster 20 feet above the water than at the surface. Because of its greater velocity, the apparent wind comes from farther aft aloft than down low. Thus the sail can be fuller at the head and can be

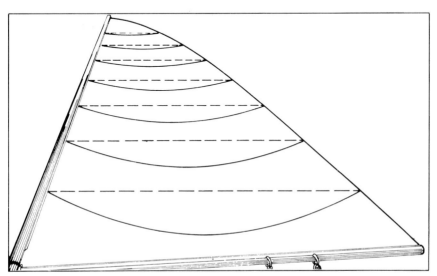

Figure 1: Mainsail with same relative draft throughout

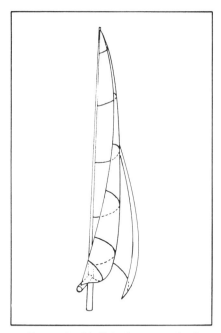

Figure 2: Shelf built into sail at foot carries airfoil

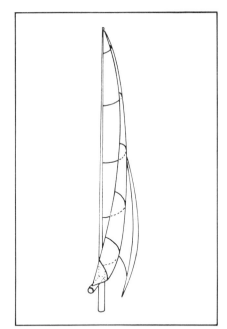

Figure 3: Shallow shelf is compromise to keep slot between mainsail and jib open

trimmed tighter with no need to ease the sheet and improve the twist of the sail so that it meets the wind at the same angle at all levels.

Most higher-performance dinghies now have a flexible transverse top batten extending over the entire chord from luff to leech. This batten allows the sailmaker to build in the maximum amount of roach allowed by class rules. The batten also allows him to put more draft high up in the sail, knowing it can be controlled by the flexibility of the batten.

Almost all modern dinghy mainsails also have a shelf built into the sail above the boom to make utmost use of sail area (Fig. 2). Without a shelf several square feet of sail above the boom would have proportionately less draft than the rest of the sail because a boomed mainsail must lose its aerofoil shape and become flat at the boom. Without a shelf this transition can encompass the bottom third of the sail which also happens to be the third with the most area and the largest possible aerofoil.

Thus a shelf permits the area with the most potential power to be more fully utilized. It also better allows this area to have the draft that such a large chord length merits and with it the sailmaker achieves the maximum amount of draft for the luff length.

Other sailmakers make sails that compromise maximum draft by making a flatter or shallower shelf above the boom (Fig. 3). However, the reduced shelf allows the jib to be sheeted closer to the centerline of the boat without backwinding the lower portion of the mainsail. The compromise may increase the drive of the lower sail section because of increased attached flow despite reduced draft. It also may improve the ability of the boat to point.

Sailmakers also differ on the shape of the leading edge they design. Mainsail shape next to the mast may range from a sharp, flat shape to a full rounded entry (Fig. 4). This is not to say that one entry or the other necessarily makes a sail flat or full. What determines whether a sail is flat or full is the depth of the draft measured from the deepest

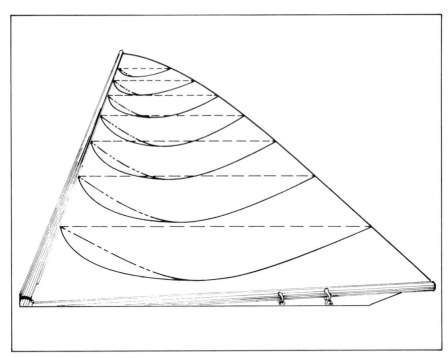

Figure 4: Full entry (solid arc) or flat entry (broken arc) does not in itself determine flatness or fullness of mainsail

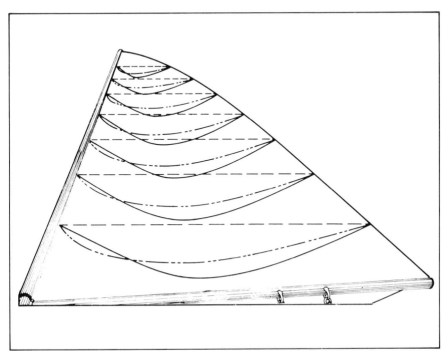

Figure 5: Full entry may lead to relatively flat sail and flat entry may lead to relatively full sail

165

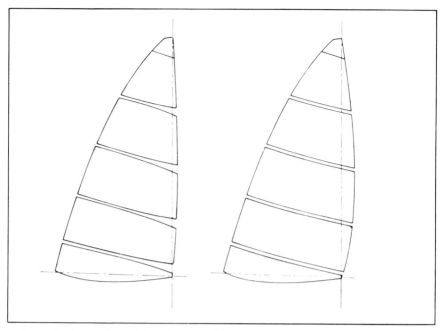

Figure 6: Sail made with broad seams (left) uses taper of seams to provide shape while another with straight seams gets draft when material in luff curve is forced back into sail when sail is set on straight mast

part of the sail perpendicular to a chord between the luff and leech. Thus the fullness of a sail depends as much on whether it is a tight or an open leech as it does on the fullness or flatness of the forward sections. A full entry could lead to a flat sail and a flat entry to a relatively full sail (Fig. 5).

One rationale for having a rounded mainsail luff is that it provides more power than a flat one and that this power is needed by light dinghies whenever sea conditions are choppy. The added power is explained by the notion that the sum of all the force vectors in a round entry are directed more forward than the force vectors in a flat luff. Thus there is a greater percentage of sail area facing forward, and as the pressure acting on a surface produces forces which act in a direction perpendicular to that surface there will be a greater total forward force.

Theoretically, this power is not so essential in light winds and in smooth water as it is in rough water. In smooth wa-

ter the added pointing ability obtained from being able to sheet the jib more tightly without backwinding the mainsail may be more desirable and a flatter entry may give better performance.

Basically, there are two ways sailmakers put curved shape into the forward half of a sail. One is by tapering the seams, or "broadseaming" as it is often called. Broadseaming is a process of overlapping the seams starting at the point of maximum draft and increasing the overlap toward the luff to produce a rounded pocket (Fig. 6).

The other method of producing such shape is to cut the luff edge of the mainsail to a curved shape rather than a straight line. When that curved shape is hoisted on a straight mast, the extra cloth is forced back into the sail, producing a pocket of cloth in the luff.

Many sailmakers prefer to create shape primarily by tapering the seams because the shape tends to stay where it is placed, whereas shape produced by cloth forced back into the sail is less

166

controllable and can drift back and forth in the sail as the wind velocity changes. Moreover, in a sail that is shaped by broadseaming the curve is gradual from the mast to the point of maximum draft whereas in a sail with a large luff curve the excessive cloth may create a bulge close to the mast in winds too light to put enough tension on the sail to pull the bulge out.

When a sailmaker designs a sail, he must be able to anticipate the shape a mast will take under different conditions. Whether that shape is the product of natural stress on the rig or of tuning by the crew, the shape will be different depending on the sail's having a flat or full entry, broad seams or a full luff curve. A flat entry does not require pre-bending the mast, a hard thing to do in many class boats and illegal in some. For sails with flat entries all forward bend in the middle of the mast section must be prevented as there is no excess cloth to accommodate the bend, and bending the spar may result in distortion and wrinkles.

In heavy air, however, a flat entry and small luff curve may be a disadvantage. The extra cloth of a full entry can absorb the force of the wind against the luff and the tension of the cunningham rig. Without enough curve such winds can cause wrinkles from the mast toward the clew.

Another aspect of high performance mainsails which varies considerably from sailmaker to sailmaker is the shape of the leech. Some appear quite free and open while others appear tight and closed (Fig. 7). Whether a leech is open or closed is a function of the overall fullness of the sail as well as the amount of tapering done to the seams aft of the point of maximum draft.

Many racing keelboats in which crew weight makes little difference to stability have traditionally gone with an open leech that permits air to flow off it easily so as not to offer an obstruction that increases the heeling movement.

Likewise the 470 class, in its early years, also went with mainsails having a fairly open leech. However, since then the leeches of high performance boats such as the 470 have become tighter as

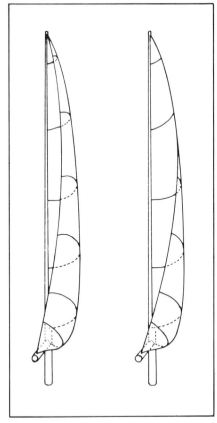

Figure 7: Mainsail with tight or closed leech (left) compared with mainsail with open leech

their crews found the boats were rarely overpowered and their weight could offset the heeling forces of even very full sails with tight leeches in windy conditions.

The maximum dimensions of mainsail roach vary from class to class, yet there is seldom any question in a sailmaker's mind how much roach to give a mainsail he designs. He gives the maximum amount of roach allowed by class rules to provide his sail with maximum sail area. A large roach is usually carried as high up the leech as possible, helped where class rules permit by a transverse batten to support the roach.

However, roaches that are too large often produce problems lower down in the mainsail. Hard spots appear in the sail cloth just inside the battens, and sometimes creases run between the battens. Just how much roach a sail can support is thus one of the major lessons a good sailmaker learns from experience.

All these aspects of sail shape are determined by the sailmaker, and are already permanently designed into the sail by the time it gets to the sailor. In turn, the sailor needs to know what factors the sailmaker considers in order to best set his sail.

Jib Shape for Windward Performance

Design factors that complicate headsail choices   Robert Bainbridge

Common complaints after a regatta are: "My jib is too flat; I had no power"; or "Couldn't point; my jib is too full." The relative fullness or flatness of jibs has taken the blame for many a slow race, but quite often such complaints are oversimplifications of the problem. Many more factors are involved in the design of a jib in addition to the depth of the draft.

One important factor is the fore-and-aft placement of the draft: is the maximum depth 35 percent of the distance from luff to leech or 45 percent or 50 percent? The vertical placement of draft is another factor: is the ratio of the depth of draft to the horizontal chord (width) of the sail the same at every height or is the sail proportionately fuller down low, up high or in the middle?

As with a mainsail, the shape of the leading edge of the jib is a critical determinant of performance. The luff can have considerable horizontal curvature or it could be flat. And in either case the designed curvature can be destroyed if the headstay sags more or less than the sailmakers designed the jib to compensate for. The trailing edge could be adversely affecting boat speed if the leech is not flat, or if it is fluttering.

The overall fullness at any point is determined by trimming the jib so that all three edges are tight, and by measuring the distance of the perpendicular from the horizontal line, or chord, connecting the luff and leech, to the point of maximum depth (Fig. 1). The distance, of course, varies depending on the height of the point measured, so it is

common to use the ratio of that distance to the length of the chord at that height as the reference of draft depth.

The amount of needed power and hence draft is one factor the sailmaker considers when he is deciding how full to design his sail. The fuller the sail, the greater the curvature of the foil which separates the flow of air passing to windward and to leeward of that sail.

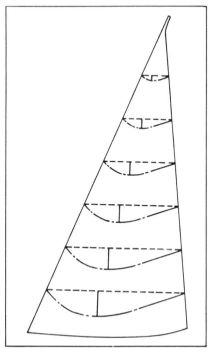

Figure 1: The overall fullness at any height is measured by length of perpendicular from chord connecting luff and leech to deepest part of sail

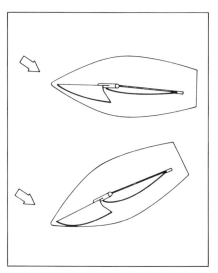

Figure 2: When two jibs are sheeted to same point, the jib with the flatter luff can point closer to wind as its luff is at closer angle of attack

The speed differential between the two flows is thus increased, because the leeward flow must travel a greater distance around the curve to meet the windward flow, which only has to travel the shorter distance inside the curve.

This greater air-flow-velocity differential produces a greater pressure differential between the windward and leeward sides, as there is less pressure in fast moving air than in slow moving air. There is then more pressure on the windward side, and the result is a greater force acting at right angles to the windward surface of the sail, and slightly greater forward drive. This added drive may be needed to drive a boat through seas in heavy air, or to power through the chop that is common in restricted bodies of water.

One drawback to a full jib, however, is that it will not be able to point as high as a flatter jib (Fig. 2). If sheeted to identical leads, the flatter jib will be at a closer angle of attack to the wind than that of the full jib. In flat water where there is little resistance to forward motion caused by chop, the extra power of the full sail may not be needed, and the better pointing ability would be desir-

able. However, in heavy air or chop, a dinghy with a flat jib would have to crack off slightly and ease the jib to aim those forces acting perpendicular to the jib more forward and create more drive.

Complicating the design factors for the sailmaker is the fact that a jib must coordinate with the mainsail as well as acting as an airfoil on its own. Besides being responsible for pointing and providing some drive of its own, the jib must channel its flow of air back along the leeward side of the mainsail. Because the power and speed generated by the mainsail is also produced largely by the pressure differential between its two sides, it is very important for the jib to direct the wind through the slot along the mainsail, and keep that airflow attached to the main for as long as possible (Fig. 3A).

A jib, then, must neither bounce the wind off the luff of the mainsail nor direct the flow off to leeward away from the mainsail (Fig. 3 B and C). To avoid these weaknesses sailmakers design their jibs so they have the right amount of fullness to function efficiently with the mainsail. A very full jib, while it may have power, must either be sheeted farther aft, or more outboard, more loosely than a flat jib in order to maintain an even slot between jib leech and mainsail luff. A flatter jib can be sheeted more tightly while maintaining the same slot but would not have the same power.

Another variable in the shape of jibs is the fore-and-aft placement of draft. Two jibs may have the same ratio of draft depth, yet have different shapes and performance and will have to be trimmed differently if their points of maximum draft differ.

Consider two jibs with the same depth of draft, one with the maximum draft located 35 percent aft from the luff to the leech, and the other with the draft at 50 percent (Fig. 4). The first will have a relatively short curve forward of the maximum draft point and a long but flatter leech after it. The second jib will have a much longer luff curve and a shorter leech section. The first luff will have only 35 percent of the chord of the sail in which to reach its maximum depth. Its angle with the chord connecting luff and leech will be more obtuse than that of the luff which has 50 percent of the chord length to reach the maximum draft point. The result is that the second jib, with its draft farther aft, will be able to sail closer to the wind than the jib with the forward draft and more abrupt luff.

The leeches on the two jibs will also behave differently. The roles are reversed however. The 35 percent with its abrupt luff will have a more gradual, less steep leech, having 65 percent of the width of the sail in which to return from the deepest point to the aft edge of the sail. As shown in Figure 4A, this leech will fall off to leeward a little more and will be able to be sheeted more tightly than the 50-percent jib. The 50-percent jib has less distance in which to return from the same depth to the leech. The result as is shown in Figure 4B is a leech which hooks slightly more to windward. These jibs would be designed by a sailmaker to set quite differently.

Jibs can also vary in the vertical placement of draft, and this too means they would have to be sheeted differently. For instance, some jibs would have big foot shelves, similar to those designed into performance mainsails (Fig. 5). Foot shelves are produced by a disproportionately large amount of broadseam in the tack seam and are sometimes accompanied by a vertical split in the bottom panel with additional broadseam, darts or take-ups in those vertical seams. They result in a large amount of fullness down low and a foot that hooks to windward. This shelf helps the foot of the jib keep its shape, and keeps the foot from falling off to leeward on a reach when the sail is not trimmed tightly.

Sailmakers also have windward performance in mind when they design such shelves. The huge amount of broadseam enables the sail to keep its ratio of depth much farther down than would otherwise be possible. Normally from the bottom quarter or so of the jib down, the draft would have to progress from its depth ratio to its straight-edge foot. However, with the shelf, the sail

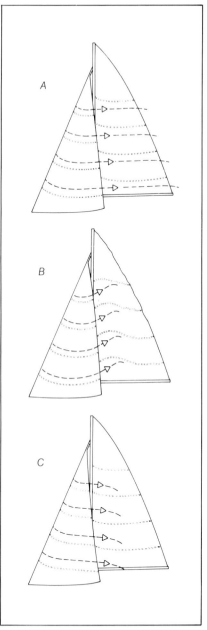

Figure 3: Jib A is functioning correctly with mainsail and is trimmed so that air flow will remain attached to leeward side of mainsail as long as possible. B and C have poor coordination between jib and main. In B jib and/or mainsail may be too full or jib sheeted too tightly, resulting in air flow off jib backwinding mainsail. In C flow off the jib falls away from the mainsail; the jib could be fuller or sheeted tighter

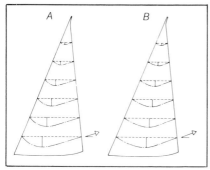

Figure 4: Two jibs with same overall fullness but with maximum draft at different points. Maximum draft of A is 35 percent; luff is short and at a wider angle and thus sail is not particularly close-winded. However, its long leech with acute angle at the chord will be free and the sail can be closely trimmed. In B with its draft at 50 percent luff angle is more acute for close-windedness but leech is tight, preventing sail from being sheeted as closely as A

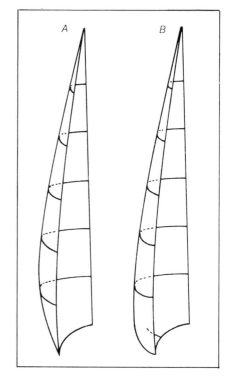

Figure 5: Contrasting shapes between sail with no shelf (A) and one with foot shelf. Shelf enables longest and potentially most powerful sections to be used more effectively but at expense of more sharply hooked leech

keeps most of its full draft all the way down until it hits the shelf. Thus some of the longest and most potentially powerful chords of the sail can be more fully utilized.

The shelf will produce a hooking leech down low, as there is no opportunity for it to fall off as does the top of the leech. However, in many dinghies, this area is primarily below the mainsail, so there is little backwind disturbing the mainsail and the sailmaker can concentrate on building power into the jib boot without concern for its effect on the slot.

Some sailmakers nevertheless still opt for the flatter foot on the theory that in light air, a closed foot which cannot be opened presents an airfoil much too blunt for the light breeze. They argue that the area stalls as the wind has not the drive to flow through or around the airfoil. Any other full area of the sail could be twisted off and freed but that one cannot.

The extremes of course are not the only possibility; there is much middle ground, and many jibs, particularly in classes which only allow one sail per regatta, make a compromise.

In this, as in most jib shape factors,

however, the sailmaker must consider the interrelationship with the mainsail. If the mainsail has an excessively large shelf of its own, a large jib shelf may not be a good idea. That of course also depends on the angle of sheeting. What may not work well on a 5-0-5 or 470, some of which sheet almost to the centerboard trunk, might do better on a Flying Scot with its jib sheeted at a wider angle.

The tendency in some closesheeted dinghy jibs lately is towards flat upper sections which have leeches that are quite free. This leech enables the jib to be sheeted without much twist, and thus keeps the entire length of the foil at relatively the same angle to the wind, making the most use of the whole sail. A flat upper section and the resulting open leech also make it much easier to

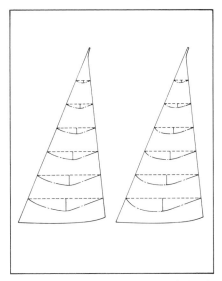

Figure 6: Two jibs with identical draft depth and position may differ in shape

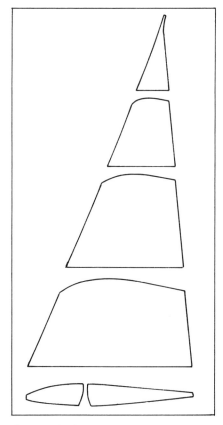

Figure 7: Draft is positioned by broadseams or tapers on one side of each seam. Luff taper ends at point of deepest draft and straight leech taper starts at or aft of point of deepest draft. Note dart in foot used to produce shelf

keep the slot open in light air. There is little difficulty in opening the slot with a full section in heavy air. The jib lead just has to be moved slightly aft and the force of the wind will do the rest. In light air however, freeing the leech is much harder, and the lead often has to be moved quite far back.

Some sailmakers, on the other hand, argue that it is almost always possible to twist the leech sufficiently, so why not have a jib which is full at every level, and have the maximum power available for when it is needed?

As with a mainsail, the leading edge of a jib has a lot to do with performance. Some jibs have a relatively flat curve from the forestay most of the way back to the point of maximum draft, and then make a fairly abrupt curve at that point before leading into the leech (Fig. 6). Others will have more curvature after the forestay, and will gradually fair into the maximum draft point and back into the leech.

A sailmaker designs his leading edges to be flat or full to a large degree by the way he tapers his panels when drawing the broadseams (Fig. 7). He puts draft into his sail by drawing tapers, or curves from some point slightly below the edge

of the cloth at the luff, and fairing those curves into the edge of each panel, wherever he wants the point of maximum draft to be.

How he draws these curves or tapers determines what the shape of the luff will be. If he starts at the luff ¾ of an inch down from the panel edge or whatever amount of broadseam he wants, and draws the taper quite straight, with very little curve, and then makes a rather large curve in the last few inches as he fairs it back into the edge of the panel at the draft point, then he is going to have a luff that is quite flat. But that luff will have a slightly more abrupt transition into the leech than will a luff that is more curved. To provide a fuller luff the sailmaker puts a relatively large amount of curve into his taper at first, with the result that the fairing back into the leech will be a more gradual transition.

The shape of the tapers can vary, of course, from being extremely curved at one end or the other and flat for the rest, to being curved at both ends and flatter in the middle, to being more gradual all the way. Some sailmakers make jibs with tapers that start out really flat to produce flat entries which will point as high as possible. Other sailmakers prefer more gradual tapers with more initial curvature on the theory that they will have jibs with more power, and a smoother transition into the leech so that the wind does not have to negotiate an abrupt angle.

The shape of the leading edge then, has a bearing on the pointing ability of a jib, and its potential for power. The overall fullness of the jib is not the sole factor. In fact, a full jib can have a flat entry, by means of having the flat tapers described above, and a flat jib can have a full entry.

Jibstay sag has quite a bearing on the shape of the leading edge too, and it is an area where the sailor can ruin the shape designed into the sail by the sailmaker. If the jibstay sags too much, then the designed draft changes. Likewise, in light air it is possible to have the rig too tight and the forestay too straight for a jib which was designed to accommodate a certain amount of forestay sag. Jibstays cannot be kept absolutely straight in heavy air, so often the sailmaker hollows out the luff of his jib somewhere to allow for that sag. If the luff wire is too tight, it will often show up by means of wrinkles emanating horizontally from the luff.

The draft in sails is constructed by a combination of luff round (or in jibs by reducing luff hollow) and broadseaming. Sometimes draft is produced, particularly in the upper sections of jibs, only by luff curve, that is, by inducing extra cloth back into the sail as the luff is pulled straight. The draft is then kept positioned by means of straight leech tapers starting at the edge of the cloth and running to a point slightly down from the edge of the panel at the leech: the same mechanics as luff tapers, only they are straight lines (Fig. 7). Incorrect jibstay sag on such a jib may not always be apparent, which means that a jib should be experimented with to find the right setting for each wind and sea condition. A jib often may be designed to be more versatile than it may appear.

There are different sailmaking theories about the leech also, although the ideal basic shape is pretty well agreed upon: as straight and flat as possible.

In big-boat genoas, leeches are cut with hollow because of the expanse of cloth between the head and the clew. If the leech were cut in a straight line or with roach, it would flutter or motorboat in the wind no matter how firm the cloth was. Putting in a concave leech greatly diminishes the fluttering.

In dinghy jibs, some sailmakers also put some hollow into their jib leeches for the same reason, to reduce turbulence created by a flapping leech. A smooth steady jib leech is important so that the wind will be directed smoothly along the leech of the main. Any turbulence will result in the flow's becoming unattached to the main too far forward. Other sailmakers feel that with such a short length of cloth they can control the shimmering, and they feel that it is worth getting as much overlap between jib and mainsail as possible to keep the flow attached to the main for the maximum possible distance.

Some classes such as the 470 allow battens in the jib. However, there are different theories as to where they should be positioned. Often they split the leech into equal parts, so that their effect of controlling leech flapping is distributed evenly from head to clew. Another thought, however, is to concentrate them in the lower half of the sail. The idea here is that if a long batten is placed one third of the way down from the head, for instance, it flattens out too great a percentage of the chord and produces a hard spot. A shorter batten could perhaps be used, but some sailmakers are now putting both well down the leech and using the full allowable lengths.

In any case, there are many more design factors in the speed and performance of a jib than just the overall fullness. They all interrelate, and a change in any one affects the others. When a sailmaker designs a sail, he has an infinite number of combinations of overall fullness, fore-and-aft placement of draft, vertical placement of draft, luff curvature, luff sag, leech shape and many ways he can arrange those factors to coordinate the jib with the main. A sailmaker's success in producing winning sails is a reflection of his ability to find a successful combination, no easy task.

Spinnaker Design and Construction

The state-of-the-art in all-around chute technology Robbie Doyle

The sail that is undergoing the most significant development today is the spinnaker. Spinnakers were originally created as bag-shaped sails to catch wind exclusively dead downwind. Now, with the help of better fabrics and sailmaking technology, spinnakers are both far more efficient downwind and so closewinded that they encroach on conventional headsails at 45 degrees apparent wind.

As spinnakers have developed even the term "spinnaker" is almost lost since sailmakers and sailors speak of spherical, tri-radials, maxis, starcuts, flankers, etc. Much of the terminology has been created by marketing wizards looking for ways to sell more sails, although there are distinctions among the various types of spinnakers. However, the key to understanding the modern spinnaker is not the language but the thinking that goes into the design and construction of spinnakers.

Today's technology is, for the first time, making exact aerodynamic spinnaker designs a reality. There have been many theories in the past, but there have been few full-scale cases in which a sailmaker could sit down and decide he would try a 4:1 depth-of-chord-ratio spinnaker and then go about making it. The technology just wasn't available. This doesn't mean that there wasn't a lot learned about spinnakers, as there are many old-time fellows who have forgotten more than many of us will ever know. If you question them as to what they felt was fast, they'd be apt to say, "Well—it has to be well rounded in

the leeches for easy trimming and flat through the middle for maximum-projected area—and, oh yeah, there has to be enough fullness in the head to lift it."

I am sure that these old fellows could tell you what was "fast" when they saw it. By contrast a number of modern sailmakers talk in terms of drafts remaining constant from head to clew. While these are impressive statements they are also over-simplifications. To maintain a constant draft or chord-to-depth ratio from head to foot is a physical impossibility given the practical aspect of sheeting a spinnaker on a boat.

When a boat is reaching with the foot of the spinnaker stretched out the foot is flatter in the middle, as seen in the photograph of *Demon* (Fig. 1). The leeches aloft, however, are still rounder than the leeches in the lower portion. For a spinnaker to be suitable running and reaching, it is essential that the spinnaker be able to assume both shapes acceptably.

One would think that today, with all the data available for parachutes and all the computer analysis done on drag shapes, there must be some very specific scientific data to indicate what makes a fast shape for a spinnaker running and what makes a fast shape reaching. Yet I have never found this information to work acceptably on a boat. One source that I thought would be very useful in learning about spinnaker construction and design would be analysis of parachute design. I did learn a great deal about spinnaker theories from analyzing parachute construction and designs, but what I learned was not so much what the shape of a spinnaker should be as the fact that the spinnaker had to be designed for a narrow set of parameters unique to a sailboat, just as parachutes are designed to a narrow set of different parameters.

The basic parachute is actually a flat plate cut with radial gores with absolutely no shaping, plus a tiny skirt around the perimeters of the parachute that serves as a lead position for the harness supports to carry its passenger or cargo. This flat shape, however, is not particularly stable and tends to slice (or yaw) through the wind in first one direction and then the other unless it is specifically controlled by the flyer. So it was found to be an unacceptable shape for dropping supplies and equipment to exact locations.

Special parachutes were then developed which were directionally more stable, and these basically were much deeper, more conical for dropping objects in a more predictable path. This is comparable to how maximum aerodynamic efficiency is compromised in spinnakers for the purpose of making a stable spinnaker. The general concept is applicable but specifics are not.

It might not be immediately obvious to most sailors, but the shape that gives the greatest amount of drag for its area is a flat plate. In fact, if one were to work out the mathematics of the drag of a hollow hemisphere with semi-equator being equal to the mid-girth width of a spinnaker (SMW) versus the drag of a flat, circular disc with the SMW being equal to the diameter, one would find the drag of the circular disc when sailing dead downwind to be nearly twice the drag of the hollow hemisphere, a finding that goes against the grain of everything any of us have ever learned on the water sailing. This fact illustrates two points. First of all, projected area is a very important ingredient in any spinnaker and, secondly, a bit of theory is a dangerous thing.

Even if one could utilize wind tunnels and computer analysis to incorporate theory into actual performing spinnakers, the process would be long, expensive, and probably somewhat inaccurate. I have often been asked by both

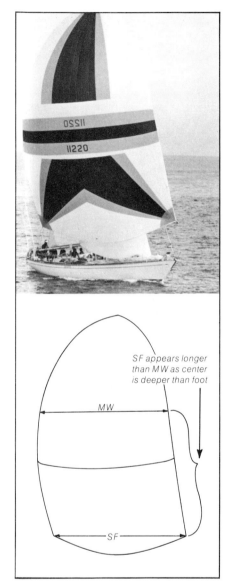

Figure 1: Spinnaker on Demon reaching has foot tighter, making SF appear longer than MW despite the fact the two measured dimensions are the same

customers and sail consultants working with me exactly what theory we are currently working on in spinnakers and why. Frankly, the answer is that the average sailor out there on the water week in and week out is conducting a much more beneficial testing program than could be set up in a laboratory.

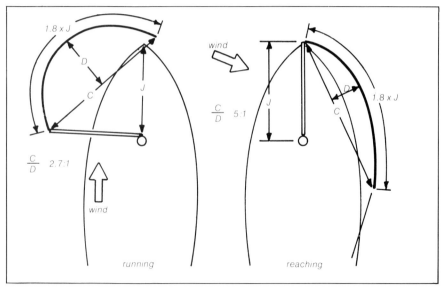

Figure 2: Diagram of how spinnaker shape (C/D ratio) varies with limitations on sheeting platform while running and reaching

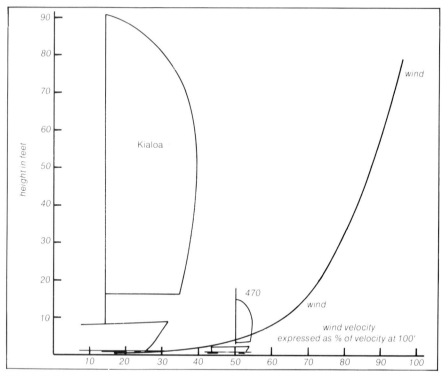

Figure 3: Graphic representation of wind gradient effect with wind velocity increasing rapidly close to water and then more slowly above 15 feet or so. Nevertheless, spinnaker on taller rig has benefit of greater velocity and makes lift important for boats with shorter mast height (from Marchaj: Sailing Theory and Practice)

Many persons may object to this type of reasoning and may say that we need much more scientific analysis of spinnakers, but, frankly, sailmakers concerned with optimum spinnaker design have the opportunity to do full-scale testing under test conditions of many different shapes, and at times we have certainly learned a great deal. However, even then the true test as to what is a good spinnaker never seems to be ultimately proved under these nearly ideal test conditions.

It is the weekend sailors who are the real test pilots for spinnakers. The average sailor often does not give himself enough credit for what he already knows about spinnakers. If one wants to learn what makes fast spinnaker shapes, he should read all the theoretical analysis of spinnaker shapes and what should be fast. But most of all, he should then take that knowledge, stick his head up out of his boat and look around him to see what's going fast, to see what is working.

Let's look at the specific parameters to which a spinnaker must be designed. First, to a great extent a spinnaker must support itself in the air. This makes it unique among the sails on a boat. Second, it must be controlled by only three different points—halyard, sheet, and guy. Third, it must operate in a wind gradient in that the wind in the lower portion of the spinnaker is not the same velocity as the wind in the upper portion of the spinnaker. Fourth, it must interact effectively with the other sails in the inventory, staysails as well as the mainsail. And fifth and most important, it must be capable of being flown optimally by a human being in some rather unstable circumstances. This human being must be able to withstand the vagaries of the wind as well as of the skipper.

Once we have the parameters, let us design the spinnaker. In order to make the spinnaker fly we need a chord-to-depth ratio through the head of the sail of approximately 5:1 for moderate air. This is a rather simple mathematical problem for a radial head design.

However, as a practical concern we find ourselves limited by the sheeting platform. The pole is only the length of J and yet the width of the spinnaker is $1.8 \times J$. There is no way we can get the bottom of the spinnaker to assume a 5:1 chord-to-depth ratio while running or broad reaching (Fig. 2).

Therefore, a sailmaker doesn't try to get the spinnaker to blossom out to a predetermined computer drag shape on the bottom but rather he shapes it so that it serves as a base for the shape he is going to design through the middle of the sail, where shape is less restricted by the sheeting platform.

The sailmaker also has the third corner to support the sail—the head. He knows this sail has to come to a point; the question is, how blunt a point? Well, frankly, the human factor comes in here, as well as the vagaries of the wind and seas. On a perfectly smooth platform head angles of 150 degrees can be supported effectively.

We now have a spinnaker that lifts and supports itself, but how high do we want it to lift? Spinnaker lift is a tradeoff. The higher the lift the more projected area is lost. On the other hand, the lift of a spinnaker gets it higher above the water where wind velocity is greater.

As shown in Fig. 3 the wind about five feet off the water is only half of what it is at 32 feet. It is significant, especially on smaller boats, therefore, to get the spinnaker up into the increased wind velocity whereas it is not so crucial for a larger boat such as the 79-foot *Kialoa.*

Lifting also helps the spinnaker fulfill its fourth parameter: by lifting it gets up and away from the shadow of the mainsail when running as well as away from staysails and from the leeward side of the mainsail on a reach.

Finally, the sailmaker concerns himself with the fifth and most crucial parameter, the need for the spinnaker to be kept trimmed by a crew despite the effect of wave motion on the boat, and momentary wind shifts on the sail. To aid directional stability the sailmaker adds round to the leeches so that the luff can fold periodically without the spinnaker's collapsing (Fig. 4). He may also take that 5:1 chord-to-depth ratio

Figure 4: Rounded leech of spinnaker permits luff to fold periodically yet prevents collapsing when sail is well trimmed

makers, we are currently designing our all-purpose spinnaker to have a chord-to-depth ratio of approximately four to one. This is varied according to aspect ratios. Tall, narrower sails seem to prefer a slightly flatter shape whereas the lower-aspect sails seem to prefer a slightly fuller shape. Our general purpose reaching spinnaker (not to be mistaken with a flanker or starcut) is designed currently with about a 5:1 chord-to-depth ratio, being varied slightly according to aspect ratio. The flanker and starcut, which are the ultimate in close-winded spinnakers and can be flown as close as 45 degrees to the apparent wind, are designed with about 6:1 chord-to-depth ratio.

The above are all numbers that come out of mathematical formulas for the design of these sails. Actual photographs have shown that the sails, when set properly, can be kept very close to these numbers. The actual chord-to-depth ratio of the sail when being flown on the boat, however, often varies according to the way the spinnaker is set. Pole height affects the amount of fullness, as does the position of the sheet, so there is no set figure that any spinnaker is tied to. And even if the ultimate chord-to-depth ratio could be determined on a computer and a sail to that design put on a boat, unless the leeches were to have the proper amount of round, the center the proper amount of flatness, and the leech the proper flatness, the sail would never perform well.

The next critical, mathematically-computed aspect of a spinnaker is the profile of the head, that is, the top 50 percent of the sail (Fig. 5). The lower half should only have enough arc to have the spinnaker set properly. A straight profile to the lower 50 percent is preferable, but spinnakers designed as such are very unstable. We currently design our profiles for our all-purpose International Offshore Rule spinnaker to have a head profile with a chord-to-depth ratio of 5.89:1. Reaching chutes have a head profile of 6.25:1 and the flankers, 7:1. Now, once again, these ratios are greatly affected by how the spinnaker is flown. Also, as critical as profile is, there is no one profile suitable

and make it a bit deeper, perhaps 4:1, so that the spinnaker won't oscillate all over the place like a disc or a parachute that is too flat.

Presto—we have the ultimate "spinnaker."

Well, not quite.

So far, in terms of aerodynamic shape, I have talked in rather broad generalities. I don't want the reader to make the same mistake that I made initially with the advent of radial spinnaker designs—to create something mathematically that looks fast on the steady platform of the roof and yet is so sensitive it can't be flown on a boat. Secondly, I am not in a position to lay out exactly the mathematics any sailmaker, including my own firm, is currently utilizing in its spinnaker designs. However, we can look at basically what makes a fast spinnaker.

First, chord-to-depth ratio is an important factor in the performance of a spinnaker. Even though it varies throughout the actual spinnaker, it is important to have it correct through the main driving area of the spinnaker, i.e., the center 50 percent. At Hood Sail-

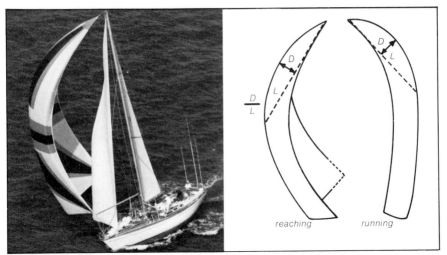

Figure 5: Profile of spinnaker on reach reveals critical shape at head and modest curve in lower section for stability. On run the L/D ratio of head shows greater fullness

for all boats. The secret of a good spinnaker is to have the vertical profile as well as the horizontal aspect complement the boat.

There is one question that may be in the reader's mind at this stage. If there is such a difference in chord-to-depth ratios and profiles between reaching and running spinnakers, how can one spinnaker be expected to do both? Well, the fact is that there is not such a tremendous difference. The difference between 4:1 and 5:1 is just not that great, nor is the difference between 5.89:1 and 6.25:1 in profile. Even the flanker, which is as close to a headsail as it is a spinnaker at 6:1 and 7:1 is not that far from a standard spinnaker in aerodynamic shape.

The reason spinnakers in the past have been hard to utilize as both reaching and running sails was distortion. The sails would often get twice as full when under the strain imposed on them reaching. Thus, if one had a good running chute with a designed chord-to-depth ratio of, say, 4:1, it would likely be 2:1 when reaching.

The tri-radial technology has largely solved the distortion problem. Perhaps there should be a greater difference between running and reaching spinnakers but only if the IOR permitted longer poles in relation to the SMW. Then the foot of the spinnaker could be spread out more when running and one could therefore better support a flatter middle section. However, as things stand today, 4:1 is about as flat as one wants to have through the center of a spinnaker, unless you plan to sail in extremely flat water when a flatter sail, say 5:1, with more projected area, can be tolerated.

In addition to the chord-depth ratio and vertical profile, there is the actual shape of the cross-section curve. Again this need not vary much between a reaching and running spinnaker. On a dead run the most important factor is projected area; shape is not all that critical. When you are reaching, however, airfoil shape is desired. So, to achieve airfoil, the center portion of a spinnaker is designed as a gentle ellipse (Fig. 6A).

When tension is pulled down on the leading edge of the sail, the luff, it becomes rounder (just as happens with increasing tension on a cunningham or halyard on a headsail or mainsail), and the trailing edge actually flattens as the sail lifts and curves out away from the boat (Fig. 6B).

Spinnaker Geometry

The first law of spinnaker geometry is the "little guy" principle: bigger is not

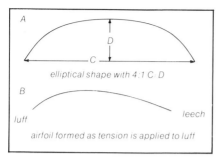

A

D

C

elliptical shape with 4:1 C·D

B

luff   *leech*

airfoil formed as tension is applied to luff

Figure 6: Elliptical shape with flattened middle lets spinnaker assume airfoil shape on reach when tension causes luff to become more rounded than leech; yet C/D ratio remains the same

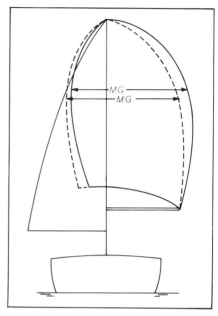

MG
MG

Figure 7: By making spinnaker (solid line) with a foot narrower than middle more area is projected to windward and less area is in the lee of the mainsail compared to spinnaker (broken line) with the same mid-girth measurement but with a foot equal to mid-girth

always better. The reasons behind this law are twofold. First of all, the spinnaker must interact successfully with the other sails on the boat, and secondly, the hydrodynamics of the hull often make it more important to sail the boat with a smaller angle of heel than to increase the sail power and increase the heel angle. This is particularly true in modern IOR yachts.

The first case, sail interaction, is perhaps best exemplified by 12-Meters. The Twelve Meter Rule permits spinnaker mid-widths or maximum girth to be 2.5 × J dimension. A typical J dimension on a Twelve is approximately 24 feet. This would mean that the SMW of the spinnaker could be up to 60 feet, but a spinnaker with a 60-foot midwidth has never proved successful on a Twelve. A more appropriate foot length has seemed to fall around 50 feet with, of all sails, the light-air floater being the smallest, falling around 44 or 45 feet. The reason for this is that the mainsail of a Twelve is so large that it interferes with spinnakers any larger than 50 feet across because pole lengths are restricted to the length of the J.

On a dead run, for example, more than half a spinnaker with a 60-foot mid-girth is blanketed behind the mainsail. This half of the spinnaker is in essentially dead air and has to be supported by the remaining half of the spinnaker which is in clear air. This dead half drags down the clear half and detracts so much from the performance

of the good half that the overall performance, despite the amount of overall area, is less. The effect on a reach is almost the opposite. These giant midgirth spinnakers come around so much they then spill their air into the leeward side of the mainsail to such a degree that the mainsail has to be overtrimmed. In overtrimming the main becomes inefficient, and the overall combination of mainsail and spinnaker is slower than the performance of a small spinnaker.

One method which can be used on boats of all sizes and shapes to help a spinnaker get out and away from the mainsail involves cutting the foot shorter and thus moving the center of the spinnaker more to windward (Fig. 7). In some respects it simulates a longer spinnaker pole. The only disadvantage of this type of spinnaker configuration is that it does not make for a really good overall spinnaker, as having a spinnaker

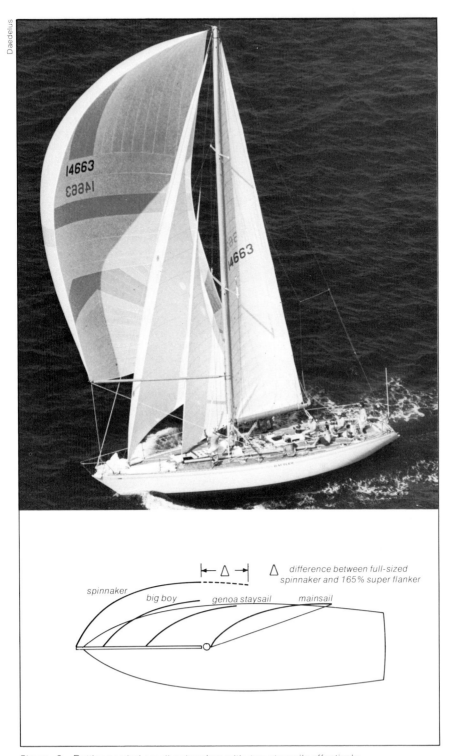

Figure 8: Rattler carried small spinnaker with two staysails effectively

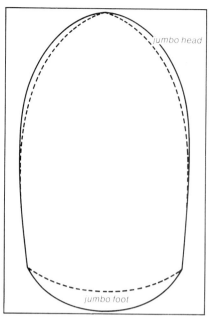

Figure 9: Periodically fashionable jumbo spinnaker (solid line) superimposed on spinnaker with more conventional shape (broken line). Jumbo head makes spinnaker harder to trim and jumbo foot tends to interfere with staysail on a reach and to pull rest of sail down in light and moderate wind strengths

mid-width much larger than the spinnaker foot tends to make a spinnaker hard to support on a reach. It works fine on a run but it makes the sail a more limited sail.

The second reason for making the spinnaker slightly smaller than the Rule permits is to keep a boat from heeling too much. This past SORC, sailing on *Rattler* we had a sail known as a super flanker which is 28 feet on the SMW rather than the permitted IOR maximum of 30.6 feet. The luff length of this sail is also short; 56 feet rather than the 59 feet maximum. The area is further reduced in this sail by a narrow head angle as compared to a standard spinnaker design. The full-sized chutes on *Rattler* carry a head angle of approximately 110 degrees, whereas this sail has a head angle of only 75 degrees. This sail, therefore, had less area overall

and what area there was was concentrated lower down.

The reason for this sail's being short on the hoist is for better interaction with other sails, the prime reason for making sails smaller. By making this sail shorter on the hoist we are able to raise our pole higher and ease the halyard off and thus get the sail out farther away from the other sails on the boat. We normally flew this sail with what we termed our triple-head rig: a combination of a big boy and genoa staysail (Fig. 8).

Two other items of spinnaker design that come and go in popularity are the jumbo foot and the jumbo head (Fig. 9). These items, like the short foot, at times exhibit small advantages, but limit the all-around performance of the spinnaker. The jumbo foot is only beneficial in rather strong winds over, say, 15 knots over the deck, 25 knots true. In all other conditions the jumbo foot tends to pull the rest of the sail down as well as to trap dead air inside the sail. The other detrimental effect of the jumbo foot is that it is simply in the way reaching. It just tends to curl up and jam the slot between the staysail and spinnaker.

The jumbo head which is often advertised for downwind spinnakers has its advantages in giving projected area aloft. However, the excess area in the head can be hard to support, as it forces the spinnaker trimmer to overtrim the rest of the sail to keep it from collapsing. The excessive shoulders also become next to impossible to support on a reach. So the sail, even if marginally effective downwind, is a severely limited sail.

Construction

The primary reason that the spinnaker design is in such a rapid state of fluctuation today is due to the revolution in the construction techniques of spinnakers. Previous to the tri-radial, spinnaker shapes were usually at the mercy of cloth stretch. This is not to say that there were not some tremendously fast spinnakers produced before the tri-radials. There were and it will be perhaps very difficult to design some faster than the ultimate in cross-cut spinnakers. Even though there was cloth stretch it was accounted for in the con-

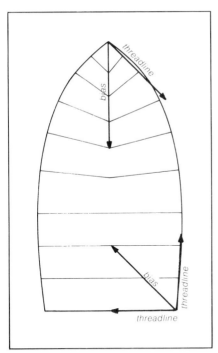

Figure 10: Cross-cut spinnaker tends to become fuller in stronger winds as center seam on bias stretches under strain while leeches closer to threadline are less subject to stretch

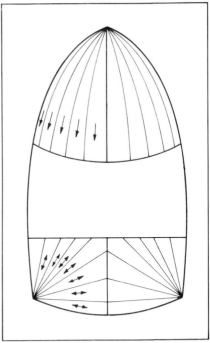

Figure 11: Tri-radial construction reduces stretch by concentrating strain close to threadline indicated by the arrows. Stretch and hence distortion in center panels is minimal and actually helps give round to the leading edge under strain

struction and seam adjustments incorporated into the design of the spinnaker. However, these ultimate cross-cut spinnakers never could exhibit the all-around capabilities of a tri-radial. If a cross-cut spinnaker was an extremely good close-reaching spinnaker, it would often be quite bad running because the strains would not be enough to stretch the sail out into shape, whereas the strains were just right to have the sail assume the proper shape while reaching.

What makes the tri-radial so distortion-free? The radial construction in all three corners is truly the most sensible method to utilize woven fabric. Conventionally woven fabrics have yarns running in two directions; the warp, which is the lengthwise, and the fill, which is across the panels. Woven fabric will without exception stretch more across its diagonal than along its thread

lines, and in the light nylons used as spinnaker material this is particularly the case. Thus if a spinnaker is laid out in the conventional cross-cut fashion, it will get continually fuller as it is strained (Fig. 10).

The tri-radial, however, because the stretch is both uniform and minimal, will not distort at all when it is loaded (Fig. 11). The obvious question is: why not continue the radial panels until they intersect on all spinnakers as they do on a starcut? There are two reasons for incorporating a center section of different construction. First of all, radial panels are not really necessary, as the strain is dissipated enough in the middle of the sails so that the stretch is minimal and, secondly, the small bit of stretch achieved in the center is actually beneficial as it helps round the leading edge when load is applied.

Like everything else, there are good

and bad methods of tri-radial construction. One common fault is to make the gores too wide so the edge of the gore has distortion, producing a washboard effect. The way to avoid this is to keep the gores narrow so that the cloth is never cut more than a few degrees off the threadline (Fig. 11). The smaller panels also give the sailmaker more seams to shape, allowing him to produce a smoother, more gradual shape.

Every sailmaker seems to have sail design aspects he takes delight in working with. With spinnaker design, though, the sailmaker can be perhaps the most creative. Modern computer and testing technology can aid him only slightly. The spinnaker once built, however, must be extensively tested afloat, and then the design can be refined to better fulfill the five necessary parameters of a spinnaker.

Finally, the sailor who gets the advantage of that design, once he understands what the sailmaker had in mind in making that sail, can perhaps trim the spinnaker more effectively so that the sail will do the job for which it was designed.

Effective Sail Care

Preventive maintenance to preserve design integrity　　　　　Steve Colgate

With the advent of synthetic sails, a new generation of sailors has grown up believing sails are practically indestructible and can be treated roughly. However, sails are the power for a sailboat and, although they are more troublefree than the power plant for a motorboat, they must be treated with a certain amount of care to extend their life. Sailmakers have some pretty beat-up sails brought back to them for repairs, so I asked a number of prominent sailmakers what the greatest cause of sail deterioration was and what could be done to prevent it. All agreed that *exposure to sun* and *chafe* are a sail's two worst enemies.

Cruising boatowners who leave their mainsail furled on the boom should not be lazy about using a sail cover. Also, sail cover material, *sunbrella* fabric, is often added to the leech and foot of roller-furling jibs to protect them from sunlight when they are not in use. Crews of smaller boats should carefully fold the sails rather than stuff them into bags. The photos show how this folding should be done: the size of the fold should be about the same as the length of the sailbag. The final roll should leave the clew exposed for the mainsail and the tack on the outside for the jib, for these are the corners that are attached first the next time you use the sails. Try to avoid folding any sail on exactly the same fold each time because eventually the crease will become too pronounced to disappear while you are sailing.

All the sailmakers I talked to agreed that sails should be washed periodically to remove dried salt. It's been my experience that a sail with salt in it absorbs moisture from the air and never does dry properly. Spinnakers end up being heavier than ones that have been washed, and they won't fly so well in light air. Rick Grajirena of Hood Sails in Florida comments that crystalized salt helps magnify the ultraviolet rays of the sun and causes the sail material to break down sooner. Both Grajirena and John Marshall of North Sails also point out that some spinnaker material colors (particularly $\frac{3}{4}$-ounce nylon) will bleed if they are put away wet. Marshall feels that all sails should be sailed dry, but if that is impractical, it's best to spread them out on a lawn rather than let them flap in a breeze on a drying pole.

Dirt in sails causes abrasion and will also weaken the sails after a time. The safest way to wash sails without damaging them is to use water from a hose, but if the dirt is very bad, you can use a mild detergent and scrub gently either with a sponge or a soft brush. Don't put your sails in a washing machine. If there are stains that you want to remove, John Marshall recommends the following:

Rust Stains. Soak the stains in oxalic acid (use rubber gloves and put a plastic sheet under the sail so you don't eat up the floor). When the stain is out, wash the area thoroughly with fresh water to remove the acid. You can purchase oxalic acid at a hardware or paint store.

Mildew. Clorox (a five percent solution of sodium hypochlorite) will bleach out light stains. If you want a stronger solution, purchase Chemex (which is a 15 percent solution of the same chemical) at a dry cleaning supply house.

Oil and Grease. Major oil and grease stains are practically impossible to remove. For minor stains, you can try Perchlorethylene. Immerse the stain in the cold chemical and try using a blotter behind the sail. Buy this chemical at a dry cleaning supply house.

Blood. Wash the spot immediately in cold water. For old stains, try a bleaching agent like Clorox if you're desperate, but don't get your hopes up.

Flogging and chafe are the other major reasons for sail deterioration. John Marshall recommends not luffing head-to-wind excessively with large genoas because of the flogging and the chafe

When folding mainsail on small boat, first hold foot over window so plastic is not crushed. (1) Next place hand on inside, take other hand and fold sail over it. (2) Pull against other person to obtain straight even fold.

against the mast, spreader, and shrouds. Rick Grajirena comments that small-boat sailors often beach their boats, and then leave their mainsails hoisted. If they keep the boom vang taut, it will tighten the leech of the sail and reduce flogging and wear.

Buddy Melges of Melges Sails puts *flutter patches* at a number of seams along the leech of sails. Each patch is a small triangle whose base parallels the leech and whose apex rests on a seam. These patches are very effective in reducing leech flutter which inevitably gets worse as the sail ages.

Jack Sutphen of Ratsey and Lapthorn has some good advice for cruising sailors. Many people think a boom vang is just a racing device, but Sutphen recommends using a boom vang to reduce twist in the leech of the sail, thereby re-ducing the rubbing of the mainsail against the spreader and shrouds. Sutphen also says that sewing complete and separate batten pockets onto the sail, rather than using the sail itself as one side of the pocket, will increase the life of the pocket. For long-distance cruising, many sailors have deleted battens entirely and cut their leech concave. Sutphen also feels that sewing elkhide up the lower part of the leech will reduce chafe from the topping lift (and from spinnaker sheets). A topping lift should be tied forward with shockcord to keep it from constantly flopping against the leech of the mainsail. Another alternative is to tie the lift with a long length of shockcord that is dead-ended at deck level and passed through a block attached halfway up the back-stay. This arrangement will stretch

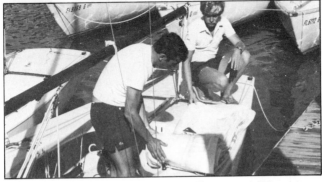

Make each fold slightly smaller than preceding one so luff lies more evenly when rolled (3). Roll sail toward clew of main (4) or toward tack of jib.

enough even if the boom is out for a run.

Sail chafe is common where spreaders hit the genoa, so be careful not to overtrim the genoa sheet and poke the spreader into the cloth. Whenever you are trimming, watch the sail at that point. Be sure the spreaders are smooth and well-protected with padding. Most wear on the genoa by the spreader tips happens when you are tacking so *don't let the sail back into the spreader.* The jib trimmer must release the sail before the wind fills it on the leeward side. Ask your sailmaker to put spreader patches on the genoa to protect the sail there. After a little use, a new sail will show dirt spots at the proper spot to put the patches, so wait until these appear before putting them on.

Many other things can hurt sails. Un-taped cotter pins or sharp edges can rip spinnakers and other sails. A broken batten can rip the pocket if the batten is not replaced immediately, and unreefing without untying all the reef points can rip a good-sized hole in a mainsail. Also, the luff of a main can be damaged by tightening the clew reefing line before you secure the tack. And here's one you may not have thought of. John Marshall points out that storing a sail in the hot trunk of a car can cause the bolt rope to shrink and damage the sail cloth.

With a little care and caution, your sails can last much longer than they will if they are abused. For a racing sailor, this can mean the difference between winning and losing. For the cruising sailor, it will ensure that you have a power plant you can trust.

Heavy-weather Genoas

Design considerations for the specialized jib　　　　　　　Charles Ulmer

Theoretically, every headsail should have a full hoist. But from a practical point of view this doesn't work too well. Manufacturing problems place a practical limit on how narrow the angle at the head of the sail can be, to say nothing of the sheeting problems, etc., that result from unreasonably tall, narrow sails.

Once you have calculated the area for a jib, distributing this area is best achieved by first using the maximum luff that is practical, then drawing an LP that will yield that area. Obviously, if the luff is longer, the LP will be shorter for any given area (Fig. 1).

There are two very good reasons for retaining the maximum luff length on any jib. First, this is the area that produces the forward thrust of the sail. If you were to pass a horizontal plane through a sail at any point, it would be

obvious from the shape of the cross-section that the forward thrust is generated up front (Fig. 2). Given this fact, and the fact that the wind gradient increases with its height above the deck, the luff area near the masthead is unquestionably the most powerful sail area on the boat and should not be cut off until all other alternatives have been expended.

Other benefits derived from a full luff sail are indirect but result from its being cut with a high clew with less overlap.

Why is a low overlap jib with a high clew desirable? As we move the clew of a jib farther and farther forward, the sheeting angle increases (Fig. 3). This means that more of the total force generated by the sail is aimed in a forward direction and less of it in a sidewards direction. In turn, this cuts down heeling moment and increases drive, both of which are important when sea conditions are aggravated.

Also, by moving the clew of the jib farther forward, the slot between the leech of the genoa and the leeward side of the mainsail is opened and the tendency of the jib to backwind the mainsail is reduced (Fig. 4). The traveler can therefore be set more to leeward which allows the mainsail to generate more forward force.

The higher-clewed jib also allows for better visibility and cuts down on the amount of water that would otherwise be caught in the foot of the sail. Tacking a boat with a short overlap sail can be accomplished much more quickly because there is less sheet to trim. A good sheet tailer on the genoa sheet can just about eliminate the grinder's job.

Finally, higher, narrow sails are subjected to considerably less distortion. The wider clew angle distributes the

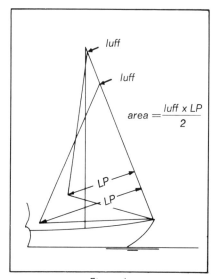

$$area = \frac{luff \times LP}{2}$$

Figure 1

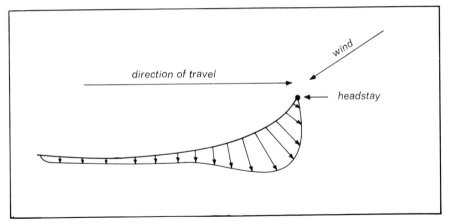

Figure 2

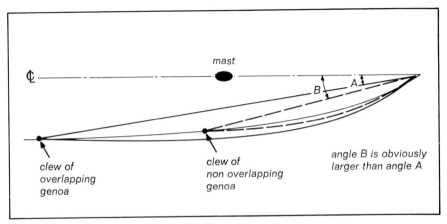

Figure 3

sheeting load over more fabric so that the load per unit of fabric is less. And a shorter LP means that less material will be loaded on the bias, thus reducing bias distortion.

The real function of this sail is windward work in heavy air. But there are two secondary roles that are also important. First, it is ideal as a cruising sail, for the high clew and low overlap provide good visibility. And a quick and easily trimmed sail is as important for the cruiser as it is for the racer. The soft resin-free cloth from which these sails are made is subject to little or no change with time so you don't have to worry about your racing sails when cruising.

Second, as a heavy-air reaching genoa, a full luff #3 can provide all the drive of any full luff sail without the heel generated by the overlap. The high clew allows for more even trimming without moving the lead much; and the sail doesn't catch water from the lee bow.

The wide slot makes it possible to set a close-reaching staysail underneath and ease the mainsail out properly. The more overlap on a jib, the more one has to overtrim the mainsail on a reach to prevent the hooking leech of the jib from backwinding it. Overtrimming the main, though, inevitably leads to more heel, less drive, and more helm; all of which do slow the boat down (Fig. 4).

A high-clewed jib has another important advantage over a low-clewed one on a reach. The high clew means that

191

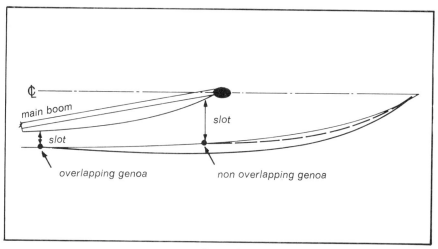

Figure 4

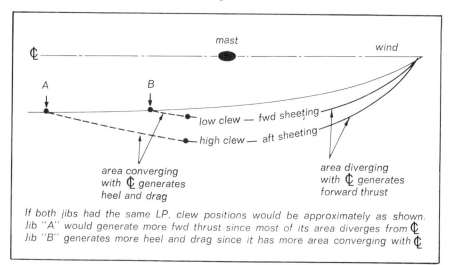

If both jibs had the same LP, clew positions would be approximately as shown. Jib "A" would generate more fwd thrust since most of its area diverges from ₵ Jib "B" generates more heel and drag since it has more area converging with ₵

Figure 5

the sheet lead will be farther aft; and the sheeting base, (the distance from tack to fairlead block) will be longer. When the sheet of any sail is eased, the combination of sail and sheet assumes an arc from tack to fairlead block. The more the sheet is eased the deeper the arc. The forward half of this arc consists entirely of the sail. Its angle to the centerline is favorable and produces forward drive. The back half of the arc is part sail, and part sheet. Its angle to the centerline is unfavorable and produces heeling and drag forces.

The longer the sheeting base the shorter the unfavorable back half of the arc is because it is sheet, not sail. This means the heeling and drag forces are lower. Furthermore, because the longer arc is proportionately shallower, the angle of the back half becomes less unfavorable (Fig. 5).

Let's look at the other side of the coin for a minute. The standard brief for having a short luff—long overlap sail is that it has a lower geometric center of area and can produce some slot effect with the mainsail.

Consider first the slot between the jib and the mainsail; in heavy weather its

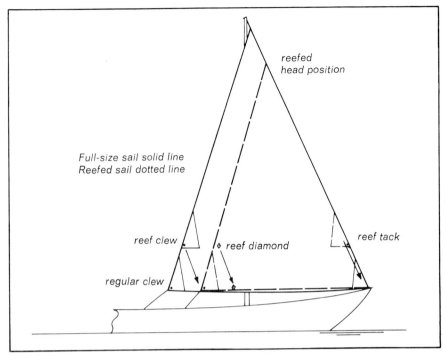

reefed
head position

Full-size sail solid line
Reefed sail dotted line

reef clew

reef diamond

reef tack

regular clew

Figure 6

importance is marginal at best. The boat generally is overpowered and the mainsail's function is more to balance the boat properly than anything else. With the traveler eased, as it usually is for heavy air, the mainsail and genoa are lying in completely dissimilar planes and the tendency therefore is for the air coming off the leech of the overlapping jib to backwind the main. This tendency is aggravated by any distortion the jib may have.

The center of area is lower than that of a high cut jib, it is true, but it is irrelevant. The important thing to remember is that the center of effort and the center of area rarely coincide. The significant comparisons are the total driving force and the total heeling force produced by a sail. The fact is that for a constant area, the taller sail produces more driving force and less heeling force than the lower one.

The difference can become greater as the lower-luffed one distorts.

What's new in heavy weather jibs?

Reefs! Actually, the idea isn't that new; I guess we just didn't appreciate what we were looking at before.

The reefable genoa offers the racing sailor a quick way to reduce sail area and an alternative to his usual heavy-air jibs (i.e., a reefed #2 genoa can have the same area as a #3 genoa). It offers the cruising sailor a way to reduce sail for those once-a-year blows without buying an expensive storm jib.

It's worth pointing out that one genoa with six reefs will not replace your racing inventory. The triangular shape of a reefed genoa is not the best (low aspect) and stretch corrections built in the clew area are largely eliminated. Also, reefs should only be installed in your heavy-air genoas (#2 genoa on down) and one reef per sail is a practical limit. Installing a reef (which consists of a new tack and clew cringle with patches) in a #1 genoa could hurt its shape and performance in light air.

To take a reef, use the following steps:

- Tie a new sheet to the new clew position and lead it through a fairlead block to a secondary winch.
- Ease the halyard so the new tack can be attached. It may be necessary to ease the old sheet a bit when you are doing this.
- Retension the halyard and trim in the new sheet.

While this does leave a lot of sail cloth lying on deck, it makes very little difference up near the tack. The area down the new clew does tend to flop around and make a lot of noise; and it also can be in the way during a tack. To prevent this, I put one reef diamond about three feet in from the clew (Fig. 6). The foot of the sail is rolled up and tied up with a light line using this reef diamond and another one through the new clew. This keeps the back end of the sail off the deck and gives you visibility. It also lets out any trapped water, and generally makes things shipshape.

Handling Cruising Sails

Modern developments in the general wardrobe   Tom Russell

Demand is what creates most of the changes that are made in any given field. When we look at cruising under sail and all the things that go with it, the principle is not much different. The explosive growth of cruising sailboats has sometimes been credited to the "energy situation," but the words I hear are challenge, fun, accomplishment and peace. It's certainly hard for me to argue with any of that philosophy.

However there are many new sailors coming into the sport who haven't been steeped in the old cruising traditions of work that is slow, difficult, heavy, done by hand and the old standby: brute strength. Today these people are asking me questions like: "Can my wife and I handle it alone?" or "How does it work in heavy weather?" and similar queries. Responding to this kind of interest, rigging and hardware manufacturers as well as boatbuilders and sailmakers have come up with plenty of new ideas that are making cruising rigs easier to work, less effort to maintain and more fun to sail.

Headsails. The time-honored badge of a dedicated cruiser has long been the roller-furling jib; its been a boon for the short-handed sailor who wants to clean up his foredeck in a hurry. Unfortunately the price for this convenience has been paid by sacrificing windward performance—sometimes as much as 25 percent—because of a sagging luff and the resulting poor sail shape. It was this particular drawback that moved designers to a furling-jib system mounted on a rod headstay that is integrated with a furling unit. With this you can point with the rest of the boats and you can even partially furl the sail without damaging a luff wire to boot.

But how do you care for it? If the genoa suffered any damage, the sail (plus rod stay) had to be removed (bosun's chair to the masthead), rolled in a six-foot circle and carted off to a sail loft. I won't elaborate on what it is like handling *that* snakelike rascal under a sewing machine!

Enter the grooved-luff headstay systems which were pioneered by the racing sailors for better luff shape, better control and more efficient sail changing. It didn't take very long for the inventors to follow what the real drift was: hoist a sail, rotate grooved stay and furl the jib. The result is that the grooved-luff furling headstay is now a proven, reliable system for any serious cruiser's foretriangle.

In working with a number of these cruising boats, I have found that versatility is the most admired quality of these stays. No longer are you confined to just one furling headsail because now all of them furl. Because most of these stays resist torsional displacement or twisting, you can partially furl headsails for heavier air service as long as the sail is built for that option.

Even though polyester is much tougher than cotton, it still requires either strategically located patches for roll-reefed tacks and heads or extra wide tablings to support tack and head loadings for variable reefed sizes. Conventional genoa reefing can also be used

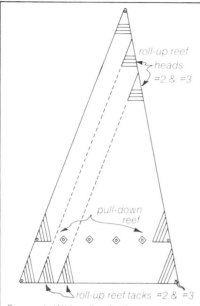

roll-up reef
heads
#2 & #3

pull-down
reef

roll-up reef tacks #2 & #3

Figure 1: With roller-furling
headsails that have been
properly constructed, reefing
can be accomplished either
by roller furling or by "pull
down" method

with the grooved-luff stay so you can reef either way (Fig. 1). Actually conventional reefing is the preferred method for long passages.

Taking care of these headsails is infinitely easier with a grooved stay than with the old roller system as there is no 1 x 19 luff wire or rod to fight. In fact, the small-diameter luff rope that fits into the stay is almost unnoticeable while the lowered sail is being folded and rolled or stuffed in its sailbag. A trip to the sail loft for repair or maintenance or even taking it up to the attic for winter storage is now far simpler than it was. There are no hanks to oil, to restitch, or to snag a vagrant spinnaker.

The diehards may mumble about sails going overboard during a hoist or a douse, but my actual experience, cruising *and* racing, shows this to be of little concern. When you douse a jib, it is pulled out of the feeder *with the halyard cast off*. The folds are gathered in place at the base of the stay and a quick turn with a sailstop secures the entire luff and, therefore, the bulk of the sail (Fig. 2). All you have to do then is roll the sail up from the clew and bag it. It is all

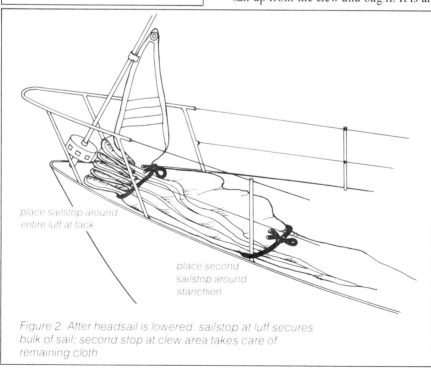

place sailstop around
entire luff at tack

place second
sailstop around
stanchion

Figure 2: After headsail is lowered, sailstop at luff secures
bulk of sail; second stop at clew area takes care of
remaining cloth

ready to be rolled out for a future set.

Mainsails. There are many exciting things that are happening in the mainsail department these days but one of the easiest and least expensive ideas is finally taking a firm hold among the cruising sailors. Jiffy, slab, speed, or California reefing—whichever term you prefer—has become the answer to the short-hander's prayer.

To some, it may seem that this return to "old-fashioned" reefing was just reinvented to displace the roller-furling boom that ran from 1930 to the late 1960s. Although it may seem that way, again it is polyester that makes this neat reefing system possible. Many people forget that to reef the real old-fashioned way, you had to lower the sail, tie in the reef points and rehoist the sail so the strain would be spread evenly along the foot. To apply the reef clew loadings used in the jiffy systems of today on the old cotton sails would have immediately and permanently distorted, if not ruined, even the best of them.

Today most new boats are equipped with the jiffy-reef system and more and more are converting each season. The heart of the system is the sail; it has a second or third set of tack and clew patches built into the sail with a few intermediate reef points to tie up the sailcloth (Fig. 3). The hardware is simple. There's a padeye, a cheekblock and a cleat on the boom for each reef. Then there's a length of Dacron braid to run through the hardware and away you go (Fig. 4). On a big boat, you add a winch to pull the clew down but with a good topping lift to support the boom while reefing, the average cruiser probably won't need one.

The benefits are numerous. First, the main sets equally well on either tack, and draft can be induced by slightly easing the clew reef line. Second, one person can accomplish the complete reefing operation without resorting to brute force. And finally, there are no boom reefing gears to jam; there is no winch handle to go overboard; there is no worm gear outhaul or boom in the cockpit. It is a highly recommended system for all cruisers whether they are alongshore or oceangoing.

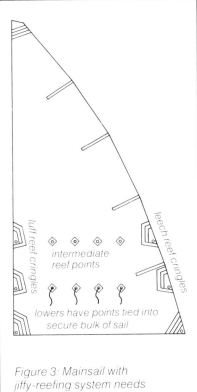

Figure 3: Mainsail with jiffy-reefing system needs reinforcing at luff and leech

(labels in figure: luff reef cringles; leech reef cringles; intermediate reef points; lowers have points tied into secure bulk of sail)

To simplify things even more, attention now is being focused on furling mainsails; ones that roll up immediately aft of their masts or completely inside them. Furling mains have been around awhile but here again, demand is the thing that is spawning so many new systems.

With these mainsail systems, battens and the roach area they support are usually eliminated. Battens are always a trouble spot for a sail and a seasoned long-distance cruiser often opts for a battenless (without roach) main. Battens, incidentally, usually mean some kind of repair work under way and it generally occurs when you don't want it to.

Light Sails. Although you hear the statement "I'm just a cruiser and don't need a spinnaker," nothing could be farther from the truth. Oceangoing cruising boats often stay away from

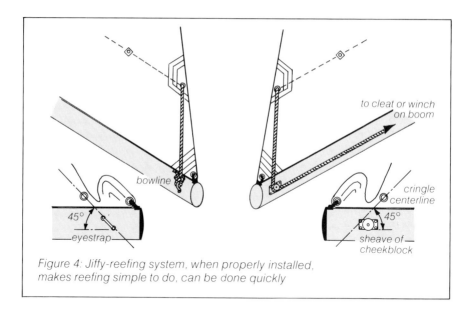

Figure 4: Jiffy-reefing system, when properly installed, makes reefing simple to do, can be done quickly

light sails because of chafe, a short-handed crew, or big seas, but this is the vast minority. Most cruising people sail alongshore and spend lots of time reaching or running. When the air is light to moderate, there is nothing more fun than rolling along at a three-to-four knot pace with a spinnaker set and the crew working on suntans.

I find that most sailors are just not familiar with spinnaker setting and dousing evolutions and once they are properly instructed, they don't have any trouble at all. Just because someone saw some racers rounding up or broaching on a brisk day doesn't mean that there aren't idyllic hours that can be spent sliding downwind on a cruising boat.

A device with rings has been developed that makes handling a spinnaker easy for as few as two people. Called a *Spinnaker Sally,* this device keeps the chute captured until it is fully hoisted and then, when all is ready, you hoist the rings and the spinnaker fills underneath it. A reversal of the procedure recaptures the spinnaker and allows you to lower it like a sausage.

Breaking away from full-sized spinnakers, other downwind light sails are popping up here and there as sailmakers seek to provide less complex rigs that produce similar results. A mod-ified *blooper* is one: it's a light and highly rounded sail which sets to leeward and complements a winged-out genoa. Another is a skewed flanker-type spinnaker which is carried without a pole, topping lift, or afterguy. It is a pretty simple rig that will allow you to reach or run with ease (Fig. 5). I'm sure all these sails have their devotees but it's still hard to beat the all-around fun and beauty of setting a "kite" and letting it coast you along to your downwind destination.

The real light-wind sails made possible with modern hardware are twin drifter/reachers set simultaneously in a double-grooved furling system. With adjustable whisker poles, these giant 180-percent LP sails can tow the serious cruising boat downwind with horsepower to burn. If the leg turns into a reach, you can gybe one sail over on top of the other one, ship the whisker poles, re-lead the weather sheet, and trim both sheets together to leeward.

At the end of the leg, the furling mechanism takes over and both sails neatly stow themselves on the stay. This type rig has been seen before but the particular construction didn't permit the adaptability that furling headstays do permit with regard to changing sails and sail uses. For example, in heavy air

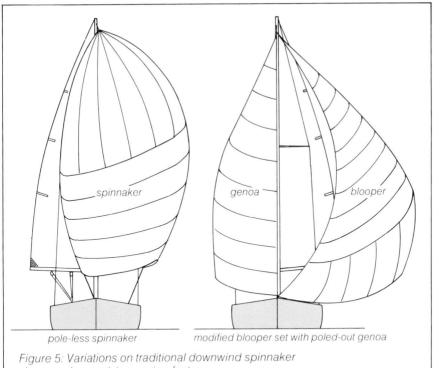

spinnaker   genoa   blooper

pole-less spinnaker   modified blooper set with poled-out genoa

Figure 5: Variations on traditional downwind spinnaker
shape makes cruising easier, faster

downwind, you may hoist a #2 genoa and working jib together for less area and for better steering control.

With much of the emphasis on ease of operation, minimum maintenance and maximum enjoyment of the time spent afloat, more new ideas pop up each day. As with everything, some are great and others not so great. However, there is more good advice around than there used to be in the old days and a little asking from "the man who owns one" can often give you a true picture of the value of some new piece of gear.

Hopefully, you will equip your own boat to make sailing fun, not a chore. A reasonable selection of sails, the gear to handle them, and a little instruction in their use is all that really is required. You'll enjoy your sailing a whole lot more if you don't let the label "cruiser" restrict you either to just two sails, or to doing things the hard way.

Sail Cloth Technology

The important role of specialized fabrics   Robert Bainbridge

By nature sailors are apt to know what type of jam cleats they have for their sheets and how their winches work. Most likely they have also carefully selected the wind pennants for their masthead. However, the chances are that they know little about the material used in their sails, other than the fact that they are Dacron and are firm or soft to the hand. The fact is that sailcloth is among the most complex and difficult fabrics to weave of any in the textile industry.

Sailcloth is a highly specialized fabric produced by a very small segment of the industry. The total number of yards of Dacron and nylon sailcloth woven in the United States in one year is probably less than the number of yards of material woven by a commercial linen weaver in a week. Moreover, less than one half of one percent of all Dacron produced in this country goes into sailcloth. That small percentage, however, turns into extremely highly engineered fabric which goes through hundreds of processes of designing, weaving, and finishing, and ends up being chosen or rejected by the sailmaker on the basis of hundredths- or thousandths-of-an-inch stretch.

Today, fabrics are routinely tested for tensile strength, tear strength, recovery, fatigue, and porosity. Tensile or stretch tests are generally done on the warp (length) of fabric roll, fill (width) and bias (diagonal) directions of the cloth, often on very sensitive, electronic cloth-testing machines. Sailmakers, in turn, choose their cloth on the basis of the firmness and stretch indicated on the graphs drawn by this machine.

Fifteen years ago there was no testing for stretch on sailcloth although the fabric was still designed to have as little stretch as possible. The way it was done was to take one thickness or "denier" of Dacron yarn, and to weave as many threads per inch as possible in both the warp and the fill.

The way to get a slightly lighter fabric was to weave the next lighter denier yarn in the same manner, in both the warp and fill. If an intermediate weight was needed between the two, then a heavier warp might be filled with a lighter fill or vice versa. For the most part, however, the fabric was sold by the weight, and little attention was paid to the fact that the stretch would be different between the one fabric with an even weight warp and fill, and the other where the warp and fill were of different deniers.

Since then this difference in stretch has been the basis of sailcloth construction. We now have different fabrics designed not only for mainsails and genoas but for high-aspect mains and low-aspect ones, for genoa jibs of different overlaps, for staysails and tall boys, for centerboarders and for small keel-boats. Although different sailmakers will have varying philosophies on stretch requirements for each sail, there are some general preferences. As a mainsail is supported along the luff by the mast and along the foot by the boom, these areas do not get much loading. The leech, however, is totally unsupported and bears the greatest loads. Every time a puff comes or the mainsheet is cranked in a little more, a greater load is put on the leech. If the leech were to stretch excessively, the entire shape of the sail would be distorted. The sailmaker, for this reason, wants to put the strongest direction of the cloth running up and down the leech.

In any woven fabric, the least stretch is in the direction of the threadlines running at right angles in the warp and fill. The greatest stretch is going to be in the bias direction, that is, the direction running at an angle of 45 degrees to the warp and the fill.

The choice then for the sailmaker is to run either the warp or the fill up and down the leech. For design reasons most choose the fill, and the panels of the sail are at approximately right angles to the leech. The best mainsail fabric then, would be one in which the fill stretched as little as possible so that the leech would have minimal stretch. Maximum fill strength can be accomplished, among other ways, by weaving a greater number of fill yarns than warp ones, by having a larger denier filling yarn than warp yarn, or by both. By using these techniques, it is possible to produce fabrics that are more than 10 times as resistant to stretch in the filling direction as in the bias. Such fabrics are often used in high aspect-ratio mainsails where the leech loads are especially high. Also in high aspect-ratio mainsails many sailmakers feel the slightly higher bias stretch that accompanies strong fill (the bias must be somewhat sacrificed to obtain the desired fill) is not objectionable as the cunningham adjustment is able to control the sail and reduce the effect of bias stretch because the cross section is so narrow.

Following the same theory, the low aspect-ratio sail would have more of a problem with bias stretch, for it has proportionately longer girths from luff to leech. However, it has less loads along the leech. Therefore, for such a sail many sailmakers look for a less extreme fabric, one with lower bias stretch and slightly higher fill stretch.

A "genoa" fabric is designed under different principles. In a genoa only the luff is supported by the forestay. The foot and the leech bear much higher loads. In fact, there are great loads on the cloth radiating out from the clew. Like a mainsail, a cross-cut genoa has panels that are aligned so that the fill runs up and down the leech. However, this means that the sheet is pulling directly against the bias. The object, then, in weaving a genoa fabric, is to have as even stretch as possible in all three directions, the bias, fill and warp. If it were possible to have equal stretch in those directions, the result would be a sail which would grow slightly but in which the shape would stay the same as there would be equal stretch along the foot, along the leech, and along the line bisecting the clew. In practical terms, what happens is that the fabric is designed with bias strength in mind. Bias stretch is minimized and threadline stretch is slightly increased to let the material stretch as evenly as possible.

There are many other factors that go into a sailcloth design besides denier, however. First of all, there is the type of fiber to be used. For sails other than spinnakers, drifters and the like, fibers made from polyester filaments are by far the most popular. One reason is because of their minimal stretch.

Dacron polyester was first used in sailcloth in around 1955. It had substantially less elongation under load than cotton, rayon, Orlon, and acrylic, some of its predecessors used in sailcloth weaving. Dacron remains today the lowest stretch-viable fiber available for sailcloth.

There have been yarns with higher modulus such as Kevlar. However, Kevlar proved in time to be too brittle and too subject to deterioration from ultraviolet rays. Kevlar-filled sailcloth generally lasted around 300 hours in the sun before the leech ripped. There are still efforts being made to improve the durability of Kevlar for sailcloth, but it remains questionable whether they will ever be practical for common use in sails. Carbon fibers and fiberglass both have lower elongation than polyester, but they are even more brittle than Kevlar.

There are other polyester fibers other

than Dacron available. English sailcloth manufacturers, of which there are several, use Terylene for the most part. Some German polyesters are Diolen and Trevira. The Japanese use Tetoran, the French Tergal. Sailcloth manufacturers in the United States prefer Dacron. Also, there are several different "types" or tenacities of Dacron which vary in performance characteristics. Several have useful applications in sailcloth. Each type has its own family of deniers, some of which have equivalents in other types, some of which do not. The denier, which is basically the size or thickness of yarn, must be decided upon for both the warp and fill, and there are several of those to choose from.

Each yarn, of whatever denier, is made up of a specific number of filaments, in much the same way as the strands of a rope are. Deniers and types vary on filament counts. The filament number can also affect performance, so that variables must also be considered in the design. Another factor is the twist of the yarn. The yarn is often given so many turns of twist per inch at the weaving mill. This is done under precise atmospheric conditions, as is every other individual process in the weaving. Twist affects the bulk of the yarn; a highly twisted yarn will have a smaller diameter than untwisted yarn of the same denier. Twist also affects the stretch and the weight. A yarn decreases in length when it is twisted. Finally it is possible to "ply" together two yarns of the same denier or of different deniers and weave them as one. This process multiplies the number of possible deniers available. During this "plying" process, additional turns of twist per inch can be put into the plied bundle.

Once the yarn has been specified the number of "ends" per inch in the warp, and "picks" per inch in the fill must be decided. This is commonly called the "count" or "construction" of the fabric and refers to the number of yarns in each square inch of fabric. All of these variables must be considered, both individually and in conjunction with each other, and the results weighed as to their effect on stretch, tear strength, weight, recover, porosity, and fatigue.

Moreover, their reactions to heat, pressure, various chemicals, and processes to come in the later "finishing" of the fabric need equally to be considered. Designing a fabric from these variables is definitely a process of building on past experience and from having conducted thousands of tests.

In designing a cloth, all of the preceding is done on paper before any weaving is done. A mill that weaves sailcloth has to be a specialty mill. Weavers like to run as few styles as possible. Large commercial mills may have several hundred or a thousand looms on one fabric alone, and they might have one person to supervise every 120 looms. A sailcloth mill may have one, two, or three looms on one style and one person to oversee every five looms. A production mill weaving fabric for bed sheets may require a warp of 200,000 yards before they will run a fabric. Sailcloth mills have often made up small warps and woven one-to five-yard test samples and put back the production fabric. This process would give fits to any large, less flexible weaver.

Sailcloth looms are very heavily built so that they can cram in the extra pick (fill yarns) needed to make sailcloth. For the more difficult fabrics even new machines have to be rebuilt after they have come from the manufacturer and specially synchronized to produce an extra-tight, dense fabric. Looms also need to be specialized. The same loom would not be used on an eight-ounce mainsail fabric in which an 880-denier fill must be hammered as on a lightweight spinnaker cloth which uses 20-denier yarn, and weaves only a few yards per day.

The plain weave has always dominated the sailcloth field for working sails. This is the simple weave in which each yarn goes over one yarn, under the next, over one, under one, etc. It uses one set of warp yarns and one set of fill yarns woven perpendicular to them. There is a possibility in the future that a triaxial weave might be used in sailcloth. Such a weave would have two warps running at 60 degrees to each other, and one fill. In a plain weave, the interstice between the warp and the fill yarns are square. In a triaxial weave, those interstices would be equilateral triangles. The result would be a fabric with three threadlines and a reduced range of bias directions.

Most of the significant developments in sailcloth, however, aside from improvements in construction, have come in the finishing process. Finish does the most to determine the stretch characteristics and other properties of the final fabric. The weaving mill will affect the designed constructions. In the finishing plant, however, the same construction can be taken and finished to achieve any number of characteristics. For instance, a genoa fabric which with the normal melamine finish might have a fill to bias stretch ratio of 1:2 might be given a "yarn tempered" finish which would reduce the ratio to close to 1:1. Or it might be given a resin-free finish which would raise the ratio to close to 1:3.

A melamine-finished fabric has been impregnated with melamine resin to the degree that it ends up having a firm or medium-firm "hand" or stiffness. Most of the sailcloth used in the United States belongs to this category. The yarns and filaments of the fabric are impregnated with the resin and during heat-setting the resin is chemically linked to the Dacron and the molecules are aligned so that the end product is not in effect just Dacron filaments coated with resin but a mass of fibers internally strengthened. The resulting fabric is durable, yet has low stretch. It retains the same properties designed into the weave, and yet is sensitive to cunningham adjustments as there is bias stretch.

In addition to a melamine finish, there are two yarn-tempered finishes—condition yarn temper and new yarn tempered, of which the latter is the firmer. Fabrics with these finishes, besides having been impregnated, have an additional treatment of resin. The result is extremely low elongation, with the bias stretch being almost as low as the threadline stretch. The "hand" on these, particularly on the new yarn temper, is very firm. They are intended strictly for racing, giving the ultimate in low stretch

properties. The leech has minimal stretch and the draft does not blow back. But sails made of fabrics so treated must be handled carefully. They must not be stuffed into sailbags, and they should not be carried in wind conditions that they were not intended for, particularly in lighter weights. For instance, a yarn-tempered finish would limit a 2.2- or three-ounce fabric to a stretch lower than the normal modulus of the Dacron. As long as the elastic limit of the resin is not exceeded, there should not be a problem, but if such a fabric were kept up at, say, 15-20 knots on a One-Tonner, the sail could blow out. On the medium and heavy weights, there is less worry, but the fabrics are still designed for performance, not durability, and they will not last as long as the melamine or the resin-free finish.

The resin-free fabrics are softer to the hands and more pliable than resinated fabrics; they are also more subject to stretch. For this reason sailmakers making sails from non-resinated fabrics need to allow for the extra stretch, but they also can depend upon excellent recovery almost indefinitely.

Different applications require different finishes. A production board boat might want a light-colored fabric, the offshore racer might want a melamine genoa, the dinghy racer might want a new yarn-tempered mainsail with a very firm racing finish, a Two-Tonner might want a high-aspect mainsail with a low stretch fill, while a 12-Meter with its lower aspect-ratio rig might want a fabric with good bias stretch as well as fill strength. Even aboard the same boat, there might be a variety of finishes. A One-Tonner might have a firm melamine or even yarn-tempered mainsail which does not have to be tightly furled or stuffed into a bag plus a resin-free light #1 genoa, a melamine heavy #1 genoa and a 1.6-ounce resin-coated nylon drifter, all in the same inventory.

Fabric that has been woven but not yet finished is called greige fabric. The weaving mill ships the greige fabric to the finishing mill. They, in turn, inspect the fabric and send it to be cleaned in what is basically a huge continuous washing machine.

The melamine resin is then applied on a multi-operation impregnation machine. This machine makes sure that the fabric absorbs the proper amount of resin and that the melamine is in contact with every fiber.

The melamine has no properties, however, until the fabric has been heat-set at high temperatures. During this process, the Dacron yarns swell, allowing the resin molecules to penetrate the fibers. These molecules are then aligned by the heat with the fiber and are thus chemically bonded. The result is an impregnated fabric. Also very important is the shrinking of the fabric from the heat. Depending upon weight and construction, the cloth is allowed to shrink a precise amount. This further tightens the weave to a point impossible to

achieve mechanically on the looms.

Some heat-setting is done on large gas-heated ovens called tenterframes. Such machines have two parallel frames which are adjusted so that they are a cloth-width apart. Continuous belts run the length of these frames with clamps attached every few inches. The cloth is fed into the end of the frame, and the edges are grabbed by the clamps and run down the frame through the oven which does the heat-setting.

Another method is to run the cloth through two thick steel rollers pressing together with many tons of pressure and heated to a high temperature.

Often the fabric goes though a machine known as a calendar. During this process the weave is further tightened, and the fabric is given whatever

Cloth-testing machine tests strips, circles or other shape samples of sailcloth to obtain highly precise quality control readings in tensile strength, tear strength, fatigue, and other properties

smoothness or surface appearance is desired, by variations in speed, temperature, pressure, and humidity.

The next step in the finishing of Dacron sailcloth is trimming. In this stage, the cloth is driven from one roll to another and over a surface to which are attached two electrically heated knives, which trim the cloth to the desired width, and leave a heat-sealed, straight edge. The cloth is then reversed and passes by another surface to which are attached two instruments which mark continuous lines just inside the edge, for use by the sailmaker in sewing the seam. Both the knives and the pens can be adjusted to handle any cloth width, and other knives can be added so that the fabric can be slit into several rolls of "tape," which sailmakers use on the edges or other places in the sail. For instance, many headsails have Teflon tape sewn onto their luffs so the sail will slide up and down grooved headstay systems easily. Several sections of Teflon are woven in one wide-width piece of cloth and then the cloth is slit into individual tapes.

Nylon spinnaker cloth goes through much the same processes as Dacron sailcloth with a few exceptions. The colors must be dyed on what is called a pressure dyer. The fabric is rolled onto a large, hollow beam with many small perforations. The beam is then placed inside a big cylindrical tank which is basically a huge pressure cooker. The dye is forced under pressure onto the inside of the beam, and out through the fabric. The fabric is then heat-set.

Pressure dyer contains one large roll of cloth through which dye is being forced at extremely high pressure

Some spinnaker fabrics are coated with a thin film of urethane, acrylic, or other chemical coating. The purpose of this film is first to reduce porosity. By use of a coating, a fabric can be made to have virtually zero porosity, in other words, basically no air will pass through it. The other physical characteristic that a coating can produce is a reduction of stretch, particularly in the bias direction. Coatings have been developed which are soft to the touch, yet can limit bias stretch to less than 20 percent of that which a similar uncoated fabric would have and still have comparable durability. The tear-strength will not be as good as on an uncoated fabric, however.

Spinnaker coatings can be applied in several ways, but one common method is called blade coating. In this process blobs of coating are rolled onto the fabric and a blade scrapes all excess coating off, leaving a thin film of predetermined thickness.

The coating is then cured under heat. Coatings are usually applied to the lighter weight spinnaker fabrics. The heavier ones have low enough stretch and porosity that most manufacturers feel that a coating is not warranted.

Although these steps described in finishing sailcloth are common, they are not standardized. There are many other machines which are used for specifically desired characteristics and finishes. Also the omission or variation of any one operation will yield a fabric with different properties. In actual practice, the schedule of operations is different for every different weight and finish of sailcloth. That is, the number of machines used, the speed of heatsetting and calendaring, the temperatures, the pressures, the humidities, the times, the chemical formulas, all differ for each fabric. As in weaving where there are a multitude of variables, all the many factors must be weighed both individually and collectively before the right finishing procedure can be reached. Possibilities and new approaches are never exhausted and the result is an endless stream of tests producing new sail fabrics.

Not too long ago weight was the only consideration in deciding what fabric to use in a sail. Now within just one weight range there are often several weaves and finishes, all of which can be used for different applications. With so much to choose from in sailcloth just as there are in winches, jam cleats, and mast pennants, it seems little wonder that sailmaking demands the knowledge and experience it does.

Mechanisms

Taking Advantage

Block-and-tackle systems for sail control   Ed Hellenbrecht

There is a truly astonishing array of hardware to control sails on today's market, and anyone walking into a well equipped marine store without having a good idea of what he or she needs can quickly be confused. So the trick is to know what you want and why you want it *before* you go in to buy.

The basic idea behind any control line on a sailboat is that something must be moved, and held, under load. On all sailboats except small dinghies, the forces needed to control the setting and shape of sails are far in excess of normal human (and, yes, even "deck ape") strength. So, some form of mechanical advantage must be relied upon.

Mechanical advantage is usually expressed as a ratio. For example, 2:1 means that the working, or moving end, of the system pulls twice as hard as the force applied by the operator. Figure 1 shows a simple 2:1 block-and-tackle system.

Unfortunately for sailors, there is a fundamental law that says what you gain in force on the working end, you as operator must make up for in distance hauled. In Figure 1, for example, hauling six inches on the sheet only moves the clew three inches. This is a basic law of kinematics and applies to all mechanical systems.

Virtually every known method of obtaining a mechanical advantage is used on the modern sailboat: screw threads (turnbuckle), levers (hyfield lever, lever vang), gears (winch), fluid pressure (hydraulic stay adjuster, vang), and, of course, the traditional and tremendously versatile pulley (block and tackle). When considered in terms of power, speed, and adjustability these methods can be grouped as shown in Figure 2.

No matter whether you have a flat-out One-Tonner, cruising ketch, or weekend daysailer, determining the

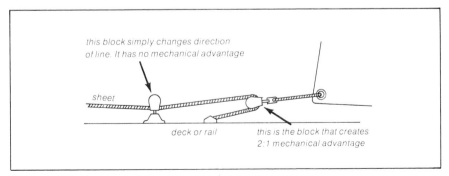

Figure 1: What a simple 2:1 mechanical advantage looks like

POWER	SPEED	ADJUSTABILITY	METHOD
Very low	Very high	High	Reverse purchase block and tackle
Low	High	Unlimited	Simple line
Moderate	Moderate	Low	Lever, simple block and tackle
Moderate	·High	High	Snubbing or single-speed winch, ratchet block
High	Low	Low	Turnbuckle, hydraulics, compound block and tackle
High	High	Unlimited	Geared winch

Figure 2: Getting proper power, speed, and adjustability often requires different methods

method first and then selecting the specific hardware depends on the answer to the following questions:
- How much adjustment is required
- How fast must the adjustment be made
- How much power is required during adjustment . . . while under a static load
- How often is adjustment required
- Is "feel" important, as on a light spinnaker sheet
- How convenient should the system be to operate, and where should its operating point be
- Are attachment points and standing rigging adequate for anticipated loads
- Is there reduced wind resistance with one system
- How much will the entire system weigh
- How much will the system cost

For every control line the *method* must be decided upon first. *Then*, the details of hardware, sizes, etc., can be

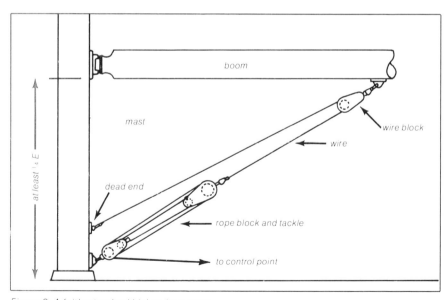

Figure 3: A fairly standard kicker-type vang

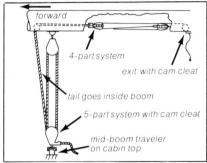

Figure 4: A mainsheet adjustment system that uses a two-way block-and-tackle system

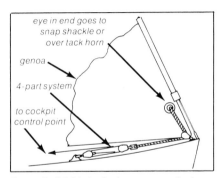

Figure 5: A fairly typical genoa cunningham system on a 35-footer

considered. Sometimes the first step is neglected and the result can be a bit misplaced, a really massive hydraulic vang on a boat under 35 feet for example.

So with that in mind, here are some guidelines for some of the more common control lines found aboard most racing and cruising sailboats.

Mainsheet

The mainsheet should be instantly adjustable under all normal conditions. It also must be able to be eased quickly, especially in light air when the wind force against the sail is small. High-quality ball-bearing blocks are highly suited for this kind of use.

On most recent stock and custom race boats booms are much shorter and the mainsail therefore is very "tall and skinny" compared with more moderate cruising rigs. These high-aspect mains require a lot more sheet tension to keep the sail drawing properly and this, of course, means more mechanical advantage is required. But extra power becomes a hindrance when the sail is eased out on a reach.

One solution is to have a kicker-type vang supply the required leech tension all the time (Fig. 3). This reduces mainsheet duties to controlling boom angle only, a task that can be done with a far simpler arrangement. However, loads on the mast, boom, and gooseneck are going to be much higher than normal and this must be allowed for.

A neat mainsheet arrangement can

use a two-way block-and-tackle system and is shown in Figure 4.

The 5:1 system down on the mid-boom traveler is used for boom-angle control. But for close-hauled work, this system is cleated, and the 4:1 system inside the boom pulls on the tail end of the 5:1 system. This type of "compound" block-and-tackle system makes the total mechanical advantage of the first system *multipled by* the system pulling on the tail end. In this case the resulting mechanical advantage is 20:1 and that gives plenty of power for leech tension adjustment when going to windward.

Traveler Control

A simple block-and-tackle system normally is all that is required to position the traveler, though a good quality roller or ball-bearing traveler is essential for really smooth operations.

Cunningham

Here is a case where plenty of power is needed but only over a very limited range. Generally, the total adjustment never exceeds one foot and this is an ideal place for the same kind of compound block-and-tackle system we've already looked at on the mainsheet. In this case, the first 2:1 system is created by leading the heavy line up through the cunningham cringle and back to a convenient point near the tack.

A valuable feature of any block-and-tackle system is that the tension on the operating end is equal to the force pro-

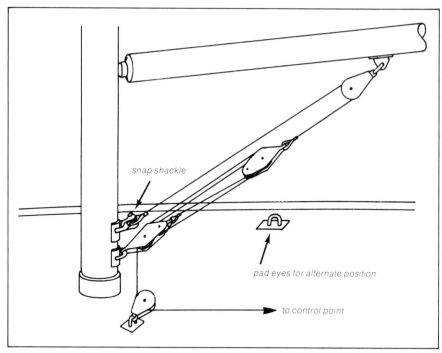

Figure 6: A combination vang shown in the kicker position

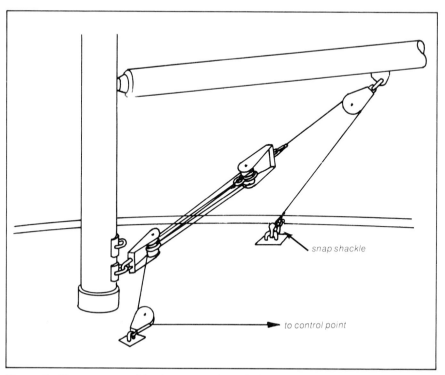

Figure 7: The same combination vang shown in the preventer position, on the rail

Length overall	up to 25:	25' to 30'	30' to 35'	35' to 40'
Rating (IOR)	up to 20.0	20.0 to 23.0	23.0 to 26.0	26.0 to 29.0
Mainsheet	**3:1**	**4:1**	**6:1**	**10:1**
	B&T	B&T	B&T	C/B&T,W
Traveler	**2:1**	**2:1**	**3:1**	**4:1**
	B&T	B&T	B&T	B&T
Outhaul	**5:1**	**6:1**	**7:1**	**8:1**
	B&T	B&T	B&T	B&T
Cunningham	**6:1**	**6:1**	**8:1**	**10:1**
	C/B&T	C/B&T	C/B&T	C/B&T
Vang-Conventional	**3:1**	**4:1**	**6:1**	**7:1**
	B&T	B&T	B&T	B&T
Vang-Kicker	**6:1**	**8:1**	**10:1**	**12:1**
	C/B&T	C/B&T,L	C/B&T,L	C/B&T,L, H,T
Genoa Sheet &	**10:1**	**24:1**	**36:1**	**48:1**
Spinnaker Guy	W	W	W	W
Spinnaker Sheet	**2:1**	**4:1**	**16:1**	**32:1**
	R,W	W	W	W
Foreguy & Lift	**1:1**	**1:1**	**2:1**	**4:1**
	—	—	W,B&T	W

B&T	Block & Tackle
C B&T	Compound Block & Tackle
L	Lever
W	Winch
H	Hydraulic
T	Turnbuckle
R	Ratchet block

Figure 8: There are different systems for every length of boat. It all depends on the required mechanical advantage

duced by the working end *divided by* the mechanical advantage of the system. In Figure 5, for example, the line leading back to the cockpit has to carry only ⅛th of the effective cunningham force. This means it can be a light Dacron rope and you can use lightweight fittings and cleats. It is the kind of thing that keeps the foredeck crew from stubbing their toes on a drum-tight wire.

Mainsail Outhaul

The biggest problem with an outhaul is not that it lacks power to pull the clew out to the band. Rather, it is the problem of easing the clew after you round the weather mark. Sometimes a member of the crew has to stand on the rail and bang the outhaul car with a winch handle. Not only is this slow but the crew could slip and fall overboard.

One solution to the lubrication problem is to wax the outhaul tack and sail slugs (or bolt rope) several times a season with paraffin, such as the kind used for home canning. It is colorless, cheap,

and won't wash off as a light oil might. Paraffin can also be dissolved in a solvent to reach that hard-to-get spot.

Vang

The boom vang probably is the least understood and poorest rigged control line aboard most boats. A good vang is tremendously important to maintain adequate leech tension after the boom has been eased out beyond the limit of the traveler. The vang only needs a limited range of adjustability, less in fact than the cunningham. But it requires plenty of power, and here is another good candidate for a compound block-and-tackle system.

A conventional vang leads from a bale, claw or strap on the boom down to a convenient point on either the rail or to padeyes on the cabin top. This type of rig still is the most common, especially on conventional rigs with long booms located down low on the mast.

Shorter booms located higher on the mast sometimes can allow a dinghy-

213

type kicker vang already described in Figure 3. If the boom is located so that the distance from the cabin top to the underside of the boom is more than about 1/4th of the boom length (to the band) then a kicker-type vang can be considered.

There are several ways to develop the required power with the kicker vang. Boats up to about 35 feet commonly use various block-and-tackle arrangements, sometimes incorporating a lever like the ones found on high-performance dinghies such as the 470 and 5-0-5. On larger boats, solid rod vangs adapted from backstay adjusters and hydraulic systems often are seen. There is one problem with this rig though, and that is that threaded or small-diameter smooth rod is great for high loads in tension. However, it is not that good in compression and a crew or even a guest could lean on the end of the boom and buckle the rod; this could require repair, or even replacement, of the unit. You have to be very careful.

For many boats, a compound block-and-tackle kicker vang system can be used quite nicely. However, if the "dead end" of the system is fitted with a snap shackle and can be attached to several points running from rail to rail as well as on the mast the system can become a "combination" vang, but can still be adjusted from a single point in the cockpit. It can be left either in the kicker position and tacked without adjustment for close reaching or in light air, or it can be shackled to the rail as a vang/preventer. Figure 6 shows the system in the centerline (kicker) and Figure 7 puts it outboard as a vang/preventer.

Well, those are a few ideas you might find useful on your own boat. And remember that while the method of operation remains the same, the specific hardware does vary according to the size of boat you are talking about. The table in Figure 8 gives you the amount of power and the type of system that is appropriate for four sizes of boat: up to 25 feet; 25-30 feet; 30-35 feet; and over 35 feet.

While nothing ever is hard and fast, you ought to be able to get a pretty good idea from this list what you might need to make your own boat sail better—and more efficiently.

Setups for Ocean Racing

Efficient deck layouts make a boat easy to sail

Rick Grajirena

Speed through the water certainly is a primary ingredient for success, but many people overlook another very important aspect of boat speed. Many boat lengths can be lost over the course of a race through insufficient placement of winches, cleats and controls. I just recently completed the deck layout on a new Peterson-designed 30-foot Half-Tonner named *Fair American* and basically our theory was to keep the boat easy to sail and concentrate the weight near the center of the boat. We looked at the boat as a large dinghy and tried to set up the deck hardware so we could sail it accordingly. The deck layout centered around the companionway which we dubbed "the pit." We had a platform built in the companionway, so that during any evolution a crewman could stand on the platform and complete any job required. All halyards, cunning-

Photo 1: Winch placement around companionway

hams, and controls led to this area. Even if it was too rough to stand in the pit, the winches were easily accessible from the weather rail.

Photo 1 shows the winch placement forward of the pit. Looking from left to right, the first winch is the port spinnaker halyard winch with a stainless-steel drum and a power ratio of six to one in high gear and 33 to one in low gear. This winch is larger than necessary for a spinnaker halyard on a boat this size but it also doubles as a secondary winch for the genoa and spinnaker sheets. We used stainless-steel drums here because the halyards all were wire with rope tails. Wire halyards were chosen to reduce windage as much as possible.

The next winch is an aluminum drum winch with a power ratio of seven to one. This is primarily used for the spinnaker pole down-guy but doubles nicely as a sheet winch for the staysails. Since no wire is on the drum, aluminum was chosen as a weight saver. The genoa halyard leads to the next winch, a stainless-steel seven to one power ratio, smaller than the spinnaker halyard winches because it isn't used for anything else.

The fourth winch from the left is an aluminum drum seven to one power ratio. This winch serves double duty, first, to tighten the baby stay when we need mast bend to flatten the main. After tightening the baby stay, the line is slipped into a large Clamcleat forward of the winch. The line was now stopped off and we could remove the wraps from the winch and use the winch for the spinnaker pole topping lift. The

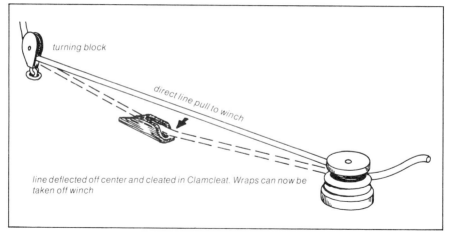

turning block

direct line pull to winch

line deflected off center and cleated in Clamcleat. Wraps can now be taken off winch

Figure 1: Maximizing the uses for a single winch

Clamcleat was just off the direct line-pull to the winch so that any time we wanted it freed, tension on the line would release it (Fig. 1).

The last winch is a stainless drum, six to one ratio in high gear and 33 to one in low gear like the one on the port side: a spinnaker halyard winch doubling as a secondary. The boat is set up with three halyards exiting at the top of the mast, two spinnaker halyards and a genoa halyard, all wire, but each can be used as a spinnaker or genoa halyard for sail changes.

Although this is certainly not an overabundance of winches, even in the most hectic situations we never needed additional winches. Again in this picture, you see three Clamcleats to the right of the genoa halyard; the first two a spinnaker pole lift and downhaul, the third a stopper for the baby stay as I have already explained. The pole lift and downhaul were easy to use and worked like this (Fig. 2).

Also shown in Photo 1 are line patches on both sides of the companionway. These are simple, pillow-type pouches with shockcord across the top to hold lines in. They are used to store the tails of halyards and sheets.

In Photo 2 you can see the boomvang arrangement. Although rapidly becoming a standard in dinghy sailing, the lever vang is just coming into its own in ocean racing. It allows for a

great deal of power with minimum moving parts and is extremely economical. In last year's SORC, the One-Tonner *Country Woman* used a vang similar to this one and it proved powerful enough to break the gooseneck the first time they used it. This particular vang was made from one-quarter-inch aluminum and was so powerful we never used a winch on it (Fig. 3).

Our technique for setting the spinnaker deserves mention here, as we were the only boat using it. The spinnaker is completely set out of the cockpit as in a Lightning or a Soling and we never "stopped" the spinnaker before hoisting. The theory here again is to keep weight out of the ends and not have a crewman running around the boat setting up the spinnaker prior to setting. This system worked easier than you might think and the only real trick, to prevent a spinnaker wrap, is getting the guy back to the pole as quickly as possible during the set. As the spinnaker is going up behind the genoa, very little air is getting to it and wraps are rare.

Photo 3 shows the cockpit area forward of the main traveler. Aluminum drum winches with a power ratio of five to one in high and 37 to one in low are used here. We have incurred frequent tacking duels and have found that winches this size are a real asset, for most of the other Half-Tonners have smaller winches for their genoa sheets.

216

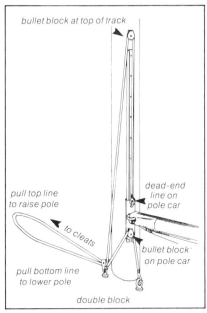

Figure 2: Double-ended pole lift and down-haul system

Here again, line pouches are used to keep spinnaker and genoa sheets in order.

With the Half-Ton Cup rules limiting the number of sails a yacht can carry on board, the selection of sails is extremely important. A Half-Tonner is allowed one mainsail, six jibs and three spinnakers. *Fair American*'s basic inventory is geared towards light air and therefore sail selection consisted of a three-quarter-ounce 150-percent drifter, three-and-a-half-ounce light number one genoa, a five-and-a-half-ounce reefable heavy number one genoa, a six-and-a-half-ounce reefable number two genoa, a three-quarter-ounce blooper, and a maximum area staysail for flying under the spinnaker.

We kept the electronics to a bare minimum, using only a log, speedometer and apparent-wind indicator. We also used a wind indicator at the top of the mast which was illuminated at night by a small masthead light. At the last minute we decided to add a digital averaging speedometer to the electronics and this, I think, helped us tune the boat faster than we might have been able to without it. When sailing to weather, for example, with the digital averager on we would move crew weight fore and aft to the optimum location and watch the speedometer go up or down accordingly.

Photo 4 is a picture of our foredeck

Photo 2: Boom-vang arrangement

217

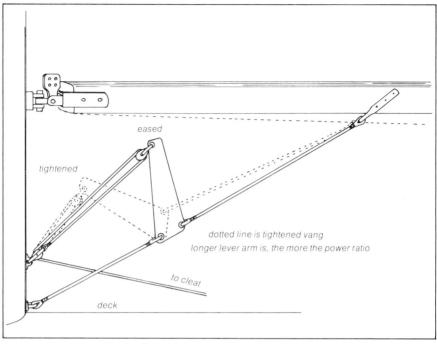

eased

tightened

dotted line is tightened vang
longer lever arm is, the more the power ratio

to cleat

deck

Figure 3: Lever-vang arrangement

with two plexiglass ports, under which is a 12-volt black light. We used fluorescent telltales illuminated by the black light for night sailing. The system worked very well in light-to-moderate air but not so well in heavy air. In heavy air, the amount of sea water coming over the forward deck and the violent pitching motion of the boat seriously affected the efficiency of the black light system.

Below decks the boat is at best, Spartan. Again, weight is concentrated amidships with absolutely nothing foreward of the mast and very, very little aft of the cockpit. On either side are two aluminum berths, one on top of each other located at the maximum beam of the boat to allow as much hiking leverage as possible even when two men were below sleeping. Just forward of the bunks, on the port side, is the navigator's station and it again is Spartan, consisting only of a chart table and a radio direction finder. Under Half-Ton rules, loran and omega are not allowed. The

starboard side, across from the navigator station, consists of the galley. Here is just a sink, a stove, and some storage beneath both. For an icebox, we used a large styrofoam cooler which slides under the pit platform.

We used wire shrouds instead of rod because we felt the loads were not great enough nor the savings in windage enough to warrant the additional expense. We did however, use a hydraulic backstay adjuster with a remote control located in the cockpit. We felt the ability to adjust the backstay quickly and accurately is very important. The remote control adjuster was decided on to, again, keep weight out of the back end of the boat as much as possible. We decided on the hydraulic after looking at a variety of other backstay adjusters. Basically, with the bridle type of backstays it is difficult to know exactly how much tension you have on the rig at any given time. Hand-cranked backstay adjusters take too much time and again you have to have weight in the ends

Photo 3: Cockpit area

Photo 4: Foredeck with black light arrangement for sail trim at night

when someone is back there adjusting it.

The boat has proved to be very easy to sail and we won the Southeastern Eliminations for the World Championships with all firsts with a crew that had never sailed on the boat prior to the regatta.

The boat has no more controls than a Soling and the fact that they are easy to use and not overly complicated contributed greatly to the success we had. It's important to remember that gadgets don't win races, people do. So keep your boat simple and concentrate on sailing it to its potential 100 percent of the time.

Fitting-out the Cruiser-racer

Think carefully before you finalize control lines Harrison Hine

In recent years, racing sailors have become pretty well versed on the exotic gear used on many of the top performing yachts. While this type of hardware does have a real value, it can lose much of its function if it's translated to boats of different sizes, sailing characteristics, and intended uses.

The primary consideration if you are planning the rig on any new boat or when you are re-rigging a boat is to make the new rigging system as efficient as possible, but still retain a simple and functional rig. If you are setting up a new boat, it would be very helpful to sail a sistership under various conditions to determine the sailing characteristics of the boat. The important characteristics you should think about are: crew position on various points of sail, the helmsman's space requirements, and general stability to windward. These points will bear heavily upon the proper final placement of the various pieces of gear and fittings needed to sail any boat efficiently.

On any cruiser-racer, the first thing to do is to take a look at the running rigging, especially the genoa sheets, to see how to best position the crew. Tacking a genoa is probably the most often performed crew task aboard and it should be the most natural and least compromised aspect of your rigging system. Until quite recently, very little thought was given to the actual dynamics of grinding a winch and putting this in the context of its placement on the boat ex-

cept on larger boats with their pedestal winches.

Lately however, designers have been incorporating crew cockpits and providing stand-up access to the primary winches to permit a crew to get far better leverage when cranking a winch. Unfortunately, most boats still are fitted with a traditional cockpit-winch base pad so it is important to make the most practical and efficient use of that space.

Here are some things you should consider when setting up your genoa jib-sheet arrangements. First, is the crew flow smooth during the tacking maneuver, and is there adequate space for the winch grinders and tailers? On many contemporary boats, the primary winches have been located either in the after part of the cockpit or up forward on the cabin top. Both configurations allow the remaining crew members to move from side to side without having to pass directly through the grinding, sheeting and letting go activities of tacking the genoa.

Once your jibsheeting arrangement is set and working, try it with your crew aboard and going through the motions before you finalize everything. Now turn to the movements of the crew members during a spinnaker hoist. Follow that with the evolutions involved in lowering, gybing and re-setting sails.

It is useful to use the deck plan for a starting point in any preliminary planning. Then sketch your initial ideas on paper. To do this either copy the deck

plan several times or use a tracing overlay. Before you start drilling holes you ought to get your crew together and walk through all the basic maneuvers. This way some of the more (or less) obvious flaws will show up, flaws that won't be noticeable on any drawing.

If it's impossible, the next thing to do is to purchase all your major hardware items such as winches, tracks and cleats and locate them where you feel they "should" go. Again, have your crew go through the motions and try them in their spots for windward work, running, tacking, gybing and so forth.

When you do this, you well may find that someone is sitting on a cleat, track, or is squeezed in an uncomfortable position. You may also find there is some advantage gained by moving a cleat or a winch to achieve a more natural grip, or to get better leverage on controlling sheets or halyards.

A common failure when thinking about rigging an ocean racer is for the skipper to think of things in terms of his position in the cockpit. Of course, he simply cannot do everything himself (unless it is a singlehander) and control lines really should be led to where the racing crew has best access to them *from their normal sailing positions.*

Check crew position when sailing to windward. If the best place for them is

Photo 1: With proper placement of the crew forward, most control lines, like the cunningham on this 30-footer, terminate near the mast

Photo 2: This 30-footer requires having the crew weight aft so all control lines are led aft to the cockpit

Photo 3: On this 27-footer, the skipper can play the traveler and mainsheet and the crew can make necessary adjustments to sail trim and shape without moving from their windward-rail positions

forward between the mast and the cockpit, locate the leads for the genoa halyard, cunningham and traveler controls so they are handy to the crew when they are properly seated (Photo 1). If the boat trims best under normal sailing conditions with crew weight aft, put the leads as far back as possible, to the edge of the cabin top if necessary, so that boat trim is not disturbed if the crew moves about to make the adjustments needed for sail control (Photo 2).

For good downwind control, remember how many crewmembers you have and think about what they are expected to do. On smaller boats, the skipper may be required to make adjustments to pole topping lifts, foreguys and so forth, and these controls should be handy for him to reach (Photo 3). On larger boats, the crew is probably more numerous and those spinnaker controls should be led to where those extra hands can most easily take care of the trimming.

I've always thought the best control line is the one that is out of sight and has a cleating point near its origin. If you can terminate a control line close to its function area you can keep the total rig simple, and that is what is important (Photo 4). And remember, not all control lines need to be cleated next to a crew member. Modern cam cleats do allow control lines to be cleated and released from quite a distance away without too much extra effort by the crew. If these can save having a maze of lines strung across either the cabin top or the deck it will certainly make your boat more pleasant to sail.

Most of us wind up rigging our boats piecemeal—adding to the rig as the need arises. The ideal situation, of course, is to have a bareboat then carefully plan the rig; and then install it—all at one time. Unfortunately, few racing sailors either have the opportunity or the funds. So I have found that the best idea, when money and time are limited, is to work out your best plan on paper, then go through the sailing evolutions I have described. Having a set plan which, of course, can be modified if the crew motions get confused, will give you a coordinated rigging system which has been carefully thought out. If, like most racing sailors, you do add some equipment on the spur of the moment, you probably will end up with a boat that looks like a piece of Swiss cheese; holes here and there, fittings in compromised positions, and an inefficient rig.

A previously-owned boat will find

Photo 4: On a 30-footer you can rig lines so that they cleat near their origins. Outlets from base of mast from left to right are: topping lift, spinnaker halyard, main halyard

you making accommodations for the thoughts of the previous owner. If the rig is poorly laid out, I would recommend removing all the fittings, filling all the holes, and starting from scratch, just as you would on a new boat. Certainly this is the best way, but it is also the most time consuming. Of course a basic deck plan of what you want to end up with certainly is called for here just as it is on a new boat.

I like to compare rigging a cruising or a racing boat to landscaping your yard. If you go down to the nursery each weekend and purchase one plant at a time, you probably will end up with a pretty sorry looking yard. You should have an overall plan, even if you do not intend to buy all the landscape items at once.

The same thing applies on a boat, but few people ever attempt to think out their total requirements. They simply trot over to the hardware store on Saturday morning and come back, with drill in hand, and start tacking fittings down without either planning the total rig or relating the various fittings to one another for best functional use. You'll find your racing will be more enjoyable if you have planned your rig both for efficiency and simplicity.

Keeping Track of Headsail Loads

How to calculate forces and angles

Frank Kurzynske

I've always had trouble finding accurate information on the actual loads that are placed on a headsail. And it seems to me that it is important that sailors have a good idea of how many pounds of force are required to position a headsail at various wind velocities. If they know this, they can install the proper size block, and also know what kinds of sheets and winches will be able to handle the imposed load.

When was the last time you leafed through a marine hardware catalog in search of a block with the required size and strength? Most manufacturers' catalogs are very clear in their application details and some manufacturers help your selection by indicating maximum line diameter. However, others make their recommendations on overall boat length, and others just leave it up to you to figure out. Guesses cost money; an oversized fitting is a direct waste of money, but an undersized unit usually means the destruction of the fitting and additional damage to gear and boat. And fortune will have smiled if no one is injured. Reputable marine hardware manufacturers, though, don't want you to buy more than you need, and they certainly don't want you to get less than you require.

How then can we reach a solution to this dilemma? The answer is make a selection based upon the strength required to carry the load. Here again, most catalogs list the strength of their products and some even indicate their suggested maximum working load (usu-

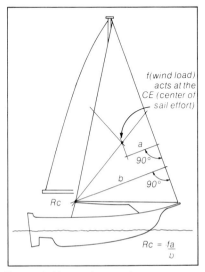

Figure 1: How to locate the center of effort of the headsail from the sailplan

wind velocity in MPH	"f" in lbs. Ft
5	0.100
10	0.400
15	0.900
20	1.600
25	2.500
30	3.600
35	4.900
40	6.400
f = 0.004AV	

Figure 2: Calculated values of wind
pressure at different velocities

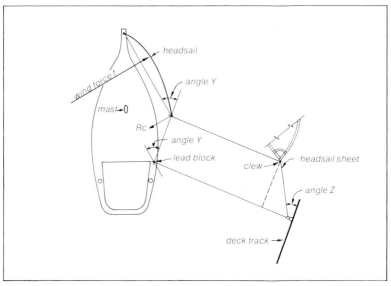

Figure 3: Force and reaction components that work on a headsail

Headsail loads can be very significant and it is important to know what kind of loads will be placed on sheets and blocks at various wind velocities

ally one half of the breaking strength). But be sure you are clear about which value is noted. Unfortunately, basing strength requirements on the size of line can also be misleading. Therefore, it is important to find some way of determining how much load the wind transfers to these jib sheets.

The first step is to draw a sailplan of your boat and put it on a workable scale. In Figure 1, I have drawn the sailplan for my own boat—I like using graph paper at ¼ inch to the foot. If you have misplaced the sailplan furnished by your boat manufacturer, you can reconstruct your own by using your P, I, E, and J dimensions. Once your sailplan is constructed, the center of sail effort can be found by drawing lines from the center of the foot to the head, center of the leech to the tack, and the center of the luff to the clew. The intersection of these lines is your center of effort.

The next thing you need to know is the value of the *wind load* that is applied at this center of sail effort. The *wind load* is a function of wind velocity and sail area. The pressure on the sail exerted by the wind varies with the square of the velocity based upon the formula $f = 0.004 \times A \times V^2$. In this formula, f is the force in pounds; A is

the sail area under investigation in square feet; and V is the wind velocity in miles per hour. To make things easier, I calculated values of f in five mph increments for wind velocities from five mph to 40 mph (Fig. 2).

The next couple of steps are a bit more complicated, but if you plug in your own numbers, you will get what you are looking for. What you are looking for now is the reaction of the sail, under load, at the clew. Just in case you want to check this out for yourself, the reaction value (Rc) is based upon the summation of moments about the headstay, assuming the wind pressure acts on a flat plate (your sail), and the wind force that is acting on the center effort also is attempting to revolve about a hinged connection. Look at Figure 1 again and scale off your own dimensions. You will find that the reaction at the clew is equal to the total wind force multiplied by the vertical distance from the headstay to the center of effort divided by the perpendicular distance from the headstay to the clew. The formula, simply stated, is Rc = fa/b.

Now that we have found the wind load reaction at the clew of the sail, we are ready to determine the sheet load. No matter what size boat you have, the

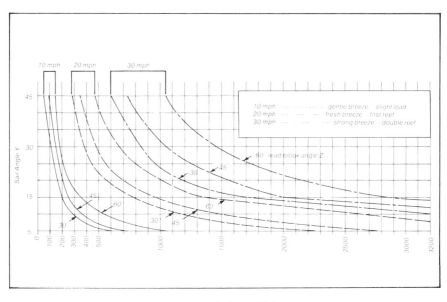

Figure 4: Calculated sheet load in pounds for a 304-square-foot genoa

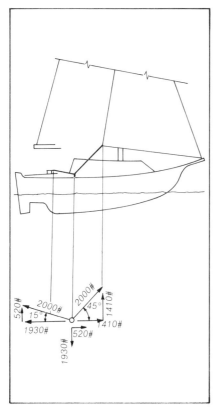

Figure 5: Detail showing stresses on lead block

diagram in Figure 3 is an accurate picture showing the relationship between the clew reaction (Rc) and the subsequent load imposed upon the sheet as a result of the relative position of the clew to the fairlead block. You can see that the sheet load is a function of the clew reaction and the angle created by the position of the sheet lead and a perpendicular to the clew reaction running through the sheet lead. If you recall your trigonometry, you will see that the horizontal component of the sheet load equals the clew reaction value divided by the sine of the included angle.

Put another way, the lower the clew is cut the nearer this horizontal component comes to equalling the actual sheet load. With a high-cut clew you must consider the "z angle" formed by the sail clew, the lead block and the deck track. To aid in visualizing this relationship take another look at Figure 3. Using trigonometry again, I have plotted, in Figure 4, the resulting sheet load for my own 304-square-foot genoa using different sail angles, lead block angles, and wind velocities. Unless you have a radically different shaped headsail, this table can be used by proportioning the loads on your own sail area from mine. In other words, if your sail area is half mine, the load will be half for the given conditions.

If you ever needed written proof of why the sheet load becomes greater as you sheet the headsail in, this figure will give you a real insight on how much the load increases as the sail angle becomes smaller and the lead block angle gets greater.

If you know what your loads *really* are, you can intelligently select your fittings and have a better idea about how much purchase you actually do need to make the working loads easier on yourself and crew.

In Figure 5, I have shown the actual component load on a lead block with a sheet load of 2,000 pounds, caused by a 30-mph wind, with a 15-degree sail angle (y), a 45-degree lead block setting angle (z) and a 15-degree winch sheeting angle. The block has to be able to resist a 520-pound horizontal force, and the deck track has to withstand a 1,930-pound vertical force. Therefore, for all practical purposes, the lead block should be selected for at least a breaking load of 4,000 pounds, using a 2:1 safety factor. By the way, don't forget that if you are using a turning block, the load on this block *is twice your sheet load.*

If you've gone through all this and you still would rather follow the manufacturer's recommendation, I suggest that you look for recommendations based upon the overall length of your boat. As a very general statement, boats of the same length do have about the same sail area. And when a safety factor of 2:1 is used, you can't go too far wrong. In most cases, you will still be on the conservative side. Which, of course, is what this exercise is really all about.

Modern Performance Rigs

Mast sections, materials, and sail-carrying devices   Eric Hall

Traditionally, the effort spent on spars and rigging on offshore racers has been disproportionately low compared to the attention devoted to hull design and sails. Today, with hull shapes looking more and more alike and with the top sailmakers in apparent agreement on sail shape and material, the best offshore efforts are now focusing on spar systems to "one up" the competition.

It is important to understand what factors make up a superior spar system. The best spar systems today are optimum combinations of structural design (strength and weight), reduced windage, and function. Let's look at each of these aspects individually.

It is no coincidence that the first concern for both the designer and the sailor is structural strength. Spars must not only stay in the boat *but also must reinforce the crews' confidence in the spars' ability to do so.*

On the other hand, the efficiency of today's high-aspect-ratio mainsail increases with corresponding decrease in the size of the mast section to which it is attached and behind which it must work. Since International Offshore Rule mainsails are characteristically long and narrow, the percentage of turbulence-affected area behind the spar is larger than with the wider Cruising Club of America Rule mainsails. With the best boats becoming more and more alike, small reductions in the turbulence-affected area of the mainsail become more and more meaningful to better performance.

Thus the dilemma: how can we reduce the proportions of the mast section to optimize the effect of the mainsail without compromising the strength and stability of the system?

Before discussing the various rigging possibilities, a brief explanation of mast loadings is in order. Although the mast supports side loads (wind on the sails), the stays "turn" the loads downward subjecting the mast ultimately to compression loads. A mast can take just so much compression, then it "pops" out of column and "fails."

There are two ways to reduce this compression load and thus reduce the size of mast section required to resist this load. The first is to maximize the chainplate base; an infinite base reduces the compression to zero. But, racing-boat chainplate widths are confined by the fact that the genoa must be trimmed to relatively close angles and the rigging must pass inside the genoa.

The second option, which in view of the constraint on the first is really the only option, takes advantage of the fact that reducing the length of slender tubes greatly increases their ability to carry compression loads. Of two masts of equal length and size the one divided in thirds by double spreaders can carry more load than the mast divided in half by single spreaders (Fig. 1). Likewise, a mast with running backstays and mid-stay can carry more load than a mast without.

Thus, the more rigging used to reduce compression by dividing the spar, the smaller the mast section required. But with more rigging comes more complication and additional weight and windage. Right now, the double-spreader rig with runners and midstay is in vogue from Quarter-Tonners to Admiral Cuppers. This double-spreader rig dates way back but its use on the smallest of racers, especially in view of its universal acceptance, is a relatively new trend.

Once the rigging system is chosen, mast size requirement is determined from righting moment and the properties of the mast material. This requirement is expressed in terms of "moment of inertia" (I), a property of mast section shape and cross-sectional area which, when combined with elastic properties (modules of elasticity, E) of the mast material, describes section strength properties (E $\times$ I).

Properly describing moment of inertia without using mathematical explanations is difficult. Simply stated, the moment of inertia of a mast section varies as: (1) the wall thickness of the extrusion; (2) the cube of its diameter.

If two mast sections have equal outside dimensions, the section with the thicker wall will have proportionately more moment of inertia and weight. If two sections have equal moments of inertia, the one with the larger outside dimensions will have thinner walls in a ratio proportionate *to the cube* of the ratio of outer dimensions. This means that the larger section for a given moment will be lighter.

If we wish to compare the weight of a stainless-steel mast with that of an aluminum, we find that because of the fact that stainless has modulus of elasticity of three times that of aluminum, it requires $\frac{1}{3}$ the moment of inertia of the aluminum section. If equal outside dimension is held, the stainless-steel section requires $\frac{1}{3}$ the cross-sectional area. But, unfortunately, stainless weighs three times as much as aluminum, so both sections end up weighing the same. The same type of thing happens with titanium: titanium has about 70 percent more modulus of elasticity than aluminum, but is about 70 percent heavier.

Applying the same thinking, it is easy to show why carbon fiber reinforcement

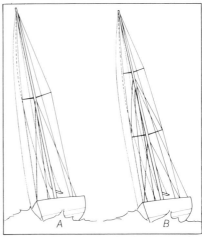

Figure 1: Single-spreader rig (A) requires larger mast section but has less rigging, while double-spreader rig (B) has smaller mast section with more rigging and complexity

works so well. Carbon fibers in a proper epoxy composite have almost twice the modulus of elasticity of aluminum and with barely *half* the weight. Thus, given equal outside section dimensions a carbon mast section would have about half the wall thickness of aluminum for comparable strength. This thinner wall combined with the lighter weight of the carbon composite section can result in a mast section weighing less than $\frac{1}{3}$ the weight of a comparable aluminum section.

Present practice is to reinforce existing mast sections rather than to produce 100-percent carbon fiber spars. A case in point was the mast of the much heralded Two-Tonner *Williwaw*, top boat in the 1976 SORC.

Her One-Ton mast section was reinforced with carbon to achieve the moments of inertia required for a Two-Tonner. If the mast were reinforced with aluminum to achieve the same moments, an increase of $\frac{1}{8}$th-inch in the wall thickness would have been required, adding about 175 pounds to the section. As it was, $\frac{1}{10}$th-inch carbon composite was used, adding only an estimated 90 pounds. The result was an extremely light spar with minimum sectional size for low-windage although playing with such exotics is expensive.

In 1970 the 12-Meter *Intrepid* used spars with varying degrees of reinforcement, using berylium, carbon, boron and titanium. Although decided weight savings were realized, the engineering, manufacturing, and maintenance costs were prohibitive and soon after the 1970 America's Cup campaign, the International Yacht Racing Union banned the use of the above materials.

Williwaw may now do the same for ocean racers. At this juncture such action would seem well-advised as carbon fibers are extremely expensive and to apply them properly is even more expensive. First, to get best results the carbon fibers should be purchased in tapes where the fibers are held together with a semi-cured epoxy "carrier." In a layup room of excessive cleanliness and climate control the tapes are applied to the mast and then, with a vacuum bag over the mast, the part is heat-cured in autoclave ovens at 350 degrees. The labor required of skilled personnel as well

as the sophisticated equipment involved result in very high manufacturing costs. Carbon can be applied in shipyard conditions to wood and fiberglass with good results, but the proper cleaning (and keeping clean) of an aluminum mast for "wet," room-temperature curing of epoxy to its surface is very difficult and the end product quality will be questionable at best.

However, as I believe that the future of exotic materials is close at hand and that the price of such materials will soon come down, any restrictions on their use should be conditional.

Given aluminum as the only practical material, the proportions of a tapered mast can be minimized by using one of the following:

1. Small thick-walled sections.

2. Small thick-walled sections chemmilled in areas of low loading. Chemmilling is a process in which an aluminum part is put into an acid tank where the acid can etch away aluminum from the surface. The amount of metal removed is proportional to time in the tank. Spars can be thinned in the upper areas by holding the tip in longer than the rest of the tube. A more sophisticated method is to mask the whole extrusion with a rubber coating, then cut and peel away the coating in areas to be etched. Where the coating is left on, no etching takes place. The latter method is used extensively in aircraft applications and is very expensive.

3. Small thin-walled sections with selective aluminum sheet stiffening. Rod-rigging expert Ken King is also an innovative and talented amateur mast builder and he has used this method on his own boats with spectacular results. His Three-Quarter-Tonner uses a section whose base dimensions are $5\frac{1}{4} \times 3\frac{7}{8}$-inches. (A conventional Three-Quarter-Ton section has dimensions of $7 \times 4\frac{1}{4}$-inches.)

4. Blunt-ended sections with normal wall thicknesses. The successful MORC racer *Pointin' Star* had a standard elliptical mast section of $7\frac{3}{4} \times 4\frac{3}{4}$-inches and weight of 3.70 pounds/feet. Her production version uses a spar section of $7 \times 4\frac{1}{2}$-inches with a weight of 3.3 pounds/feet and 15 percent higher mo-

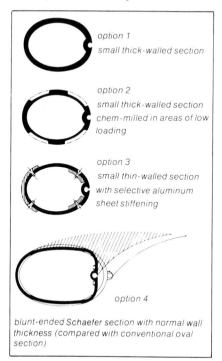

option 1
small thick-walled section

option 2
small thick-walled section
chem-milled in areas of low
loading

option 3
small thin-walled section
with selective aluminum
sheet stiffening

option 4

blunt-ended Schaefer section with normal wall thickness (compared with conventional oval section)

Figure 2: Four options used to minimize proportions of tapered mast sections

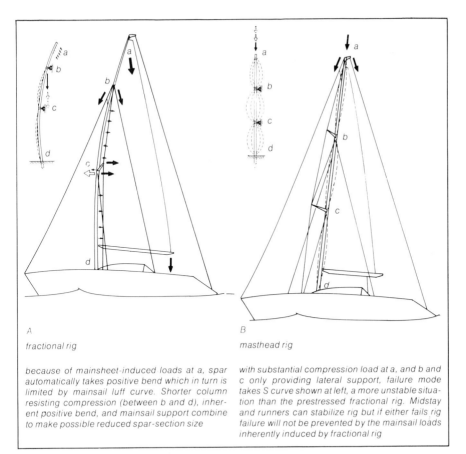

A
fractional rig

because of mainsheet-induced loads at a, spar automatically takes positive bend which in turn is limited by mainsail luff curve. Shorter column resisting compression (between b and d), inherent positive bend, and mainsail support combine to make possible reduced spar-section size

B
masthead rig

with substantial compression load at a, and b and c only providing lateral support, failure mode takes S curve shown at left, a more unstable situation than the prestressed fractional rig. Midstay and runners can stabilize rig but if either fails rig failure will not be prevented by the mainsail loads inherently induced by fractional rig

Figure 3: Comparison of the loading on fractional rig with masthead rig

ments of inertia. Both use identical rigging plans.

Option one is very heavy, two and three very expensive. Option four provides a comparatively inexpensive spar system with equal load-carrying ability for less weight and size when compared with traditional ovals (Fig. 2). Although improved aerodynamics have been claimed for such sections, their real secret lies in presenting less projected area ahead of the mainsail than conventional sections.

A novel approach to spars recently is the Bergstrom and Ridder rigging system which has chosen option one. These systems use small sections with very thick walls. The sections thus are heavy and require a complex swept-back spreader support system relying on a bow-mounted tensioning device. To date, these rigs have been most successful in medium air round-the-buoys racing in that the one great advantage with the B & R rig is that, because of its aft-mounted shrouds and lack of midstay, quicker tacking is possible. In heavy-weather situations where the added mast weight may be detrimental to motion in a sea and where the extra rigging may add to windage, performance has been less spectacular. The B & R rig once tuned does not "pump" or bend. This yields the advantage of minimum headstay sag and the disadvantage of minimum mainsail draft control through mast bending.

After a few false starts, $^3/_4$, $^7/_8$, $^{15}/_{16}$, etc., rigs seem now to be finding increased usage. The rating advantages with such

233

rigs seem to be complemented by the fact that sections for such rigs tend to be smaller because of inherent positive bending and support induced by the larger mainsails such rigs use (Fig. 3). The smaller sections in turn allow boats with such rigs to "depower" the main without reefing as the mast tip bends off to leeward. This property has been put to especially good use on the ultra-light dinghy-shaped level racers of Bruce Farr, which seem to perform best at minimum heel angles. Twelve-meters, on the other hand, have not had to rely on tip bend-off to reduce heeling moment as their somewhat larger heel angle can be tolerated up-wind. Use of these highly flexible "dinghy" spars on larger boats is relatively new territory and more development can surely be expected.

As a general trend, winning boats are also using spars with lower moments of inertia. This seems more a result of very precise tuning and higher tolerance of mast motion in a seaway by those sailing the boats than any new developments in rigging these lighter sections. These lighter, "whippier" rigs do cause, with each "pump" of the mast, resultant increases of jib-stay sag, but proponents seem to accept this compromise in favor of less mast in front of the main.

The other aspect of the structural design of the ocean racing rig, standing rigging, has improved. Although spar sections have become smaller, the standing rigging required to support them has not. Generally, on masts with minimum section size rod rigging is a must as the low stretch keeps the spars in column. Rod rigging is becoming increasingly available and many of the early problems with fatigue have been virtually eliminated.

Streamlined rod, however, has yet to catch on. Special vibration/fatigue problems associated with streamlined rod which may have caused one spar failure during the 1976 SORC still have not been solved to universal satisfaction. This vibration seems worse in the very streamlined sections over 4:1 width-to-thickness ratios and diminishes in rods as the elliptical shape approaches round.

Windage has always been a prime consideration in the design of spars and rigging, and although much progress has been made over the years, the rate at which it continues has not lessened.

We have already discussed the use of smaller mast sections as related to structural design. The most recent improvements in reducing windage along with spar proportions are evidenced in the mastheads. In the last three years the mastheads with cranes with spinnaker blocks hanging from them have been replaced with craneless mastheads with fixed-orientation sheaves and chafe guards to protect wire halyards during side loading. The basic system uses three headsail sheaves as shown in Figure 4, and reduces windage and weight by removing the blocks and the halyard tails which pass into the mast somewhat below the masthead. This system allows genoa changing with double-groove headstay systems and maintains the option of two spinnaker halyards. However, this type of masthead does present chafe problems; halyards do have to be replaced more frequently. The compromise here has, however, been made in favor of the advantage of reduced weight and windage advantages of the craneless rig. It may not be advisable to use such a masthead for cruising or extended offshore races such as the Transatlantic or the Transpac where long periods of downwind sailing prevent continuous halyard chafe inspection.

Internal tangs reduce windage substantially over external tangs but only when exit openings are taped over. If exit openings are not covered, especially on some of the spars with oversize exit holes, the appearance of a low-windage mast may actually be an illusion—such holes can be *adding* windage.

Another source of windage is spreaders and most spars are fitted with airfoil-shaped spreaders and have been for some time. More recently, spreader details at the roots and tips have shown improvements, however. Additional fairing and more precise engineering are reducing projected area at the roots. An idea which now seems to be gaining acceptance reduces tip windage on the lower spreaders by leading both cap

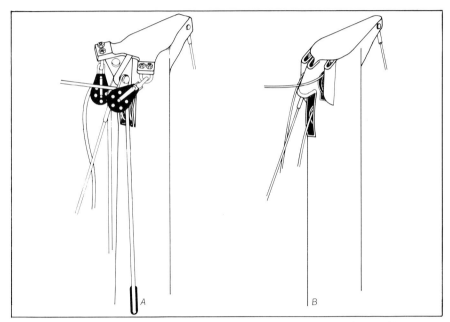

Figure 4: Comparison of offshore cruising extended racing masthead fitting (A) with modern offshore racing masthead with reduced windage and weight

shroud and intermediate to deck turnbuckles. This allows both shrouds to be tuned from the deck and requires no adjustable spreader end fitting. Shrouds still have to be properly seized to the spreader and yet the shrouds must be free to move through the spreader and relative to each other. This is not so simple as it sounds and extra care is required to keep the spreader at the proper upward angle.

Spar tapering in addition to reducing weight can reduce windage aloft. Tapering is most effective when done in the same proportions athwartships as fore and aft and to maintain symmetry. If symmetrical shapes are not maintained, there is an increase in turbulence because of the proportionately wider mast section.

The function of a spar system is to provide the mechanism to optimize the use of the sails it carries. As we have discussed, it must have the strength to carry the sails yet provide minimum aerodynamic disturbance around the sails.

The spar system must make it pos-sible to design the sails to fit any situation. It is also in the area of function where the spar system and deck system become inexorably interrelated.

Beginning with the mast's input on sail control, spars must be outfitted with rigging to induce bending to flatten mains in the higher wind ranges. In a bent condition, the mast is more vulnerable to buckling so adequate adjustable staying in the form of baby stays and running backstays is essential to keep the mast from bending farther out of column. As a bent mast is "shorter" a proper backstay tensioner is required. On smaller boats a bridle system does adequately; on the larger boats hydraulics are required.

The simplest and most basic of sail-handling operations is the hoisting of sails; ideas and refinements of ideas new just a few years ago now abound. All winches on racing layouts are either on deck or attached on or near the mast below deck. In the early 1970s many boats had deck-level exits which "replaced" double-sheave exits located six to seven feet above deck. The halyards

235

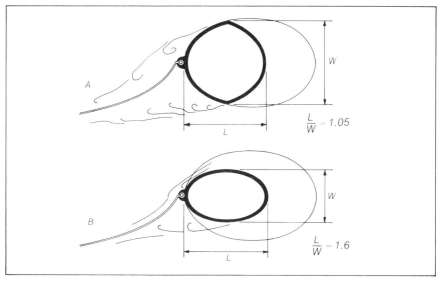

Figure 5: A common mistake in mast tapering is to remove a section only from the sides (A) yielding virtually no reduction in athwartships size. By maintaining symmetrical shape (B) turbulence is reduced

then led to turning blocks on deck which in turn led to respective winches. These deck level exits proved in some cases sources of weakness in spars and many caused cracks if not downright spar failures. Spar makers are now back to the high exits for strength and to enable a crew to get an extra hand on hoisting a headsail while using a double-groove headstay. The friction between the sails during a headsail change can be very high, especially in wet going, and extra muscle is required at times for fast changes. Halyard exits no longer have sheaves in them but are now slots with stainless-steel rubbing pieces. This idea, the origins of which can be traced to an idea originally tried by Sparkman and Stephens on *Valiant* in 1970, is a substantial improvement over the old double-sheave exits which sooner or later jammed up, which had to be removed to reeve a halyard, and which actually increased wear on halyards because of sharp directional changes caused by the opposing sheaves.

Although halyard lockoffs have been in use for several generations of Twelves, the extent to which they have been used on offshore racing boats never has equalled that of the past year. It is now common to see lockoffs for almost every halyard. The biggest reason for the more extensive use of lockoffs on halyards is that the crews now trust the wire-rope splices to the point where they will lock off on the rope tail. Although the wire-rope splice is not considered to have the strength of the wire itself, it comes surprisingly close. Furthermore, the wire itself is usually loaded at most to 50 percent of its breaking load as higher loads will induce rapid wear on the wire rope at masthead sheaves or turning blocks at the deck. Lockoffs which adequately hold wire without excessive wear on either wire or lockoff cams have as yet not been developed.

The acceptance of lockoff has opened up new deck layout possibilities where winch placement and use can be made more flexible. For instance, with lockoffs, the same winch can be used to service two or more halyards during sail changes. Once sails are changed the halyard in use should be put back on the winch to prevent the consequences of an accidental opening of a lockoff and to enable the crew to make immediate luff tension changes if required.

It is difficult to imagine significant improvements over present rigs as one lists the refinements existent today. However, as one traces the equipment advances even over just the past five years one can only project additional advances. The near future will not only show further refinements in present ideas but will bring fresh new ideas in all areas of spars and rigging, many of which will represent quantum jumps which five years from now will have seemed inconceivable today. The common ground rule will remain: the optimum compromise of structural design, windage and function.

Racing with the Moon

Equipment and techniques for sailing at night   Tony Parker

Many people who day race competitively are reluctant to try overnight racing. They are intimidated by the extra gear they feel they must buy, and they have little confidence in their ability to do well at night.

However, many regional ocean racing fleet championships now include one or two overnight races during the series. Because these races often are longer, they are weighted more heavily, and this puts a premium on placing well. We are going to take a good look at some of the equipment and various techniques that should be included along with your ordinary day-racing set-up.

First, a couple of general thoughts on night racing. Sailboat races are won the same way at night as they are during the day, by alert, aggressive crews who drive their boats and themselves to the limit and who capitalize on their competitors' mistakes.

There are three ways darkness affects your sailing. First, and most obvious, you can't see as well; second, it is easier to lose your alertness, and therefore concentration; and finally, though it's not so obvious, your depth perception is severely reduced. Helmsmanship is therefore more difficult and proper sail shape is harder to judge. All three problems are intertwined but the net effect, of course, is slower boat speed—and lost races.

Let's take a look at how to set up your boat and organize your gear to minimize the restrictions darkness can place on you.

The first step is to mark *everything* for easy identification and calibration.

Start with your sails and mark every corner with a black indelible Magic Marker. Any simple system will do, but keep it simple. Don't use a tricky code for you run the risk that someone on board won't know or remember it (Fig. 1). Never use red ink for it will not show up if you use a red-lensed flashlight.

Also mark the sailbag clearly on the bottom and on both sides so when someone goes below to find a new headsail or spinnaker he won't have to fumble with every sailbag. Make a sail stowage chart and post it where it can be seen easily. This will cut down on rummaging. Make sure the crew puts the sails back where they are supposed to be on the list.

On deck go to the mast and mark each exit sheave and cleat with the name of that halyard; again use a black Magic Marker on white adhesive tape for maximum contrast. Put the white tape beside the cleat as well as on top of it so you can find the correct cleat even when a line is on it (Fig. 2).

Mark your halyards by marking the halyard shackles with tape. If you don't mark them, it is easy to use the wrong halyard. You then could cross and possibly jam both halyards. This is hard to spot in the dark and might be impossible to straighten out without sending a man up the mast. Again, rather than the

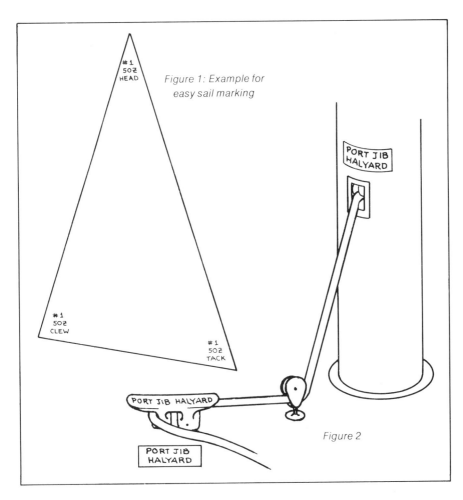

Figure 1: Example for easy sail marking

#1
5OZ
HEAD

#1
5OZ
CLEW

#1
5OZ
TACK

PORT JIB HALYARD

PORT JIB HALYARD

PORT JIB HALYARD

Figure 2

more common red tape for port and green tape for starboard, use either no tape for starboard and adhesive tape for port or put adhesive tape on both sides but color the port halyards black. The contrast will be easier to pick out at night (Fig. 3).

Proper halyard tension is extremely important for draft control. To "calibrate" your jib halyards, first hoist your number one genoa until the shackle fitting is just about to make contact with the masthead sheave. Have a person aloft at the masthead to see precisely when this happens. Now cleat the halyard and place a ruler on the mast in a vertical position. Take white adhesive tape and run it lengthwise vertically up the mast, and mark off 12 inches at one-inch intervals, again using a black

Magic Marker. (There are preprinted labels that do the same thing.) Mark on the "ruler" when the halyard is two-blocked (Fig. 4). To mark the wire halyard itself, I like to use fingernail polish to make a spot on the wire opposite the first mark. You can also take a small piece of wire and thread it through the halyard itself to establish the proper point. Seizing or tape that is merely wrapped around the outside of the wire won't work because it slides up and down after you have run it through the sheave once or twice.

Also mark your mainsail traveler and mainsheet for typical settings when going to windward. These will provide you with benchmarks to work with at night.

Now that everything is marked I

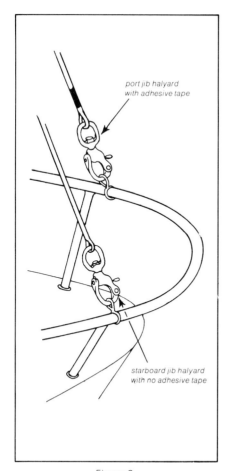

port jib halyard
with adhesive tape

starboard jib halyard
with no adhesive tape

Figure 3

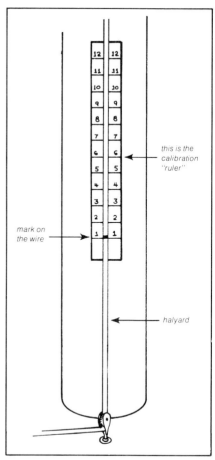

this is the
calibration
"ruler"

mark on
the wire

halyard

Figure 4

would like to turn to the problem of sails. Sail folding and proper stowage take on very important roles in night sailing. There is nothing more tiring or discouraging then having to go below in the middle of the night and heave each sailbag out of the way to locate the proper sail. Each sail has to have its proper place. If your sail locker is toward the bow you might think about having a hook placed just above each sailbag. Mark each hook clearly, then hook the appropriate drawstring of each bag over the proper hook.

Folded sails are also more important at night. A folded sail is easier to stow, is easier to carry around; and third, and most importantly, is much easier to put up.

After a headsail has been taken down, it should be dragged to the weather rail and folded in two-foot folds that are parallel to the foot. Then it should be rolled from the luff to the leech (Fig. 5). It sounds like a lot of work but it can be done while the crew is sitting in their normal positions— which should usually be on the weather rail.

If a sail is folded in this manner it can be pulled out of the bag quickly and set down on deck where the clew should be right on top. It is then a simple task for the hookup man to unroll the sail to the headstay. This system reduces the manpower needed for a sail change and keeps the weight in the bow to a minimum.

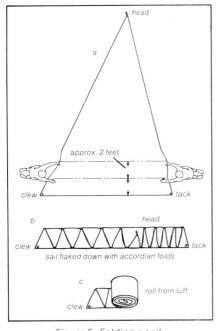

head

a

approx. 2 feet

clew   tack

b   head

clew   tack

sail flaked down with accordian folds

c

clew   roll from luff

Figure 5: Folding a sail

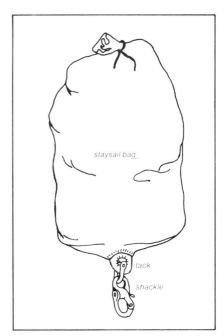

staysail bag

tack

shackle

Figure 6

Spinnakers always should be re-packed down below right after a take-down. Staysails, on the other hand, should receive a different treatment. I like to cut a hole in the bottom of the staysail bag. This allows me to push the tack of the sail down through the hole. Then I sew the bag to the tack, and attach a snap shackle to the tack (Fig. 6).

Then, when you decide to set the staysail, it is an easy job to attach the snap shackle to the proper place on the foredeck. If you have a sheet permanently attached to the staysail clew, you can run it to the proper lead on deck before hoisting (Fig. 7). When you are ready to set, just pull the bag down around the tack and hoist. When you want to take the sail down, drop it, stuff it back into the bag along with the

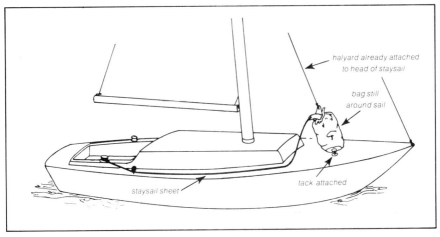

halyard already attached
to head of staysail

bag still
around sail

staysail sheet

tack attached

Figure 7

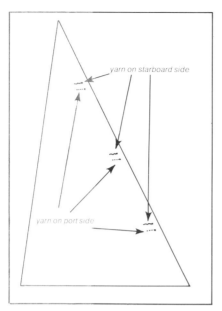

Figure 8: A standard method for telltale placement

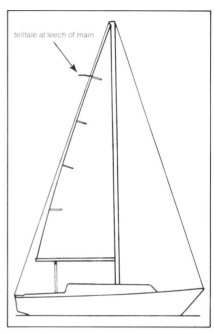

Figure 9: If telltale is streaming aft it means wind is flowing evenly off leech of the main. If it is not it means the upper part of the mainsail is stalled

sheet. It is then ready to go the next time you need it.

Make sure you have telltales on your genoas. An excellent material is black yarn. The telltales should be about 10 inches long, about 10½ inches behind the luff with the port side above or below (it makes no difference—just don't have them directly opposite) (Fig. 8). Standardize this staggered setup for all sails so you get used to it. The reason for staggering the telltales on the two sides is because it is difficult at night to tell which telltale you are looking at—the windward or the leeward.

Another telltale that is preferred by some sailors is a telltale trailing off the upper batten on the leech of the mainsail. It is an excellent way to judge whether the mainsail is stalling (Fig. 9).

A third major area about night set-up is lights. As a general rule the less light used the better off you are because it impairs your night vision. The only exceptions to restricting light usage is when checking sail trim, and then here it should be used almost continuously. You will also need a red-lensed compass light that is bright enough to be

seen but does not blind the helmsman. In addition, all speed and wind instruments must have adequate but not blinding red-lensed lights. A white spreader light two thirds of the way up the mast is most helpful in taking care of a major snafu that can sometimes occur on the foredeck.

Down below you should have at least two cabin lights that can convert to red lenses: the light over the galley and the light over the navigator's table. A light can be converted easily by painting a thin coat of fingernail polish on the inside of the lens. You can also buy two lens covers, one white and one red. Then substitute the red lens for the clear lens any time you are night racing.

There are three separate types of hand-held flashlights used in night racing. The first is used to spot racing and navigational buoys, to clear halyards, and to illuminate the sail in case of impending collision. The second type is used to check sail trim and the third is used to clean up or find loose gear on deck. The first type requires a powerful hand-held spotlight. An ordinary flashlight is just not powerful enough to do the job. It should be stored down below near the hatch but out of the way.

The second and third types require an ordinary two-cell flashlight, a white lens for sail trim, and a red lens for deck clean-up.

Many top sailors have a white flashlight on the luff of the jib at all times. Some tape the flashlight to the shrouds, others assign a crew to hold the flashlight. I have found having a crew hold the flashlight is better for two reasons. First, by having him call the trim continuously while sitting on the weather rail by the shrouds it keeps him awake and alert, and it will also keep the helmsman on his toes.

Another crew should be assigned to check mainsail trim constantly. Because of the reduction in depth perception, a particularly good way of looking at mainsail draft is to look at it from underneath the boom.

There also should be several red-lensed, two-cell flashlights for work around the deck. These flashlights should be stored at a particular location, perhaps one by the mast and the other back by the cockpit. Anywhere is fine as long as it is always there when not being used. You might try putting day-glow stripes on your flashlights to aid in their location if they get mislaid (which always seems to be the case).

The oncoming watch ought to make it a routine part of the relief process to make sure the flashlights are located in the places where they are supposed to be. There is nothing worse than having an emergency, or just releading a sheet, and finding that the flashlights are down in the jacket pockets of the watch that has gone below.

These are some ideas you can utilize to set your boat up. Remember the goal in night sailing is to minimize the effort in every evolution so the maximum amount of energy can be given to keeping the boat sailing fast.

Theory

Visualizing Wind Patterns

Aerodynamic flow around sail rigs   Eric Twiname

Most of us take for granted dirty wind and lee-bow effects without having much of an idea what the wind pattern set up by a sailing rig looks like. Inevitable really, because for one thing we can't see the wind and for another, sailing aerodynamics is a very complex subject. But so is the aerodynamics of flying and there are countless pictures of smoke flowing over airfoils in wind tunnels. When it comes to visual representation of air flow, sailing usually seems to be a very poor cousin.

To get a clearer picture of disturbed wind patterns around sailing rigs I conducted a series of tests with water flowing past static plates with the help of Dr. Dave Hardwick, a Canadian working at Imperial College, London. The results are the photographs reproduced here. For several reasons they break no new theoretical ground in sail research; their value is that they illustrate *clearly* some of the basics of wind flow round sailing rigs. In talking about the pictures, therefore, emphasis has to be on their relevance to wind patterns in the light of experience and other research rather than on making any attempt at quantitative analysis of the experiments. Their value lies entirely in their striking visual representation of known wind behavior.

The "sails" are curved rectangular pieces of aluminum which stand vertically in a steady stream of water about

three inches deep. On the surface of the water a light powder is scattered, and its particles, supported by surface tension, trace the movement resulting from the deflection of the stream by the sails. After minimizing the effect of surface tension on the flow pattern by smearing the plates with a soapy liquid, the water surface is illuminated and photographed from directly above, using a fifth-of-a-second time exposure.

During the time the shutter is open single particles of powder trace short lines (some of which are individually identifiable) and give the overall hair-like appearance to the flow picture. The patchy black and white texture of the photographs has no significance to the wind pattern and is due entirely to uneven distribution of the trace powder, while the hull shapes are superimposed photographically.

The most striking picture is Photo 1 and it shows just how severely the wind behind a running rig gets churned about. Big eddies fill the space immediately to leeward and move off downwind to be replaced by others; there is a constant downwind movement of the eddies, though this is not apparent from this still photograph.

The effect of such a highly turbulent wind pattern felt by a boat passing through the disturbance close-hauled is like a hole in the wind: the boat gives a sudden heel to windward as though the

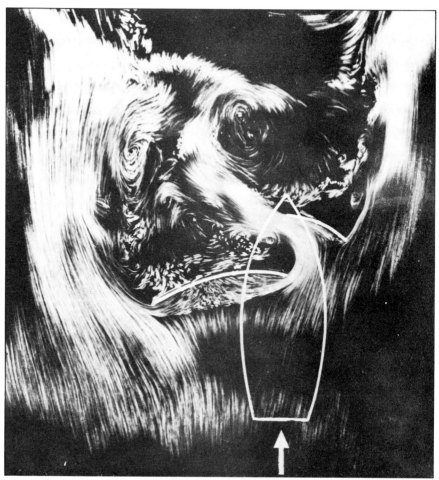

Photo 1: The traumatic turbulence caused by a boat on a dead run. The area on the left of the picture immediately downwind is clearly a bad place to be! A pressure build-up shows up to windward of the sail, while around the outside of the leech and outside the boomed-out jib the flow accelerates

wind has been switched off. It is not difficult to see from the picture why this happens.

A wind shadow as powerful as this works extremely well when used as a brake on a boat a few lengths ahead, provided it is made to sail right in the center of turbulence. A masthead wind indicator marks its line, so if you are close astern on a run you line yourself up to slow down the man ahead by using the wind indicator as a gunsight—a well enough known but often neglected tactic.

On the windward side of the mainsail a pressure build-up can be clearly seen. This cushioning of the air flow was first noticed by Dr. Manfred Curry in the 1920s during his famous series of experiments using smoke to show how air flows round spinnakers. He even tried putting a hole in the center of the spinnaker to release the static air, for this cushion was thought to decrease the efficiency of the sail. With modern spherical spinnakers and the tendency to fly them high there is a downward draft in the sail which probably prevents forma-

248

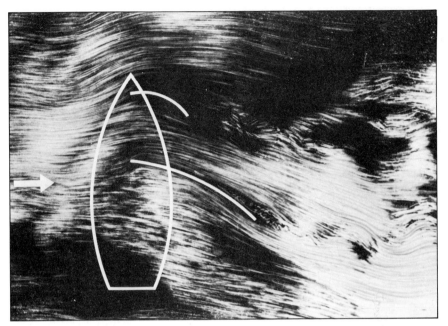

Photo 2: Reaching: Although there is a fair amount of turbulence, the flow is reasonably smooth over the "sails" themselves. Notice that the curvature of flow actually begins before the air has reached the sails

tion of any stagnant cushion of air. To-day's spinnakers tend to confirm Dr. Curry's theory though no one was able to prove any racing advantage by making holes in the old-style spinnakers to release the air cushion.

Returning to the water model picture of a running rig, notice that the flow bends around the rig and a marked deflection extends a surprising distance to either side. Where the streamlines close up, the speed of flow is increased. Where they diverge the speed is decreased. So there is a significant increase in wind speed close to each side of a boat on the run, and in this accelerated airstream a nearby running boat sails faster than it does in undisturbed wind.

The effect is magnified by two boats running parallel. With about a boat's length clear between them they appreciably accelerate the wind flowing through the gap. When the gap is between two bunches of running boats the wind is accelerated even more, which is why a single boat merely by keeping its

wind clear sometimes can draw many lengths clear ahead of a big fleet starting on a run. The phenomenon is known as the venturi effect and most coastal sailors will recognise it on a larger scale: the rise in wind speed by as much as three to five knots when sailing into a hill-bounded estuary with the wind blowing down its length.

There are interesting points to pick up from the series of reaching photographs if you look at them closely. With the jib and mainsail properly trimmed there is a fair amount of turbulence, though it's certainly not excessive (Photo 2). The flow bends significantly over most of the photograph and actually begins to deflect upstream of the sails.

When the mainsail is sheeted in too hard amazing things happen (Photo 3). Vast eddies behind the mainsail now make the area to leeward of the boat an almost impossible place to sail in (cruising skippers please take note). Oversheeting can consequently be used in

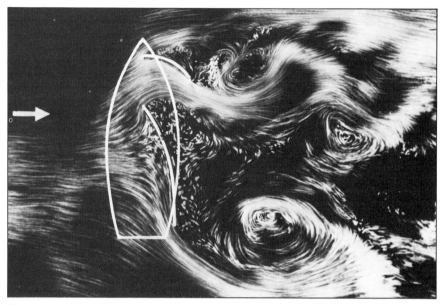

Photo 3: The same reaching situation but with the mainsail deliberately over-sheeted. The flow in the area immediately downwind has now broken down and big eddies make this boat very difficult to pass to leeward

team racing to slow down a boat trying to overtake you to leeward. The technique is to sweat in your mainsail, which slows you to about two-thirds normal speed, and the hole in the wind to leeward prevents your opponent from breaking through.

This particularly nasty wind pattern also can be used for breaking overlaps at reaching marks. Let's say a boat behind you has put its bow to leeward on a beam reach. This entitles the boat to inside room at the next mark unless you break that overlap. You can do this by first slowing down to allow the boat to become almost parallel to leeward. Then, preferably as a gust is just approaching, haul in the main hard, but allow the jib to set properly. The leeward boat will now be in appallingly dirty wind and will not accelerate with the gust—if you're really close, the turbulence can actually swing his boom into the middle of his boat. At this moment you let out the mainsail, accelerate away and break the overlap. If you don't believe me, try it!

On a beat (Photo 4), the flow pattern clearly shows why the familiar tactics of lee-bowing and covering are a result of the deflection of the air flow. The change in direction of the lines means that any boat sailing on the same tack immediately downwind will sail in a continual header, which is why a covered or lee-bowed boat can't point high, and falls away to leeward.

Close upwind and slightly astern, the effect of this header is really powerful and even a boat's length away the flow deflection is noticeable. Downwind the flow is slower too after the upwind boat has tapped the power supply. Notice the line of maximum turbulence; it is farther aft than many people imagine.

But it's not all bad for a boat behind on the beat. For a boat on the opposite tack crossing astern, the loss of wind-power is more than offset by the benefit of the wind curve which is now a lift—a useful little bonus to remember when crossing behind a beating boat. This lift is most clearly felt after a gate start (or rabbit start as they're sometimes

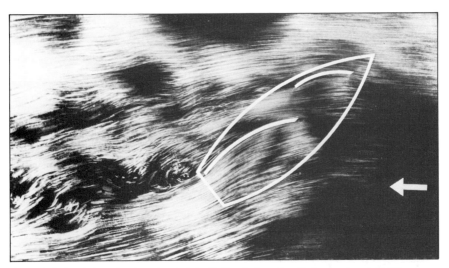

Photo 4: A simulation of a close-hauled rig. Notice that any boat to leeward and slightly astern will suffer a permanent heading wind shift. The airflow is appreciably curved well away on the windward quarter at the bottom left of the picture

known). With the whole fleet on starboard tack a steady lift of about five degrees is available to anyone who goes onto port tack early after messing up his start and crosses close behind the rest of the fleet. So after a bad attempt at an early start it is possible to sail the whole length of the line on port behind the starting fleet and lose no more than five or six lengths. Championship races in 140-strong fleets have been won by helmsmen who did exactly that.

The part the jib plays in close-hauled sailing becomes fairly obvious when you compare the photographs of a jib and mainsail rig beating with that of just a mainsail set at the same angle (Photos 4 and 5). Instead of a relatively smooth flow behind the mainsail, there are *bigger* eddies and *more* turbulence downwind when the jib has been removed. The mainsail has stalled, is less efficient and therefore provides less driving power to the hull. The sail can be unstalled by letting it out so it makes a finer angle to the wind.

One point the pictures do not illustrate (because they are two-dimensional) is the vertical movement of air over sails—upward at the top of the rig, and downward at the boom when sailing upright. Once the rig heels, though, there is a continual upward flow and this releases some of the pressure build-up which curves the wind flow on the windward side of the boat, so the lee-bowing effect is reduced. But heeling has more undesirable consequences than that.

The center of effort of the sails is displaced from its position (for an upright rig over the centerline of the hull) to a point over the water to leeward. This displacement of the point of drive to one side creates a turning movement on the hull which is the prime cause of excessive weather helm when a boat heels. But the direction of the resultant driving force changes too. On a heeled rig it is acting partially downwards, increasing displacement so that the boat is effectively heavier in the water.

Already I have moved from the two-dimensional model to three-dimensional reality. That doesn't reduce the value of the water model, but it does show the limitations. Sail shape assessment or any quantitative analysis of water models can be meaningless, for inevitably the tests have to be made in air.

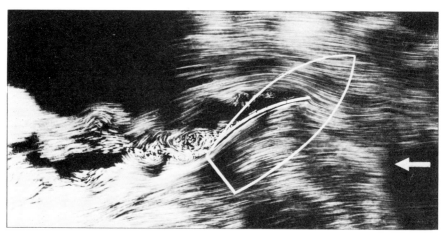

Photo 5: The same close-hauled situation but with jib removed and the mainsail at the same angle. The rig becomes considerably less efficient. Turbulence develops behind the latter part of the mainsail

One method of looking at wind flow relies on a phenomenon we all are familiar with but in quite a different setting—snowflakes in a car's headlights. Air is made to flow past a model rig in a darkened wind tunnel and fine ice crystals are released in the airstream upwind to make a miniature snowstorm. A thin plane of light now picks out a slice of the snowstorm, and that plane can be photographed in much the same way as we photographed the plane of particles on the water surface at Imperial College.

To my knowledge no one has used this technique in the aerodynamics of sailing.

Get the Most from the Wind

A practical examination of how sails work

Norman Smith

The youngster had just finished a sailing lesson when I asked him if he understood how a sail works. He shook his head.

"Not really," he answered, "but I don't know whether that's because it's hard to understand, or because they don't explain it very well."

I would hasten to reassure him, and any reader who may have the same problem, that it is the latter reason. A bewildering variety of explanations for how the sail does its job appear in books and articles on sailing. The differences among them suggest that all of them cannot be correct. The obvious confusion and inadequacy in many of them give rise to the feeling that there *must* be a better way!

As sailors, we don't need to know the mathematics or the minute details of the encounter between wind and sail, but we do need to understand the overall process of how the sail takes energy from the wind and uses it to propel the boat. We should also have an appreciation of how—and why—sail forces change as we try to wring out maximum speed with sheets and tiller.

Many popular explanations say no more than "the wind exerts pressure on the sail" or that the wind provides "not only the pressure on the windward side of the sails to push the boat but also causes a partial vacuum on the side of the sail to pull her forward." Such explanations are not incorrect, but are quite inadequate because they say nothing about *how* these pressures are created.

Some authors attempt to explain *how* by saying that the air has farther to go around the leeward (convex) side of the sail than around the windward (concave) side and must therefore travel faster around the former than around the latter, thus producing a pressure differential. This reasoning is incorrect on two counts: (1) it is *not* farther around one side than around the other (only the thickness of sail cloth separates the two routes); and (2) even if the distances were different, there is no physical law requiring the wind to make the longer passage more quickly. In spite of their inadequacy and inaccuracy, such explanations virtually dominate the literature on sailing.

The correct explanation not only is more useful to sailors but also is more plausible and easier to understand than discussions in the popular literature. This explanation says that the sail is an *air-deflector*. The sail produces all of its thrust through the simple action of deflecting the wind. The wind is not just deflected momentarily while it is passing over the sail, but *permanently,* and is discharged from the leech of the sail with a direction different from its approach.

This view is not speculation or theory, but a fact that we can confirm by watching the flow directions shown by telltales hung on windward and leeward shrouds. It is also based upon the scientific principles of momentum that are well known in fluid mechanics and aerodynamics and have been substantiated by experiment.

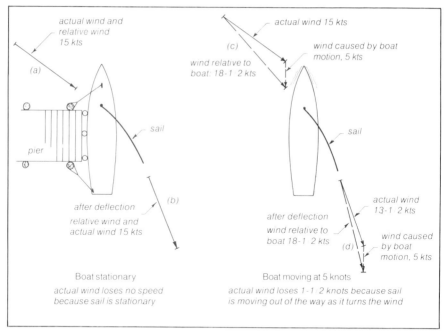

Figure 1: Two situations that illustrate what happens to actual wind when boat is stationary, and when it is moving

When we examine the deflection of wind by the sail, we can see how energy is transferred from the wind to the boat. Energy has become a household word in the past few years, as a result of the energy crisis. We have come to appreciate that energy cannot be created out of nothing—it can only be changed from one form to another. This principle tells us that when the sail acquires energy (or power) to move the boat, it must do so by taking energy from the wind, leaving the wind with less energy than it had before it met with the sail.

To see how this happens, let's first imagine a boat that is under full sail, but tied firmly to a pier (Fig. 1). The actual wind blowing past the pier approaches at (a) and is turned by the stationary sail to a new direction at (b), approximately parallel to the sail at the leech. If we assume no friction between sail and wind (a valid assumption for our purposes), the speed of the wind will be the same at (b) as it was at (a). The moving air has been turned, but has lost no energy of motion because it

has not been slowed down. The wind produces a force on the sail, as we shall see later, but the sail in this case has not taken any energy from the wind because the boat is not moving.

Now imagine the same boat no longer tied to the pier but sailing close-hauled at five knots into the same wind. The boat no longer feels the actual wind, as most sailors will recognize, but instead experiences the *relative* wind, a combination of actual wind and wind because of boat motion. (The two can be added by drawing each as an arrow, or "vector," with a scale length and proper direction; the sum, or relative wind, is the arrow that closes the triangle.)

The sail takes this relative wind at (c) and turns it to a new direction at (d). If we assume no friction, again, the sail turns the relative wind but does not slow it. The speed at (d), however, is still the speed relative to the sail. To find the speed and direction of the actual wind *after it has left the sail*, we must subtract the wind caused by boat

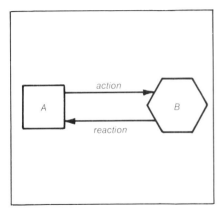

Figure 2: Newton's Third Law of Motion says that for every action, there is an equal and opposite reaction

motion from the relative wind. This diagram—which is simply the reverse of the diagram at (c)—yields the actual wind speed with respect to the ground (or perhaps we should say with respect to the pier). When this is done, using carefully scaled vectors, we find in our example that the final actual wind speed vector measures to be 13½ knots, 1½ knots less than the original actual wind speed of 15 knots. This loss of speed represents a loss of energy; in other words, when the wind is turned by the moving sail, the wind gives up some of its energy of motion to the sail. *This is the energy that drives the boat.*

To reassure ourselves that this really happens, we can look again at the difference between the actions of the fixed and moving sails. The fixed sail simply stands there and firmly turns the wind. The moving sail, on the other hand, is sliding out of the way while it is turning the wind. It, therefore, does not turn the actual wind firmly but lets it lose some speed in the process. As it slides away from the turning process, the sail takes away some of the wind's energy and uses it to move the boat. If we were to somehow measure the energy lost by all the wind that the sail turns, we would find that it is equal to the energy used to move the boat ahead (a small amount would, of course, be lost here and there because of friction).

It is well known that the wind from our sails is a good weapon to hurl at a rival in a race. Figure 1 shows why: not only has the wind's direction been altered adversely, but also its energy has been diminished.

Having used the turning idea to trace the exchange of energy from the wind to the sail, we can now look more closely at the details of the turning process to learn useful things about the forces we control with sheet and tiller. We need only a couple of simple scientific laws about how things move that may already be familiar to you from school science or other experiences.

The most important physical law we need was stated by Sir Isaac Newton 200 years ago. This law says that when one object, A, pushes on another object, B, there will always be an equal and opposite reaction force from B pushing on A (Fig. 2). Forces always occur in pairs, Newton was saying, equal and opposite,

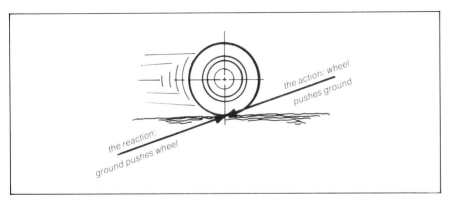

Figure 3: Forces always occur in pairs: equal and opposite

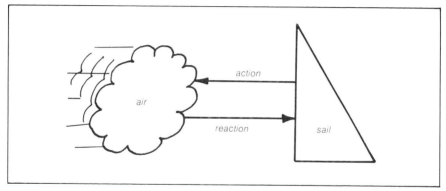

Figure 4: If the moving air is to produce a force on the sail, the sail must push the air in the opposite direction

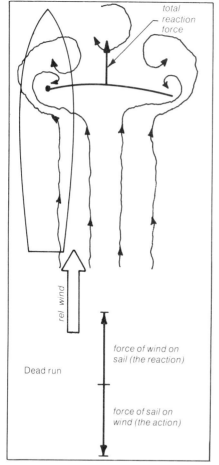

Figure 5: A sail on a dead run acts on the wind to slow it and turn it aside, and incurs a forward reaction force. Flow on the lee side is completely separated

action and reaction. A wheel driving an automobile pushes back on the ground (the action) and the ground pushes forward on the wheel (the reaction) to propel the car (Fig. 3).

The action-reaction encounter between sail and wind is more complicated, but we can diagram it schematically, as in Figure 4. This diagram tells us that if a sail is to be hung out so that the wind will push on it, it must be hung so that the sail pushes the wind with an equal force in the opposite direction. Because the wind cannot stand still and push back, like the ground under the wheel, the wind will be deflected. It is in this deflection that the thrust force is created, and, as we have seen, the propulsive energy is transferred from wind to sail.

Using Newton's Law of "action and reaction" we can see what happens between sail and wind on all tacks. Moving downwind on a dead run, the sail is operating in the simplest way (Fig. 5). The wind approaches from behind and the sail slows it and deflects it to both sides as shown in the diagram. Because air has weight, the sail must exert a sternward force on the moving wind to slow it and turn it aside. That's the *action* Newton tells us about. Simultaneously the wind produces a forward force on the sail that billows it and pushes the boat along. That's the *reaction*.

The air flow over the lee side of the sail on this tack is not smooth, but separated and rough—a kind of swirling

256

dead-air-region. This kind of flow is unavoidable here, but can (and should) be avoided on other tacks, as we shall see later.

As the tack is changed toward a beam reach (Fig. 6), the sail begins to do its deflecting job a bit differently. The separated region is swept away and the wind begins to flow smoothly over both the windward and leeward surfaces (Fig. 7). The sail now is deflecting the wind with greater efficiency than for the downwind case, because *both* sides of the sail are turning the wind. Since the

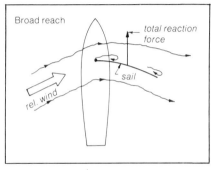

Figure 6: As the tack changes to a reach, the lee side begins to deflect air efficiently

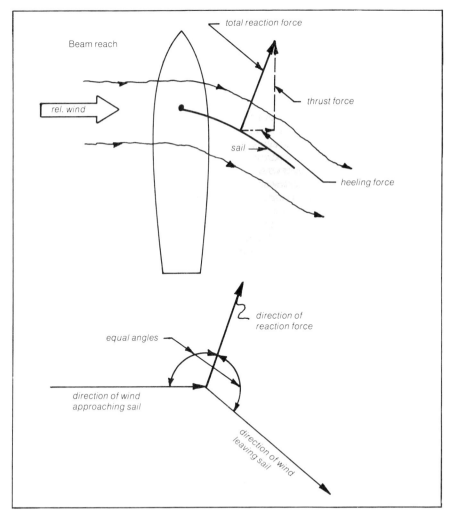

Figure 7: On a beam reach both sides of the sail are working, and the direction of the total reaction force can be found from the direction of the wind approaching and leaving the sail

sail now affects a larger amount of air, a larger reaction force will be produced.

But for the reaching case, the action of the sail becomes more complicated than for the dead-run case. The sail wind, and boat are all pointing in different directions. How can we tell the direction of the force on the sail? Most books on sailing seem to guess at the answer. But any fluid-mechanics textbook will give the exact answer, which seems almost obvious when you think about it: when a moving fluid (such as air) is turned by some device, the reaction force produced will have a direction halfway between the direction of the fluid approaching and the fluid leaving the device (Fig. 6). This principle holds whether the turning device is a turning vane, a turbine blade, or a sail assuming no friction, a legitimate assumption for this analysis.

The reaction force on the sail, drawn in this way in Figure 7, is at an angle to the direction that the boat is moving, and therefore is partly forward, and partly to the side. One more step is needed to break it down into a forward force and a sideways force. By drawing a line in the fore-and-aft direction from the tip of the arrow and another line in a beamwise direction from the foot of the arrow, we can create a "force triangle." The resulting shorter arrows show the amount of forward and sideward forces that are contained in the total reaction force. The forward force, of course, is the thrust force that drives the boat, while the sideways force is wasted in heeling the boat.

By looking at the sail as an air deflector, with the help of a few ideas from the science of fluid mechanics, we have seen how energy is taken from the wind by the moving sail and used to drive the boat. We also have the tools to draw the force diagrams for any tack and any sail setting.

Why Proper Trim

Factors that affect sail power   Norman Smith

Considering the sail as an air *deflector* allows us to trace the energy as it is transferred from the wind to the moving sail. If we draw a diagram showing the wind vectors approaching and leaving the sail, the direction of the reaction force on the sail can be determined and broken down into the more meaningful thrust force and heeling force.

Now we can proceed to draw the force diagram for any tack. The total re-action force and its forward and side-ward components have been drawn from a beam reach (Fig. 1), and for a close reach and a close-hauled condition in Figures 2 and 3. (A total-reaction-force vector of the same length has been assumed for all three conditions to show more clearly how thrust force and heeling force vary with tack.) The diagrams show that as the boat is turned toward the close-hauled condition, the

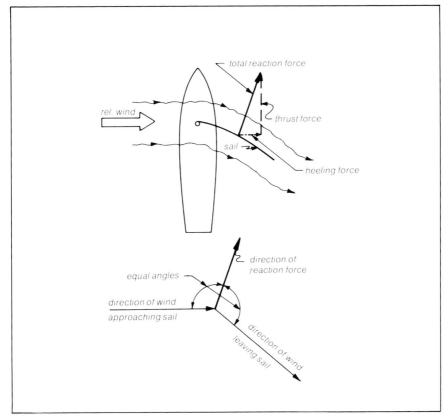

Figure 1: On a beam reach both sides of the sail are working,
and the direction of the total reaction force can be found
from the direction of the wind approaching and leaving the sail

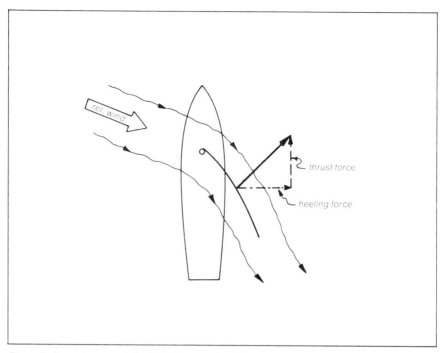

Figure 2: On a close reach the total force on the sail
is turned more toward the side

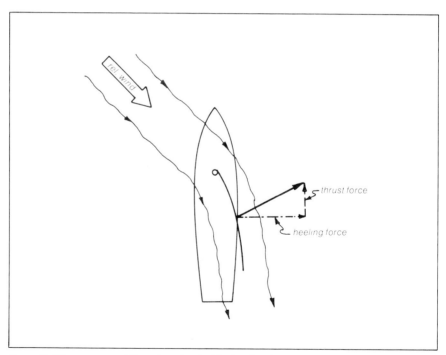

Figure 3: When you are sailing close-hauled the heeling force
reaches a maximum and the thrust force decreases

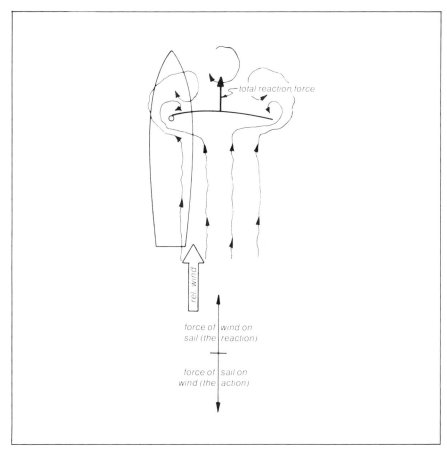

total reaction force

rel. wind

force of wind on
sail (the reaction)

force of sail on
wind (the action)

Figure 4: When you are sailing on a dead run the sail acts on the wind
to slow it and turn it aside, and incurs a forward reaction force

total force on the sail is turned more and more toward the side. The forward thrust force, which was the entire reaction force for the downwind case (Fig. 4) now becomes smaller and smaller. The sideways heeling force, which was zero for the downwind case, grows larger and larger, reaching a maximum for the close-hauled case. The hull, along with the centerboard or keel, resists this sideways force, and the boat heels to leeward more and more as it approaches close-hauled.

With most boats, the fastest sailing is done near a beam reach. When a boat is pointed higher into the wind, the sail force is turned abeam, which reduces the forward thrust. When a boat is pointed downwind, relative wind de-creases and the flow over the lee side of the sail may begin to break down, both of which will reduce forward thrust.

From these diagrams it is clear why a boat cannot be sailed directly into the wind. With a boat pointing into the wind, there is no way a sail can be trimmed or shaped to deflect air in a way that will give a total reaction force that has a component in the forward direction. You can prove this for yourself with pencil and paper.

The fore-and-aft sail is often described as being "entirely different" from the older square sail, even operating on a different principle. Actually, the operating principles of all sails are the same. The square sail is a relatively crude device, for all its picturesqueness,

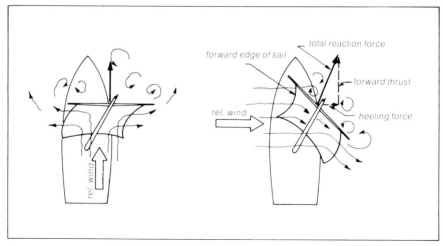

Figure 5: The square sail acts on the same principle as the fore-and-aft sail: deflection of air. But the square sail cannot be trimmed and shaped to deflect air efficiently enough to go to windward

designed to sail best downwind. It catches the wind from behind (Fig. 5), slows it and turns it aside, and incurs a reaction force forward, just as a fore-and-aft rig does on a reach. But the square sail doesn't do that job very well, because the forward edge of the sail is not shaped well enough to permit the wind to make the sharp turn around the lee side. The wind trips over the edge of the sail and swirls around the lee side without being deflected very much. Only the windward side of the sail is deflecting wind in a reasonably efficient manner. Because the square sail is not an efficient deflector of wind, ships built with this rig cannot sail to windward to a useful degree.

The principal improvement that the development of the fore-and-aft rig brought was a good "entry" for the approaching air. With the leading edge of the sail neatly and tightly held by the mast, the air can pass smoothly over *both* sides of the sail to provide usable thrust all the way up to the close-hauled condition.

The reaction forces I have described here are within everyone's experience. If you extend your hand flat against the wind from the window of a moving car, you will feel a force pushing your hand

back. Turn the palm of your hand so that it will deflect air downward and you will feel a force upward as well as back. If you carry a panel of plywood on a windy day, you must keep it pointed into the wind or the reaction force may knock you down. Note that neither your hand nor the plywood deflect air by bouncing it off their under sides like so many grains of sand. Because molecules of air are very close together and bump into each other constantly, air acts as a fluid, like water, and will flow around *both* sides of an object just as water will flow around a rock in a stream.

The wind blowing past a sail, too, will follow both sides, given half a chance, and will be deflected by the sail to a decreasing degree for a considerable distance from its surface—perhaps as much as a mast-length away.

In order to bring the deflection idea to bear upon trimming sails for best efficiency, we need to look further into the detailed factors that govern how large a force a sail produces. To do this, we need another one of Newton's Laws of Motion. This law says that the force produced by deflection of air depends upon only two things: (1) the amount (mass) of air deflected per second; and

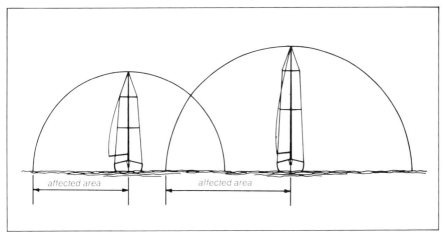

Figure 6: A tall slender sail (as represented by the mast height) will affect a larger area of wind than will a short, wide sail of the same area

(2) the amount of acceleration (which means change of speed or direction) given to that mass. This is Newton's famous equation:

$$\text{Force} = \text{mass} \times \text{acceleration}$$
$$F = m \times a$$

Of course we can't readily see or measure either of these items aboard a boat as we sail. But that doesn't matter—if we know what these items are, we can get a kind of feel for them. We can think about them and try to get F: (the product of m and a) to be as large as possible and to act in a direction that will give the boat the most thrust.

What factors control m, the mass of air deflected? Wind speed, first of all. The faster the wind is blowing, the larger quantity of air that passes (and can be deflected by) the sail each second. Sail area is a second factor. The larger the sail, the more wind it should be able to deflect. Sail dimensions (width, height, etc.) are a third factor, and are so closely connected to the second that they should be considered together. A tall, slender sail (called a high aspect-ratio shape) will affect a larger area of wind than a short, wide sail of the same area (Fig. 6).

What factors control a, the amount of acceleration (deflection) given to the air? Wind speed, again, is one factor. The faster the wind is blowing, the larger the force that will be produced by changing its direction. The angle between sail and wind (called angle-of-attack by aerodynamicists) is another key factor. We can vary this angle to control the turning action of the sail. But here other factors enter to complicate the picture. The turning must be done efficiently to avoid *stalling* or separation of the flow over the lee side of the sail. Also, the geometry of the whole boat-wind-sail arrangement must be taken into account.

Using the principles developed above, we can draw accurate (qualitative) diagrams that illustrate the effects of sail angle-of-attack at four positions of the mainsail, from luff to stall, all for the same wind direction and the same direction of boat travel (Fig. 7). The reaction force on the sail has been broken down for each case to show the relative size of the forward thrust compared to the sideways (heeling) force.

At the left in the first diagram, the sail angle-of-attack is too small. The sail is luffing and producing too little reaction force because it isn't deflecting the wind through a large enough angle.

In the next diagram, the sail has been sheeted in until it is well filled. A larger total reaction force is produced. Although this force points slightly more to starboard, the forward thrust force is

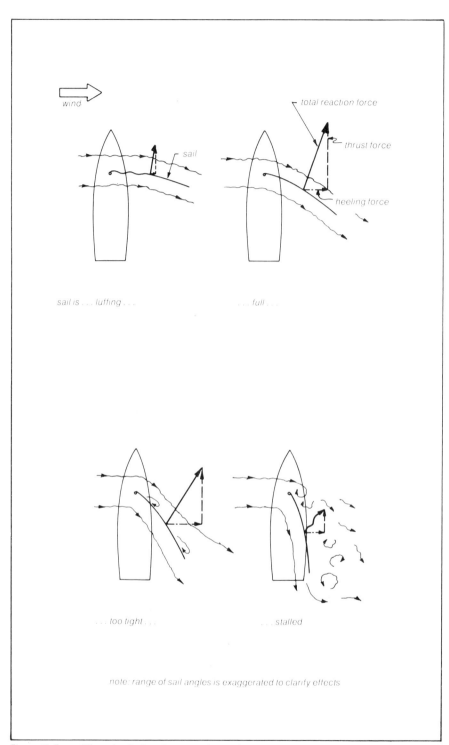

wind

total reaction force

thrust force

sail

heeling force

sail is . . . luffing . . .

. . . . full . . .

. . . too tight . . .

. . . stalled

note: range of sail angles is exaggerated to clarify effects

Figure 7: Four different sail directions are shown for the same course and wind direction.
The range of sail angles is exaggerated to clarify the effects

greater because the reaction force on the better trimmed sail is greater.

In the third sketch, the sail has been sheeted in still tighter. Now the total reaction force on the sail has turned still farther to starboard. If this total force is assumed to be roughly as large as the one for the sketch just to the left, the forward thrust is less while the sideways force is greater. This diagram illustrates how a sail that is too tightly sheeted wastes potential sail force by putting it into heeling force at the cost of forward thrust. Also, areas of stalled or separated flow may begin to appear over the lee side of the sail because the air may not be able to negotiate the sharp turn around the lee side of the mast. Any separation of the flow quickly reduces the sail's ability to deflect the wind efficiently over that side.

The fourth sketch shows what may happen if the sail is sheeted still tighter. The turn that the air is asked to make around the mast to the lee side of the sail is now much too sharp. The flow over the leading edge of the sail has completely separated and the wind is swirling across the lee of the sail in disarray. Because the wind is not being smoothly deflected by that side of the sail, the total force has decreased. We can only guess the average direction of the erratic flow leaving the sail, and cannot accurately draw the direction of the reaction force. However, it really doesn't matter, because we know that stall reduces the total reaction force so drastically that it should be avoided under all conditions.

These four sketches in Figure 7 are almost a summary of what the art of sail-trimming is all about. If you can view the sail as an air deflector, you can see what you must do in trimming the sail. You must fill it well to deflect as much air as possible, yet not get the angle of attack so high that force is wasted in heeling the boat instead of driving it forward. Nor do you want the angle of attack so high that the flow stalls over the leeward side.

I emphasize once again that these diagrams are schematic and the range of sail angles has been exaggerated in order to clarify the effects. The actual geometry will be somewhat different for every boat, for every part of the sail, and for every tack, but the principles shown here do apply to all situations.

So far we've considered only the mainsail, but now let's look briefly at the jib. The jib is an air-deflecting, force-producing surface in its own right, of course, but it does another important job in helping to guide and control the flow over the mainsail. By helping to turn the air around the lee side of the mast without stalling, the jib can make possible a slightly higher angle of attack for the mainsail and larger thrust. Also, with the mainsail and jib properly trimmed, the large mass of air flowing through the channel or *slot* between them is smoothly and efficiently turned to produce propulsion. This mutual assistance between jib and main can give the combination a greater propulsive thrust than the sum of the thrusts that each could produce by itself. The job of trimming two sails is more complicated than trimming only one, because each must be trimmed not only to do its own job, but also to give the maximum help to the other.

In the literature on sailing the slot between jib and main is sometimes compared to a *venturi,* with extra thrust explained by a speeding up of the flow (and reduced pressures) through the constricted area. This view is clearly incorrect, since reduced pressures would "pull back" on the jib as much as they "pull forward" on the main. The thrust produced by slot flow is a reaction to the turning action, and appears as generally more positive (push) pressures on the rear side of the jib, and more negative (suction) pressures on the forward side of the main.

A lot of good material has been written about techniques for maintaining good flow over sail surfaces by controlling sail shape and trim. All these techniques have a common goal: to produce smooth flow and even loading that is entirely consistent with the deflection-of-air concept.

I should say that while this discussion may be a "fresh look" at how a sail works, it really uses processes and principles that are quite old and are well known to the fields of physics, fluid mechanics and aerodynamics. Unfortunately, they are not often used to explain how a sail works. Complicated mathematics or abstract notions of aerodynamic theory, such as "circulation," are unnecessary when you are talking about sails, as are nebulous remarks about venturis, Bernoulli's Theorem, pressures, etc.

It is perfectly true, of course, that there are low (suction) pressures over the lee side of a sail and higher pressures over the windward side. The sum of all the local pressure forces is equal to the total reaction force on the sail.

But these pressures are *not caused* by tricking air into speeding up and slowing down over a specially-shaped sail. They are caused as a *reaction* to the sail's *action* of turning the wind that moves over it. By turning and slowing the wind, the sail incurs a propulsive force and captures energy from the wind to use in driving the boat.

The action-reaction view of the sail is not only correct physics, but it also yields a useful qualitative picture of the size and direction of sail forces, and how these forces vary with design factors and with the motions of sheet and tiller.

Delaying Flow Separation

An experimental method of improving sail effectiveness   Arthur Slemmons

Of the many challenges associated with sailing, perhaps the most challenging is the trimming of sails for maximum hull speed. Great skill is required to find the best combination of hull attitude, sail trim, and angle of attack of the sail foil to the relative wind velocity. Going up-wind, the goal is to maximize the boat's upwind velocity component (velocity made good—VMG). By decreasing the sail's angle of attack, the optimum set-ting is already passed before the time the sail starts to luff. By increasing the angle of attack, the optimum is ex-ceeded by the time the leech and bat-tens start to vibrate because of vortex shedding associated with aerodynamic stall.

Because the winds are constantly shifting direction, the waves and swells are continually rocking and turning the hull, and variable wind speeds are changing the heel angle and altering the balance of the boat, the helmsman has the demanding task of maintaining the optimum angle of attack relative to the wind. The problem is compounded by the difficulty in knowing what the opti-mum combination of angle of attack and heading is in the first place. As a re-sult, effective sailing includes the tech-nique of constantly changing the head-ing and the setting of the sails in relation to the wind direction to achieve the highest effective boat speed. In ad-dition, both mainsails and jibs have flexibility in the cloth that results in a twist of the airfoil shape from the foot

to the head. This twist creates variations in the angle of attack over the entire sail. The combination of improper set and the unavoidable variation in angle of attack over the entire sail because of twist often allows the airflow on part of the sail to diverge from the convex con-tour on the lee side, a condition called *aerodynamic stall.*

Stall reduces the sail's driving force or *lift* in conventional aerodynamic ter-minology. Stall can be observed several ways. Evidence of stall and the associ-ated backflow of the wind on the lee side of the sail can be observed by watching *telltales* or tufts on the lee side near the leech. During stall, they gyrate or fly in a direction contrary to the fore and aft flow. Pennants on the trailing edge curl behind the sail. These phe-nomena are often accompanied by an audible buffeting or fluttering of the *leech.* This vibration is caused by the vortex shedding associated with flow separation. Battens along the leech are used to control the shape of the sail. Battens are sometimes justified to ac-commodate a large roach, but more im-portantly, battens are used to stiffen the leech in the direction of the airflow and to reduce the flexibility of the sail along the trailing edge where separation be-cause of stall first occurs. This stiffening is important because analysis has re-cently confirmed that flow along a boundary is destabilized by the flex-ibility of the boundary. Because flutter-ing is recognized as being associated

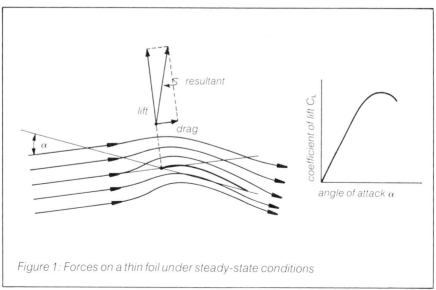

Figure 1: Forces on a thin foil under steady-state conditions

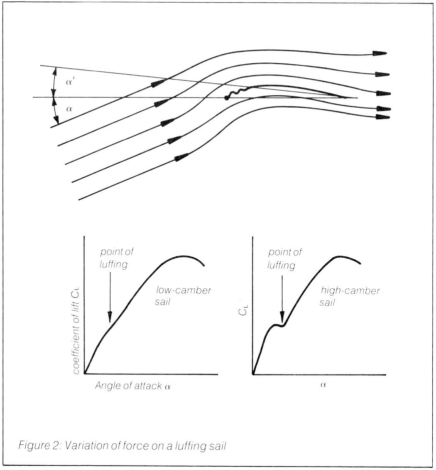

Figure 2: Variation of force on a luffing sail

with intermittent separation and reattachment of the boundary layer, it is a visual and sometime audible symptom of the loss of performance because of improper flow past the lee side of the sail.

To better define the problem of optimizing racing sail performance and to describe a recently developed solution, an analysis of the diagrams of the flow of air past the sail airfoil is in order. Figure 1 shows the ideal flow past a sail under steady-state conditions. The coefficient of lift, C_L, increases almost linearly with an increase in the angle of attack until stall occurs. As stall is initiated along the leech or trailing edge, the lift still increases but at a decreasing rate. Lift reaches a peak and finally falls off as the angle of attack is further increased.

Figure 2 shows the effects of the other extreme, *luffing*. When the angle of attack decreases to the point where the local up-draft angle near the mast is tangent to the curvature of the sail at the luff or leading edge, incipient luffing occurs. As the angle of attack is further decreased, the forward part of the sail waves like a flag and the remaining part of the sail forms a foil of decreased chord. Note that the angle of attack of the remaining filled portion of the sail now has an angle of attack larger than the previously incipiently luffed sail. This causes a hump in the C_L curve (Fig. 2a). Interestingly, it is possible for a full sail with the maximum camber far aft to be stalled by the act of luffing.

A few sailors believe that stall starts at the luff. There may be a local separation of flow from the sail along the mast because of the local increase in updraft angle along the mast. A local flow of discontinuity is also caused by the thickness of the mast relative to the sail. However, the airstream will normally re-attach itself forming a "bubble" of backflowing air. True stall, in contrast, is always initiated at the trailing edge where the airstream leaves the sail, never to re-attach itself, unlike the case of the bubble along the luff.

In Figure 3a, the graph recording the relationship of C_L to α, demonstrates the effect of stall. As the angle of attack, α,

increases, the coefficient of lift, C_L, falls off from a straight-line relationship and finally decreases. The variation of the negative pressure coefficient, C_p, on the lee side along the chord of the sail is shown in Figure 3b for conditions with and without a bubble. C_p is the ratio of the pressure change on the sail surface to the dynamic pressure of the free airstream. The pressure is negative (below atmospheric) on the lee side of the sail. C_p is positive (above atmospheric) on the windward side of the sail.

Aerodynamic stall is well known in the aviation industry and has been alleviated on certain airplanes by the use of vortex generators consisting of many small foils located in a linear array about midchord. These small foils are set at an angle to the free airstream, and they alternate in their angles to the airstream.

The effect of these foils is to initiate a trailing vortex at the tip of each foil. The trailing vortex mixes the free airstream with the turbulent boundary layer. This mixing prevents the boundary layer from slowing and finally reversing direction. The trailing vortices re-energize the boundary layer by mixing in faster air from the free airstream, thus preventing or delaying stall and the associated flow separation (Fig. 4). By arranging each adjacent vortex generator at alternating angles to the free airstream, the adjacent trailing vortices have opposite directions or rotation. Each vortex is allowed to augment its adjacent vortex. The vortices thereby derive greater stability than if they were opposing each other at their point of tangency. The mean diameter of each trailing vortex grows linearly with the distance traveled.

Each vortex is extremely stable and continues to re-energize the boundary layer far downstream from its generator. The positioning of these generators at mid-chord of large airplane wings gives an indication of the vortices' stability and effectiveness of mixing all the way to the trailing edge of these large foils. Interestingly, the trailing vortices do no decay by simple diffusion, as one might expect. Usually, they finally undergo a symmetric and nearly

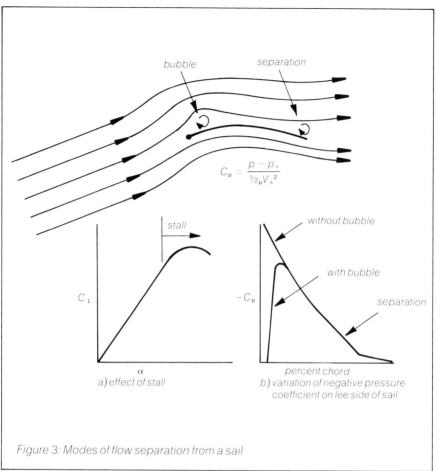

$$C_p = \frac{p - p_\infty}{\frac{1}{2}\rho V_\infty^2}$$

bubble

separation

stall

C_L

α

a) effect of stall

$-C_p$

without bubble

with bubble

separation

percent chord

b) variation of negative pressure coefficient on lee side of sail

Figure 3: Modes of flow separation from a sail

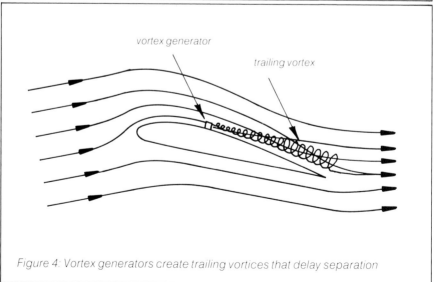

vortex generator

trailing vortex

Figure 4: Vortex generators create trailing vortices that delay separation

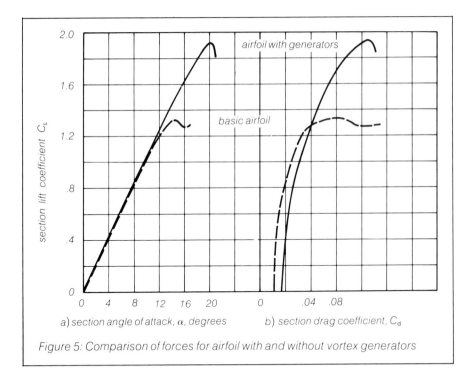

Figure 5: Comparison of forces for airfoil with and without vortex generators

sinusoidal instability until they eventually join at intervals to form a train of vortex rings.

A foil without the vortex generators begins to stall at an angle of attack of approximately 11 degrees and the coefficient of lift, C_L, begins to fall off from an almost straight-line relationship with α (Fig. 5a). It is also known that sails with aspect ratios of five or six also begin to stall when α is about 11 degrees. The same foil with vortex generators has its stalling point delayed until the angle of attack, α, reaches about 18 degrees. This gives a 45-percent increase in the maximum lift obtainable from the same foil without vortex generators. On the graph of C_d versus α (Figure 5b), it can be observed that in the high-lift range corresponding to separated flow on the basic foil the drag on the foil with vortex generators is less than the drag on the basic foil. This provides a higher lift/drag ratio for the modified foil under these higher angles of attack.

These data demonstrate how the air adjacent to the lee side of a foil with a high angle of attack slows down as it progresses rearward and sometimes does not follow the contour of the foil as a unidirectional stream flowing smoothly to the trailing edge of the foil. The flow also separates from a sail airfoil; eddies form; and the air near the leech of the sail flows back again toward the front of the sail with the lift of the sail decreasing.

By similarly mixing the high-speed stream of free air flowing past a sail with the slower boundary layer of air flowing next to the lee side of the sail, the boundary layer of air would be induced to maintain its rearward flow. Separation of the free air from the lee side of the sail would be prevented right up to the trailing edge of the sail. Vortices generated on the lee side of the sail could mix the faster, free airstream with the slower air near the sail and prevent or delay the separation of the free airstream from the lee side of the sail. Greater lift could thereby be obtained from the sail.

A row of discrete air jets penetrating into the airstream on the lee side of the sail and disposed at an angle to the free

271

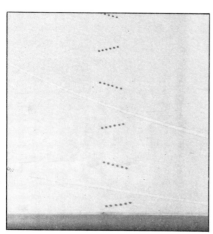

Rows of holes through mainsail form experimental discrete jets that serve as vortex generators. Zigzag configuration is designed to impart twist to reinforce and stabilize vortices

airstream direction would act as a deflector of the main airstream to impart a local twisting motion to the main airstream. The stream would be deflected over the row of short, discrete air jets, thereby generating a stable trailing vortex in the airstream.

The rows of air jets can be provided simply by forming short rows of small, flat-edged holes in the sail. The rows of jets would be disposed at alternating angles to the airstream with each row of jets penetrating into the main airstream, thus forming an "aerodynamic fence" which acts as a vortex generator. The converging ends of adjacent rows of holes or jets should be substantially spaced. Because adjacent vortices of opposite twist would be provided by the converging aerodynamic fences, the adjacent vortices in the mainstream would reinforce and stabilize each other.

This principle was first tested by using smoke to visualize the jets, their penetration into the airstream and the resulting trailing vortices. The tests were visually satisfactory, with the $\frac{1}{4}$-inch-diameter jets penetrating into the free airstream about one inch. The trailing vortex action was clearly visible.

Additional tests with a jib modified according to the concept and using orange smoke again showed the vortex mechanism. On completion of these simple encouraging tests, a 505-Class mainsail and jib were modified in accordance with this concept. Each discrete row was made by punching holes in the polyester sailcloth with an electrically-heated hole punch. The melted polyester plastic around the edges of the holes joined the fiber ends into a "grommet" that inhibited fraying and ripping of the sailcloth.

The modified cloth is devoid of the drag that would result from projections such as nozzles or vanes. Furthermore, the vortex-forming action is equally effective on both port and starboard tacks, with no manual adjustment or mechanisms from tack to tack being necessary. Two or more zigzag arrays of these vortex generators could have been used with locations at two or more diverging lines from the head to the foot of the sails. Additional arrays may be desirable for sails of large camber such as spinnakers and reaching genoas.

The modified 505-Class sails were tested against other 505s under controlled conditions and during races. The modified sails show an ability to point higher and still maintain the same boat speed as boats with unmodified sails. Apparently the loss in lift because of air's leaking through the small holes is more than compensated for by the higher lift because of delay of separation. No significant difference was noted off the wind. Further testing with additional array locations farther forward on the chord is indicated to improve crosswind performance. The improvement has also been demonstrated on a Santa Barbara Class radio-controlled sailboat and a Catalina 27. The question naturally arises whether the holes are legal. The International Yacht Racing Union (IYRU) rules do not prohibit the holes. However, certain one-design class rules do prohibit sail modifications of any kind.

Vortex generators over the outer portion of an airplane wingspan have been found more effective than the same extent of vortex generators over the inner portion of the wing. This would not necessarily be true in a sail, however. The twist in the sail tends to give its upper portion a lower angle of attack and less tendency to stall. However, when the forward velocity of the boat is considered, the naturally greater wind speed near the top of the mast tends to mitigate the effect of this twist, and vortex generators should also be effective in the upper portion of a sail.

The location on the chord, the size, and the number of holes of the vortex-generator array on sails has not been optimized. Wind-tunnel tests show a position of vortex generators on wings to be optimum at 25 percent aft of the leading edge. The position of vortex-generator arrays on commercial airplane wings and stabilizers is usually nearer the center of the chord, however.

The improved experimental upwind performance of the vortex-generator sails may be understood by a closer analysis of curves of a foil with and without vortex generators. Figure 6 shows two C_L curves, one without vortex generators, and another with vortex generators.

The boat with unmodified sails has a maximum lift at an angle of attack, α; the boat with a modified sail develops the same lift at a smaller angle of at-

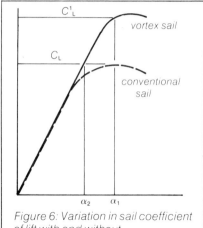

Figure 6: Variation in sail coefficient of lift with and without vortex generators

tack. The modified sail can point higher at the same hull speed, achieving a higher velocity made good.

The process of further experimentation to develop and to exploit this interesting development is continuing. Sailors are always looking for ways to get that extra margin of speed, and this low-cost improvement seems well worth further experimentation.

Light Air and High Performance

Theories and techniques for sailing in drifters   Frank Bethwaite

Like all fluids, air has a natural internal friction (viscosity) of its own, and it takes work to keep the boundary layer stirred into turbulence. The frictional energy of the wind's speed over water just isn't enough to sustain this stirring when the wind speed is less than about six knots. In the case of sails, the critical speed is even a little less—about three to four knots. But when apparent wind speed falls to this critical speed or below, the whole flow pattern over a sail changes. Figure 1 shows some of the details.

The best way to visualize the flow pattern is to imagine a series of layers of progressively lighter fluids such as water, oil, paraffin, alcohol, which are flowing slowly over a surface and over each other. They do not mix, and the water always stays next to the surface. The oil always stays next to the water, but no oil ever penetrates through the water to touch the surface—and so on. Above all, there can never be any "scrubbing" of the surface by any high-speed parcels of alcohol. There is nothing to stop the water from flowing in a direction that is different from that of the alcohol; this is exactly what is happening in Figure 1. The undisturbed

wind is flowing from b to d, but the surface flow is, if anything, from the higher pressure at c toward the lower pressure at b. This flow builds up a wedge of "dead" air which acts as if it were a part of the sail itself. The undisturbed wind flows not around the sail curve (abc) but along the much straighter surface of the wedge (abd). The same thing happens on the pressure face of the sail—instead of flowing in the curve (efg), the wind blows almost staight along (ehg).

The "power" of a sail depends upon how much it can curve the wind. Clearly the deeply curved sail in Figure 1 is so wrapped up in its thick cocoon of stagnant air that it isn't curving the wind very much at all and there cannot be much power until the Figure 2 situation is restored. This phenomenon, called *laminar separation*, can always be spotted by the action of *leech ribbons*. In the attached flow of Figure 2, these ribbons stream downwind, fluttering in "live" air. But in the "dead" air of Figure 1, they hang limply.

The cure for laminar separation is to flatten the sail until the leech ribbons stream again (Fig. 2). In very light air, this flatter sail with its attached flow will give substantially more curve to the

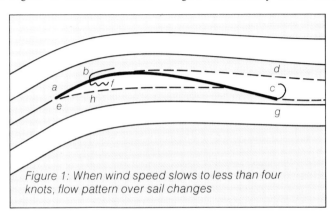

Figure 1: When wind speed slows to less than four knots, flow pattern over sail changes

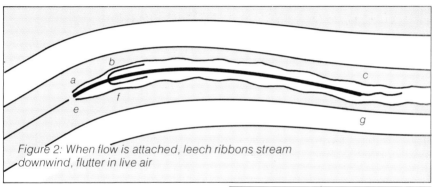

Figure 2: When flow is attached, leech ribbons stream downwind, flutter in live air

wind, and therefore more power, than any fuller sail from which the flow will separate. If this sounds strange at first, just reflect that all slow-flying creatures (butterflies, moths, dragonflies) have almost flat wings. In boats, this principle of flatness applies in calm water only. In waves, the fragile flow cannot remain attached to the unsteady sails, and fuller sails will then always prove to be faster. So the first technique for sailing fast when you are reaching in very light air is to *flatten* the sails whenever the leech ribbons are indicating laminar separation.

Also be guided by the leech ribbons when you are trimming the sails because these gentle flows cannot follow a sail that is sheeted at more than about 10 or 15 degrees to the wind. Compare this with the 30 degrees and more that is appropriate with a turbulent boundary layer.

A second technique that can increase light-air reaching speed substantially is pure physics—mass, force, acceleration, and time. From Figure 3, it is clear that in all winds of less than about four knots, a boat will sail most quickly on a close-reach heading of about 70 to 80 degrees from the true wind direction. The drive force developed by the sails on this heading is about 25 percent greater than that developed on a beam reach because the apparent wind is stronger.

Imagine two high-performance boats sailing for a mark directly across the wind in a light breeze. The wind blows at one knot for 30 seconds, at 2.5 knots

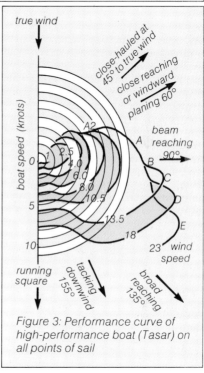

Figure 3: Performance curve of high-performance boat (Tasar) on all points of sail

for 30 seconds, then drops to one knot again. One helmsman heads straight for the mark, and at the end of the lull he is moving at about 1.4 knots (Figure 3). As he enters the increased wind of 2.5 knots, the apparent wind increases by only 1.1 knots initially but this increases the driving force from 1.1 pounds to about 3.1 pounds (Tasar calculations). Then, as the speed builds up and the apparent wind increases because of the increased boat speed, the drive force progressively increases to about 7.1 pounds and boat speed stabilizes at 3.5 knots for the duration of that peak.

In practice, much of the duration of the peak wind will be occupied with the acceleration process itself. Even ignoring the increasing water resistance, when a two-pound additional force is applied to a 500-pound mass, there is only a maximum of about 30 seconds before the next lull occurs.

A second helmsman heads up 15 degrees as the next puff approaches. In this way he increases his apparent wind by 10 percent, from 2.9 knots to 3.2 knots, and thus he enjoys not only an immediate 25 percent greater accelerating force but also a continuing 24 percent increase which is available sooner because of the more rapid acceleration. This won't go on for too long—eight or 10 seconds is about right in these conditions. Having attained his full speed very much earlier than his competitor, he should bear away a little in the remainder of the peak to regain the rhumb line.

Quite spectacular gains (in light-air terms) can be achieved by employing this technique, but this is a high-performance-boat type of technique. As soon as you start thinking in terms of applying additional forces of only three pounds to a 2,000-pound trailer-sailer or a 3,000-pound yacht, t' e resultant acceleration over periods as short as 10 or 20 seconds, let alone the differences in acceleration, is too trivial to be of any real advantage.

I'd like to correct one popular misconception. The technique of sailing a little more closely to the wind in lulls, and heading a little farther off the wind in puffs is exactly right in all winds greater than about four knots, but it is *exactly wrong* for high-performance boats such as the Tasar in all winds of less than about four knots. By inspecting the one-knot and the 2.5-knot curves of Figure 3, you will see why. Ignoring all acceleration effects (and here again, bearing away in a light-air puff will reduce the resultant acceleration even further), the loss in speed from bearing away in the stronger wind will be much greater than any possible gain in speed gotten by heading up in the lighter wind. This is because the shapes of the 1.0-knot and the 2.5-knot curves are so similar; in both cases, the highest speed is achieved on the same point of sail. Note, however, that the curves for stronger winds are not the same.

The only situations where this principle will be valid are conditions in which the puffs are persistent and visible. Then the winning boat will be the one that zigzags so it spends the greatest time in the strongest wind. Very light airs are tricky.

The second area where a helmsman can significantly increase his reaching speed occurs when the true wind is fluctuating between 2.5 and five knots. In these conditions, the speed of the apparent wind across the sails of a boat that is heading straight across the wind may occasionally fall below the critical three or four knots where laminar separation occurs, so the performance of that boat will be greatly reduced.

The best technique in these conditions rests on the principle that any helmsman can increase (or maintain) the speed of the apparent wind by heading up. If in fluctuating conditions a helmsman heads up in the lulls just enough to keep he speed of the apparent wind fast enough to maintain turbulent flow with its increased power, then bears away as necessary in the puffs to regain the rhumb line, he will keep his boat moving much more quickly in the lulls so that the extra distance sailed will be trivial compared with the advantage gained. The leech ribbons will be the first things to signal any onset of laminar separation.

Contributors

William Allen manages Murphy and Nye Sailmakers in Chicago, where he is involved in one-design and offshore sail design. He grew up in a sailing family in Minnesota and has acquired an impressive racing record, racing his own boat at age nine and participated in two Sears Cups at 14 and 16. Bill has won many E Scow championships, including four national titles, as well as a gold medal as crew on Buddy Melges' Soling in the 1972 Olympics, and a gold medal in a Finn at the Pan American Games in 1975.

Robert Bainbridge oversees sailcloth production at Howe & Bainbridge, Inc., in Boston. He previously worked for three different sailmaking companies as well as making sails for himself. His sailing experience includes five years of teaching and offshore racing on One Tonners, Three-Quarter Tonners, and some smaller boats, but his concentration has been in dinghies. He campaigned a 5-0-5 for three years and a 470 for six years. During this time he has won and placed in several national and world championship events.

Robert Barton started sailmaking in 1971 with Murphy and Nye, becoming Vice President two years later. He founded Horizon Sails in 1975, now reportedly the third largest sailmaking organization in the world. His sailing career began at four years of age and he has raced with varying intensity ever since. He has participated in all common one-design boats at one time or another and more lately has been racing on offshore boats of all sizes. Bob participated in two 12-Meter campaigns as well as campaigning his own One Tonners, *Country Woman* and *Agnes.* He won the 1977 season championship of the Offshore Racing Club of America.

John Bertrand, an Australian, began sailing at eight. He holds a Bachelor's degree in Mechanical Engineering as well as a Master's in Naval Architecture. Over the years he has won the Nationals in Sabots, Vee Jays, Lightweight Sharpies, Finns, Solings, and Half-Tons. He was main trimmer aboard the 12-Meters *Gretel II* and *Southern Cross.* He has also participated in Olympic and World Championships. In 1977 John was named Australian and Victorian Yachtsman of the Year. He began and still manages the North Sails loft in Melbourne.

Frank Bethwaite built his first sailboat in 1930 and won the New Zealand Junior National Championships in 1939. For the next 20 years military, civil, and scientific flying precluded sailing. During these years he designed and flew model aircraft and established several model aircraft world endurance records. In 1958 Frank moved to Sydney where he returned to dinghy sailing and became part of a design movement which has produced lighter, faster, and more responsive dinghies in Australia. He has designed a whole series of champion dinghies, most recently the Tasar. Having won several state and open championships in Australia, he is a member of their Olympic team as meteorological officer and assistant coach.

Christopher Bouzaid is President of Hood Sailmakers. Originally from New Zealand, he grew up in a family of sailmakers and learned to sail at about the same time he learned to walk. He has attained a strong racing record on his own and has been a member of two winning New Zealand Southern Cross teams and captain of an Admiral's Cup team. In 1966 he built his first One Ton ocean racer, *Rainbow II,* and went on to win many races; he was the first boat, other than an Australian to win the Sydney-Hobart Race and he also won two World One Ton Cups. In 1969, New Zealand named Chris Yachtsman of the Year and Sportsman of the Year and the Queen honored him with the "Member of the Order of the British Empire." Chris and his brother, Tony, made sails under the Hood name in New Zealand and developed the South Pacific market so well that Ted Hood finally asked Chris to come to Marblehead as President of the Hood Group.

Stephen Colgate is president and owner of the Offshore Sailing School, Ltd. Founded by Mr. Colgate in 1964, the school offers sailing courses on all levels at seven resort locations. Steve has wide experience in both one-design and ocean racers. He crewed in the 1968 Olympics on a 5.5 meter and in two America's Cup Trials—1967 on *American Eagle* and in 1970 on *Heritage.* He has also participated in five Transatlantic Races and eight Bermuda Races, as well as Olympic trials, Admiral's Cup races, Pan American Games, and Mallory Cup races. He has won numerous class championships and distance events and presently owns and races the 54' aluminum, Frers-designed sloop, *Sleuth.* He has authored two books and two sailing manuals and is a regular contributor to SAIL Magazine.

Robert Doyle manages Hood Sailmakers in Marblehead, where he is the chief sail designer. At ages 14 and 15 he won the Sears Cup and has had an outstanding racing record ever since. He was a two-time winner of the Boston Bay Challenge Cup in 110's, a member of the U.S. Olympic Finn Team, and a winner of Intercollegiate and North American Single-Handed Championships several times. He was also tactician aboard Canada's Cup winner *Dynamite*, watch captain and skipper on SORC and Admiral's Cup race winners, and skipper of *Obsession* in her victories in the 1978 Stamford-Vineyard Race and ORCA Fall Series. Robbie was Sail Trimmer and Sailmaker for *Courageous* during her successful 1977 America's Cup campaign.

Richard Grajirena is manager of Hood Sailmakers in Florida. His sail designs have won numerous small- and large-boat championships. Rick started sailing in 1957 and has participated in eight SORC's, the Congressional Cup, and the Ensenada Race, and has won the Tampa Bay MORC Championship, the Spring Florida Ocean Racing Circuit, the Southeastern Half-Ton Championship, and the Clearwater Yacht Club Kahlua Cup. He has also won 19 Florida or district championships in various classes of dinghies. He was 470 North American Champion twice and National O.K. Dinghy Champion three times. He is currently the coach of the U.S. 470 team.

Benjamin Hall is Product Manager of spars and hardware for Kenyon Marine. He previously worked as sail designer and manager for Hard Sails' Connecticut loft. Starting at age seven, he has done extensive cruising and racing. He has raced in Halifax, Bermuda, Transatlantic, and Admiral's Cup races. Ben sailed in Flying Dutchman races for years, and was Junior National Champion three times, later becoming National Champion. More recently he has been successfully skippering Half-Tonners, Quarter-Tonners, and MORC boats. In 1978 he won class II of the MORC Internationals. For three years he was course director for *Yacht Racing*'s offshore racing clinic and is a contributing editor of that magazine.

Eric Hall is general manager of Schaefer Spars. He holds degrees in Aeronautical Engineering and Naval Architecture. In 1970 he was project engineer on America's Cup defender *Intrepid*, and in 1973 he supplied spars to the victorious German Admiral's Cup team. His own sailing experience includes the 1964 Finn semifinal Olympic Trials as well as crewing on Flying Dutchmen in the 1964 Junior Nationals, 1971 Nationals, and the Olympic Trials in 1964, 1968, and 1972. He is currently campaigning a Flying Dutchman and a Laser. Also on his record are many offshore events: Transatlantic, Fastnet, Bermuda, Halifax, SORC, Admiral's Cup, and One-Ton races as well as numerous other distance events.

Edward Hellenbrecht began sailing as a cadet at the U.S. Coast Guard Academy, where he was a member of the yacht squadron and sailed aboard the 71' S&S yawl *Petrel*. Ed worked for a year setting up an East Coast branch for a marine hardware and fiberglass boat manufacturer. This included intensive training in fiberglass boat construction and repair as well as marine hardware design and its application. He then became a designer for Van Zandt Sails, Inc., in Connecticut, where he was responsible for much of the sail design work and computer programming for both flat sails and spinnakers. Mr. Hellenbrecht was most recently employed as a senior project engineer for Cheseborough-Ponds, Inc., and races his own Morgan 27, *Hellion*, out of Mystic, Connecticut.

Harrison Hine is president of Seaway Supply Company, manufacturers of marine hardware in Los Angeles. He has actively competed in many sailing classes and won major championships in Endeavors, Finns, Tornados, Solings, and Stars. These include District, National, North American, European, and World championships. Harrison was also a member of the winning crew for the USYRU Prince of Wales Interclub match racing championships and competed five times in the Congressional Cup as a crew member.

Jeremy Howard-Williams was born at Cowes, England, and started sailing almost before he can remember. He served as night fighter pilot in World War II and remained in the RAF afterwards, which gave him the chance to sail in Singapore, Ceylon, and the Baltic as well as his home waters of the English Channel. In 1958 he left the RAF and joined the sailmaking firm of Ratsey & Lapthorn at Cowes for six years before going into the boat building business. In 1974 he became Managing Editor of Adlard Coles Ltd., publisher of nautical books. He has been in Olympic trials in a single-handed dinghy, held the record for the Fastnet Race in Baron Rothschild's *Gitana IV* (until Ted Turner took it in *American Eagle*), and raced in Edward Heath's *Morning Cloud*. He has written six books on sailing, including *The Care and Repair of Sails* (Adlard Coles Ltd., and SAIL Books, Inc.) and holds the Royal Yachting Association's certificate of Yachtmaster (offshore).

English sailing writer *Jack Knights* has been a regular contributor to SAIL for the past six years. He has had a long and successful career in a wide variety of one design classes, including the Finn, Star and Soling. He also races offshore. Knights lives on the Isle of

Wight, the Mecca of English yachting. His present boats include a Laser and an Aphrodite-101 one-design offshore racer.

Fred Kurzynske is president of Kurzynske & Associates, consulting engineers in Tennessee. Over the past 25 years they have participated in design projects that include rocket test facilities used in the development of the U.S. space program. Frank first became interested in sailing while in high school, crewing for friends in Snipes and Scows. A few years ago he purchased a 25' Irwin 10/4 and has enjoyed cruising around the inland waters of his home state. He and his family have also chartered boats off the coasts of Maine, South Carolina, Puerto Rico, Central America, and Hawaii. He has written many articles, published here and abroad, about various facets of sailing.

Philip Marriner's early racing was in Comets and Stars in Western Long Island Sound. Through the years he has won regional, national, and international competition in Comets, Penguins, Stars, Thistles, Lightnings, and Sunfish. He began MORC sailing in 1962 and has won numerous regional regattas and races. His offshore racing includes the SORC, Annapolis-Newport Race, Block Island Race Week, Edlus, and Vineyard Races. Philip has been affiliated with the marine industry for many years and is now associated with Howe & Bainbridge, Inc., sailcloth manufacturers in Boston. He was sail fabric consultant in the 1962 and 1967 America's Cub campaigns.

Anthony Parker is in private law practice in Washington, D.C., but in the past has managed to find a lot of time for sailboats. At one time he was Junior Sailing Champion of New England and later captain of the Harvard Sailing Team and named All-American sailor while still in college. He came in second, three out of the four times he entered the Congressional Cup. In 1967 Tony sailed on *American Eagle* in the America's Cup Selection Trials and in 1977 sailed on *Independence, Courageous,* and *Mariner.* He also skippered *Mariner* when she was being used as a trial horse for *Enterprise.* Tony tried out for the Olympics in 1964, 1968, and 1972. In 1974 he was the Three-Quarter-Ton National Champion. He has sailed in many long-distance races and was the ocean racing coach at the Naval Academy from 1970 to 1972.

Thomas Russell sailed Penguins as a child and then joined the U.S. Navy for a 20-year career in submarines. During this time he raced occasionally with his father and became active in racing again when he got out

of the service. During the period from 1969 to 1977 Tom owned several different boats, including a Morgan 24, a Morgan 27, and a C&C 33 Three-Quarter-Ton sloop, and won over 200 trophies. He has sailed in numerous SORC series, Halifax Races, North American One-Ton Championships, and more. In addition, Tom and his family have done extensive cruising. In 1971 he was named Production Manager of Van Zandt Sails and in 1974 became owner and president of that company.

Michael Saunders was born in South Africa and brought up in Mozambique, where most of his free time was spent in a variety of little boats, from trading dhows to stitched-bark canoes. Later while living in Rhodesia, Mr. Saunders and his wife built a 20' trimaran and sailed in the Mozambique Channel and on the Lakes of Rhodesia. In 1972, as a result of the political scene and other circumstances he gave up his job, sold all his family's possessions, and bought an old 33' ketch. The boat was called *Walkabout,* and with his wife and four children he set sail around the Cape of Good Hope to St. Helena, South America, the West Indies, and Azores, and finally England. The voyage took two years and is related in Mr. Saunders' book, *The Walkabouts.* After arriving in England, the Saunders continued to live afloat, first on *Walkabout* and later on a converted trawler. They are now building a 45' ferro-cement cutter, specially designed for a long voyage. Mr. Saunders writes for a living and makes yacht deliveries, which has provided thousands of miles' experience in many craft. He also runs a firm that offers design and consulting service.

Paul Schreck, who sailed his first race at age six, comes from a family of naval architects, boat builders, and sailmakers. He became a sailmaker in 1939 and six years later went into business for himself in New Orleans. He has won the Scot North Americans three times, the Scot Mid-Winters three times, the Windmill Mid-Winters once, the New Orleans to Gulfport Race six times, and the Havana Veradero Race. Paul has also sailed in two Mallory Trials and many ocean races as well as participating in the district championships of various classes. He owns seven sailboats, including a One-Tonner and a Half-Tonner.

Arthur Slemmon's sailing experience began at an early age on Lac Labelle in Wisconsin, racing Class "C" scows. He designed and built his own "skeeter" class ice boat and later sailed dinghies while receiving his Mechanical Engineering degree from M.I.T.

While in Detroit designing and building automobiles and automotive gas turbines, he sailed in Lightning Class races on Lake Sante Claire. Art is now with SRI International in California, where he is Senior Research Engineer and the Solar Thermal Energy Program manager. He has 15 U.S. and foreign patents, with others still pending. His family is made up of avid sailors who enjoy racing their 32′ sloop on San Francisco Bay.

Norman Smith was introduced to sailing in a Herreshoff 12 when he was a teenager. He worked for NASA for 29 years as a research aerodynamicist. He also has a "second career" as a freelance writer of science books which specialize in explaining technical topics to young people and laymen. Norman now lives on the Champlain Islands of Vermont and has discovered the delights of cruising in his 32′ ketch.

Eric Twiname is a sailor by inclination and a writer by profession. He began sailing when he was 9 years old and his successes include the British Laser National Championship as well as the British National Team Racing Championship. The British Olympic team, Admiral's Cup team, and America's Cup syndicate have all drawn on his specialist knowledge and experience of racing tactics and rules. He lectures and coaches extensively and his articles are published world-wide, as are his books: *Dinghy Team Racing, Start to Win,* and *The Rules Book.*

Charles Ulmer is the son of the founder of the sailmaking firm of the same name. He is a graduate of the U.S. Naval Academy, where he was a member of the sailing team, one of the top eastern teams at the time. He was singlehanded collegiate champion on several occasions and skippered the Navy team that won the McMillan Cup in 1961. Charles is also the former National Champion in International Tempests and Mobjacks. He is currently president of Charles Ulmer, Inc., which has five lofts on the eastern Gulf coast.

Index

Other Adlard Coles titles of interest

The Best of Sail Trim:
Edited by Charles Mason
ISBN 0 229 11843 7

This is an anthology of authoritative articles from one of the world's major sailing magazines. Containing a wealth of invaluable advice, tips and opinions from leading yachtsmen, sail designers and manufacturers, it represents current ideas and practice for cruising and racing sailors alike from dinghies to ocean racers.

By means of this anthology, information which the experts take for granted will help the ordinary sailor to keep abreast of the times.

Sails – Sixth Edition:
Jeremy Howard-Williams
ISBN 0 229 11824 0

An encyclopedic volume covering both cruising and racing sails. This new edition discusses the impact of film laminates, the use of Kevlar, Mylar and Melinex and computers on the sailmaker's craft, and even includes a section on the Thames sailing barge. Autoplotters, new theory, latest design, sailboards and the Chinese junk rig are all looked at and their worth assessed. Many new photographs and drawings.

'Highly recommended.'
Practical Boat Owner

Small Boat Sails:
Jeremy Howard-Williams
ISBN 0 229 11786 4

The rapid development of sailboarding has led to increased sophistication of sail design. No longer is brightness of colour the principal factor – for as the sport becomes more competitive the use of high-tech materials has entered the arena. Now available in paperback, this rewritten edition of a classic text contains the essential information for dinghy and boardsailors, and surveys the state-of-the-art in both racing and cruising sails on dinghies and day-boats to approximately 20 feet LOA.

Rigging: Enrico Sala
ISBN 0 229 11817 8

This guide, fully illustrated with colour diagrams, will help all DIY sailing enthusiasts to maintain and improve all aspects of rigging on their craft. From splicing to mooring lines, from leather chafe protections to mast tuning, from fixing deck hardware to the description of various types of block, right up to preparing for an ocean crossing, this book – technical but easy to consult – gives advice on how best to confront an infinite number of operations in the most practical way.

If you would like a catalogue of the complete list of titles published by Adlard Coles, please write to: The Editor, Adlard Coles, 8 Grafton Street, London W1X 3LA